Jewels and Ashes

ARNOLD ZABLE
Jewels and Ashes

HARCOURT BRACE & COMPANY
New York   San Diego   London

ISBN 0-15-146348-4
Printed in the United States of America
A B C D E

For my dear mother and father,
Hoddes and Meier;
and for all those who seek refuge,
regardless of race, nation or creed.

Author's Note

Except for members of my immediate family, the names and some personal details of the people described in this book who are still living have been changed so as to protect their privacy. All place-names and historical events have been thoroughly researched and, wherever possible, authenticated. But this is not primarily a book of history. Instead, it is concerned with the way in which family stories become, in time, ancestral legends. And as the author, recreating such stories, I am, of course, a part of this process.

I am indebted to many friends who offered advice and encouragement. To Tony Knight, John Larkin, Lily Rigos, Jenny Rigos, Ursula Flicker, Jenny Wajsenberg, Ida Sokolowski and Yehuda Medownik — thank you. To my publishers, Henry and Margot Rosenbloom of Scribe, I owe much for their discerning editing and constant support. And I especially want to thank my wife, Dora, who has continually urged me to go deeper within, to that uncharted territory wherein reside both unresolved fears and the most durable of joys.

— *Arnold Zable, Melbourne, April 1991*

Part One

Chapter One

IT BEGAN EARLY IN LIFE, his love of trees. He traces it to Zwierziniec, a forest on the outskirts of Bialystok — a city within the
empire of Nicholas 11, Czar of Poland and Autocrat of all the Russias.
It was a time of prosperity for the Zabludowski family. In summer
they would retreat to the dachas, cottages that were hired for holidays
within cool forests, well away from scorched and dry city streets.
And in a forest called Zwierziniec my father made his first acquaintance with trees.

There was one in particular, many centuries old, a massive chestnut
tree. While describing it father climbs onto a kitchen chair. 'Its trunk
was solid and thick', he says, and lifts his hands from his stomach
in an expansive gesture. He spreads his arms as if about to take flight;
its canopy was so broad and high it exploded towards the heavens.
Underneath, lovers sat on summer nights while bands played on
stands in the clearing that surrounded the tree. Children ran about
in circles, their excitement barely under control, and gathered
chestnuts that had fallen to the ground. When prised from their
husks, the nuts emerged as smooth as lacquered furniture and were
used as marbles and currency. Three were worth one sweet, father
recalls with accuracy over seventy years later. Boys stuffed their
pockets with nuts, and their homes became so littered with them
that people tripped over, and exasperated mothers would yell, 'Get
those accursed chestnuts out of here'.

When father tells a story he enters into it and becomes the object
he describes. There is a chestnut tree growing in the kitchen,

3

sprouting from a chair, branches spreading, outstretched limbs reaching towards the ceiling. He is on his toes now, an eighty-year-old man trying to grow taller. 'Be careful', I warn him, 'or you'll topple over.' I don't fancy the prospect of an uprooted chestnut tree sprawling across the kitchen floor.

'I can see it now, as if it were in front of my eyes', mother tells me. She conjures images of childhood on a distant continent. Father draws maps of a city for me. Streets flow into a central square, and he recalls their names as if he still lived in them. It is almost half a century since he last walked them. 'I can see it now, as if it were in front of my eyes', mother says. She describes scenes at random. An epic unfolds in fragments: tales of flight through snow-laden fields at night; a wagon piled high with cucumbers drawn by a pair of horses plodding towards a village market in the pre-dawn darkness; an isolated town caught in the crossfire between rival kingdoms; a ragged band of paupers ransacking an abandoned palace; a boat they called the Wild Mama, rolling and swaying on stormy seas — countless images evoked at the kitchen table of a Melbourne house by two ageing parents for a son about to leave on a journey.

It is not often that I walk with mother nowadays through the streets of the neighbourhood she has lived in for forty years. She remains, most of the time, secluded at home. For hours on end she sits quietly by the kitchen table. The radio drones in the background tuned to talkback shows, classical music, and the proceedings of Parliament. The hours are punctuated by news bulletins. The days revolve around the meals she prepares slowly, as she summons her last reserves of energy, moving from sink to cupboard, fridge to stove, navigating her kingdom of bare necessities. Between chores she sits quietly again. When I come across her at such times I am soothed rather than saddened. The room is permeated with solitude. In mother there is a gentleness, a feeling that life's struggle is almost over, a sense of twilight and long nights that extend towards eternity.

We walk together through the familiar terrain of my childhood on a day of seamless blue skies. The sun hovers on the northern horizon; winter light in Melbourne radiates softly, with a clarity that reveals objects and people in transparent detail. I notice how much mother has aged, how slowly she walks, the streaks of grey that thread through her once pitch-black hair. Frailty is edging in at the limbs. She is, it seems, becoming smaller, succumbing with quiet resignation.

We enter the waiting room of a doctor's surgery. The afternoon sun filters through lace curtains, spreading uneven pools of light onto a coffee table stacked with magazines. Mother's hands tremble as she reaches for something to read. Several years earlier I had noticed this shaking for the first time. She was handing me a cup of tea: the cup rattled, tea spilled into the saucer, and I was shocked into the realisation that mother had crossed that imperceptible border which divides us from the realm of old age and fragility.

While we wait, an elderly woman enters the doctor's rooms. When she glances at mother a strong current of recognition passes between them, something far more powerful than a warm greeting between good friends. They are 'ship sisters', having met over fifty years ago in the port of Marseilles. Soon after, they had boarded the French boat the *Ville d'Amien*; after the first storm they began to call her the Wild Mama, because she bucked and rolled on wild seas.

Their bond is as strong as any ties of blood. They are on the threshold of the ninth decade of their lives, but in this moment of surprise encounter they stand outside time. They are ship sisters who left behind them a way of life, an indelible intimacy, family and friends they were never to see again. As they sailed from Marseilles in January 1933, the passengers heard the news that Hitler had become Chancellor of Germany. 'We knew enough to be disturbed', mother has told me. 'But how could we know what was going to happen and how immense it would be?'

The Wild Mama was steaming away from Europe, wrenched free from a continent that was beginning to seethe and boil. Cauldrons of ancient tribal hatreds were being fanned towards an explosion; and between the Old World and the New, the Wild Mama ploughed through a furious sea.

'Do you ever think about those you left behind?', I ask father. 'Not often', he says. 'Such memories are a luxury I can't afford.'

He guards himself, in his day-to-day existence, from sinking into reveries on the past. Many times, during the years since he retired, he has told me that each day of added life is a miracle. There are mornings he awakens as if paralysed; with sheer will he propels himself out of bed, shakes his limbs and, slowly, with increasing vigour and precision, he sets about his daily chores.

'Just put one foot in front of the other', he tells me: out to the bathroom to wash and shave; to the shops to buy food and newspapers; into the kitchen to make breakfast. In old age he has been able to make the kitchen a part of his domain, at least in the mornings, when mother usually sleeps. He chops onions, grates potatoes, shreds cabbage, and fries them with whipped eggs into thick cakes until they are blackened on the outsides. 'That is when you know they are ready on the insides', he claims, in defence of his method. He has developed his formulas and sticks to them. They are his recipes for survival. But he may also throw in a few raisins or almonds — 'to keep my imagination alive', he explains.

He has an explanation for everything. He reads newspapers, 'to keep myself alert'. He studies chosen articles, underlines sentences in red biro, and scrawls commentaries in the margins like a talmudic scholar interpreting a sacred text. He extracts philosophical comments from even the most mundane of news items, and copies them onto scraps of paper which he gathers eventually into notebooks.

'Just put one foot in front of the other, and don't stop moving until you have extracted your full measure of life from the day', he tells me, and moves into the backyard. He points proudly to this season's tomatoes, radishes, and silver beet, as he waters his patch of soil. It measures two metres by about ten, and is divided into segments marked off by primitive fences made of wire mesh. 'I love form', he says. 'This is why I garden: to experiment with form and to create symmetry.' He takes up a shovel and deepens the hole he is preparing for his next batch of compost; and I recall a time when I was coming into my first focussed view of the world, and milk was still delivered by horse-drawn cart. Father would go into the street to collect the fresh manure that had been left behind the previous night, and would spread it over the same backyard plot he is now tending for the fortieth year.

He guards himself from disturbing thoughts and memories, and has done so for many years; as he must, for he is the sole survivor of his once large family. 'There are not enough hours in the day for what I want to do', he has told me many times. 'Why waste them in recalling things that have long since gone?'

Yet there is one way, at least, in which father does maintain links with the past. He is a hoarder, especially of old documents, newspapers, magazines, letters. The newspapers pile up, and he spends many hours sorting and rearranging them. Occasionally he gets rid of some, but only after he has gone through them carefully again to make sure he is not losing something of great importance.

'Do you ever think of those you left behind?', I persist. Father responds by going into his bedroom and emerging with the yellowed pages of a Yiddish newspaper stained with brown pock-marks of decay. The disintegrating pages are held together with strips of transparent tape which track through headlines, news commentaries, features, radio timetables, advertisements, reviews of concerts and lectures, and notices of births, engagements, marriages, and deaths. The date is March 17, 1936. On the masthead is printed the proud claim that *Unzer Lebn* is the oldest and most widely-circulated Bialystok daily. Towards the lower right-hand corner on the front page, within a space four inches by two, framed in black, is printed the announcement:

> To our beloved son, brother and brother-in-law Meier. On the occasion of his departure for New Zealand, we wish him a heart-felt bon voyage and a happy future in his new homeland.

In his customary red biro, father has reinforced the black frame to isolate this insert from those that surround it. Directly below is a notification of the drawing on this day of a lottery conducted by the orphans' welfare society. Above it is advertised a forthcoming series of lectures by the renowned pedagogue Sholem Broide of Warsaw: 'Be enthralled by his slide-illustrated talks about his recent journeys to ancient cities of the Mediterranean! A rare insight into other worlds for the people of Bialystok!'. To the left is the news that Celina Sandler, 'for many years a Professor at the Université de Beauté in Paris', no less, will be giving advice from her suite at the Hotel Ritz, for absolutely no cost. And to the right is a proclamation of a special unbeatable quality Passover matzos, now available from Messer Brothers Bakery.

Over the matzos advertisement is attached a note, on a scrap of paper which apparently father had inserted several years ago, indicating how the various signatories to the farewell notice were related to him. Yet again he had written in red, as if to alert any curious descendants who might stumble across the newspaper in years to come, and to provide them with a means of deciphering this clue to branches of the family tree.

On March 17, 1936 father bought *Unzer Lebn* for the final time. That night he boarded a train to begin a one-way journey to the other side of the globe, his newspaper tucked away in trunks crammed with books and journals. Decades later they were to become the decaying reminders of the world he had left behind.

December 26, 1932. Mother stands by the Warsaw express at the Bialystok station. Her closest friends are clustered around, conveying their final farewells; among them is Meierke, her husband of a day. The luggage has already been taken to her compartment; the train is warming up. At this moment, mother catches sight of Reb Aron Yankev in the distance, on the platform, running frantically towards her. The black caftan he is wearing trails down to his ankles and flutters by his side as he rushes beside the train.

When mother had left the family apartment several hours earlier, Reb Aron Yankev had, as usual, maintained his silence towards her. In his eyes, the daughter who was about to depart had long since strayed from the righteous path of Orthodoxy, lured by modernity and worldliness. He broke his silence for just a moment, as she was leaving, to remind her to kiss the mezuzah attached by the door. Chane Esther, the matriarch of the Probutski household, also decided not to accompany her daughter to the station. She was too ill and, I suspect, much too upset. What my mother recalls is that Chane Esther's last gesture was to insist on her drinking a glass of milk to fortify her for the journey. 'Five weeks at sea?', she had queried. 'You'll die of hunger.'

Mother tells stories in fragments. Over the years she has retold the same anecdotes many times. Her experiences flow through her, always liable to leap out unexpectedly in moments of unguarded reflection. The sight of Reb Aron Yankev dashing along the platform of the Bialystok station is one of these recurring images; as too is the glass of milk.

From such lean and Spartan clues I have reinvented her journey.

On the Warsaw express she had wept incessantly. A pair of lovers sat in her compartment whispering to each other until they disembarked and disappeared into the night at a provincial station. Warsaw was a dream shaded with heartbreak at the loss of Bialystok. After staying overnight at her brother Joshua's, she arrived back at the Warsaw station to pandemonium and a sea of farewell tears as hundreds of immigrants resumed or began their journeys to the West. The train departed at midnight, and for the first time since leaving Bialystok she gave way to exhaustion and fell into a deep sleep.

She was woken at dawn by the voices of German border-police asking for passports and papers. She ate breakfast in Berlin, crossed the Belgian border at night, and waited for several hours at the Paris station, shivering in a hall crowded with passengers falling asleep against each other. Mother recalls a collective meal to which fellow immigrants contributed salami, sardines, and schnapps; and many times she has told me about her first-ever glimpse of the sea, as the train emerged from the night and rushed towards Marseilles. Wonderful pictures began to form before her eyes: green fields; a ring of mountains with their summits covered in snow; and then the glistening ocean, aflame in the morning sun. Over the water's surface there glided an aeroplane, and at the docks the Wild Mama was waiting.

The living quarters, when mother first saw them, seemed like crowded pigsties. In the first few days she was confined below deck, nauseated, as furious storms whipped up heavy seas. In Alexandria she disembarked and bought a gift — two black elephants carved in wood — for the sister who awaited her in Melbourne. And as she sailed through the Suez Canal she was riveted by what was to become the most indelible of memories: Bedouin boys diving for coins that flew from the decks of the boat.

Yet throughout that voyage, even as she succumbed to the adventure, to the breath of unlimited freedom that wafted across open seas, and to that special bond that develops between immigrants thrown together by chance to become ship brothers and sisters with a common destiny, my mother could not shake off her vision of Reb Aron Yankev, running frantically along the platform of the Bialystok station, desperate to make one last contact with his estranged daughter. He had paused for a moment when he reached her, to steady his voice, before he said, somewhat hesitantly, 'I wish you a safe journey and a successful future in your new home. And I forgive you'.

When she recalls this moment, mother invariably adds, 'And how could I have known that I would never see them again? Not only my father, but almost everyone who stood there on the Bialystok station farewelling me?'.

His parents were not informed. Her father had no idea at the time, although Chane Esther the matriarch knew, and one of her brothers was a witness. From father's family there were no witnesses. The minyan of ten males required by traditional law had to be rounded up; there were always people on hand to make an extra zloty as witnesses on such occasions. The rabbi performed the ceremony quickly. Bishke Zabludowski happened to pass by the marriage bureau soon after.

'Mazel-tov', the office workers exclaimed. 'And why should I be congratulated?', he replied. 'Don't you know?', came the shocked answer. 'Your son Meier has just been married.'

'We didn't confide in our parents', father has told me. 'We never discussed our personal affairs with them. In the pride of our youth we saw ourselves as being far in advance of previous generations. We were freethinkers, breaking away from stifling traditions; at least, this is what we thought at the time. Many of us didn't bother getting married. The major problem was finding a room. Once you found one, you could begin "married" life.'

They were officially married because, they hoped, the papers would enable him to receive a permit to the New World after his wife had settled there. They didn't require a room because she went home immediately after the ceremony to pack. She had received a permit from a sister who had migrated several years previously. The newly-weds were not to see each other for over three years.

My father loves words. It is a passion that still grips him at the onset of his ninth decade. The discovery of a new word — its origins, precise meaning, nuances, and variations — can make his day. Father's most prized possessions are his dictionaries, among which are the rare ones he took with him on the sea voyage from Europe half a century ago. Instead of clothes he packed books and dictionaries: Polish-Yiddish, English-Polish, Russian-Yiddish, German-Russian, Hebrew-English; all the permutations of the six languages he has mastered over a long lifetime.

Father claims he knows what his first words were, his first naming of things, the earliest labels he attached to the world. It is 1907. A two-year-old boy dressed in a sailor's suit runs beside his mother through a town square. Above him looms the clock-tower of Bialystok. He points to the tower and at an object moving through the streets. He names them, and his naming becomes a refrain he repeats over and over again:

> A zeiger, a konke
> A zeiger, a konke.

The zeiger is the town clock, and the konke is a horse-drawn tram that ferries passengers within the city and beyond it as far as the Zwierziniec forest. 'You see', father remarks triumphantly, 'even then I was already a philosopher, and my first poem was about time and space.'

They lived on the edge of time and space, my ancestors, always on the verge of moving on, continually faced with the decision: do we stay, persist, take root within this kingdom, or do we take to the road again? Perhaps it is safer, greener, beyond the next river, over the next mountain-range, across yet another border? Often enough the choice was made for them, and they fled for their lives in the wake of expulsions, inquisitions, and massacres to seek a new place of refuge. At other times they were welcomed, initially, for the skills they had accumulated as wanderers; centuries on the move had made them masters of the ephemeral. They knew how to serve as middlemen, entrepreneurs, navigators and astronomers, court advisers and healers; even though their hearts longed for some soil to till.

So it was in Eastern Europe one millennium ago, when they began to arrive in flight from the Crusades. Later they came as guests of noblemen, who invited them to settle in their fiefdoms to become conduits between aristocrat and peasant, town and countryside. They traded as pedlars and merchants, transformed forests into slabs of timber, and shaped the timber into expanding towns, where they could set up workshops to weave, sew, hammer, cut, and shape future destinies.

Towns and villages sprang up like mushrooms after rain. Over the centuries they expanded in all directions: north to the shores of the Baltic Sea; south into the Carpathian Ranges and towards the Black Sea; west into obscure pockets of the Austro-Hungarian empire; and east, deep into Czarist Russia, beyond the banks of the River Dnieper. Settlements emerged as far and wide as the horizon and shifting foreign borders would permit them.

Yet at no time were these communities entirely secure. Arbitrarily, a charter or privileges they had been granted could be repealed, and their function, place of residence, and status redefined. There was always the threat of a sudden whirlwind, a madman on the rampage full of drink and misdirected rage, inciting the mob to join in and take out its frenzy on these peculiar people who had settled among them with their private God and the countless prayer-houses in which they worshipped Him.

So they maintained their talent for movement, travelling within the prescribed boundaries as itinerants, eking out a living from limited opportunities. Foremost among them, or at least this is how I once loved to imagine it, were the troubadours, storytellers, cantors, and bands of Klesmorim who toured obscure hamlets trading tales for a meal, songs for a drink. Wandering preachers, scribes, scholars, and wonder workers exchanged Hebrew and Aramaic scriptures, amulets, and talismans for precious roubles and zlotys to send home to their impoverished families. Their gifts and messages were borne along dusty roads and country paths by horse-drawn wagons. 'We will return soon', they wrote, 'by spring, in time for Passover; or by autumn, for Rosh Hashonah and the Days of Awe.' Sometimes they would break beyond the limits completely to steal over the horizon, murmuring: 'Enough! It is time to find a new haven with greener pastures and the possibility of redemption.'

When, as a child, I had my first intimations of these ancestral wanderings, I saw them initially as a romance. I imagined myself the descendant of Gypsies and nomads. I tried to retrace their steps. I would catch glimpses of footprints and hooves etched in mud and dust within the pages of Yiddish novels that I read voraciously. My interest waxed and waned, and sometimes the footprints would peter out. Old volumes I found in the recesses of forgotten corners in our house would revive my flagging interest with an unexpected photograph of a forefather walking absentmindedly through a village, crooked cottages visible in the background, cobblestones underfoot. They drew me, these volumes, in spite of myself, back to the search.

One particular page stood out. In the wake of the Annihilation, the survivors had assembled photos, snatches of history, glimpses of what had been until so recently their beloved hometown. They did it in haste, as if building a moat against the ravages of memory loss. Within six years it was published, in New York: a massive volume encased between hard covers of dark crimson on which were embossed, in gold lettering, in Yiddish on the right-hand side and English on the left, the words, 'Bialystok — Photo Album of a Renowned City and Its Jews the World Over'. Copies were sent to countries around the entire globe, to every corner where Bialystoker had fled and recreated their lives.

A random flip of the pages revealed scenes of a thriving metropolis and its citizens, both prominent and obscure. Other more faded photos and paintings depicted an era when Bialystok was merely a village enclosed by field and forest. But the pages could just as easily fall upon images of ruin and desolation, with buildings aflame or reduced to rubble. Then there was one particular page: after I discovered it I would always turn to it first, skimming over the ruins, not quite seeing or allowing myself to focus fully upon them. Recently I returned to that page which had once held me so captivated; and even though it was years since I had last seen them, the images retained their haunting quality and hinted at mysteries I had not quite penetrated.

There are five photos under the heading, 'Memorable Bialystoker Characters'. Above, to the left, stands Yankel the Organ-Grinder, holding aloft a wooden box from which a parrot is drawing out a lucky envelope with its beak. They are in a market-square surrounded by a crowd watching this poor man's lottery. Yankel's hair is white, as too are his ample beard and moustache. He has the bearing of a fierce patriarch, a communal elder rather than a pedlar of cheap dreams.

Alongside Yankel, to the right, is a photo with the caption: 'A Bialystoker urchin from the Chanaykes'. Wrapped in a ragged overcoat, he leans against a timber door, clutching a cigarette to his mouth. He squints at the camera defiantly from beneath a peaked cap that perches crookedly on his head — a little rascal from the alleys of the neighbourhood where my mother once lived.

On the lower half of the page there are three passport-size photos. One of them remains as sinister today as it appeared when I first saw it and began to realise that, at a certain point, the romance wore thin and there were darker forces that could obliterate it. On the face of the 'Boy Layser', we are informed, the anti-Semite Dr Granowski had burned the words 'ganev', 'dieb', and 'wor' — all meaning 'thief'. The words can be seen clearly, tattooed several inches high, one plastered across the forehead, one etched into each cheek. This incident took place in 1888. Almost a century later the face of Layser stares out, frozen and trapped within a square-inch prison that bears witness to the day he had been irreversibly branded and bound to his fate.

For relief from the intensity of Layser's gaze, I would turn my attention to the photo of Faivel Lilliput. A turban wrapped around his head, a white robe draped over his shoulders, a hand held against his chest in a Napoleonic gesture — Faivel was a dwarf, a circus performer, and a distributor of theatre placards throughout Bialystok.

I knew Faivel. In the 1950s he resurfaced in Melbourne. His inflated head, muscular shoulders, and rolling gait were a familiar sight. He seemed to be everywhere: a jester at weddings; a guest at circumcisions; a mourner at funerals; an odd-job man in the run-down houses of newly arrived immigrants. He loved to play pranks and always put aside time to play with us, the children, as we darted about the communal functions that our parents often attended. He played with the abandon of someone who had long ago resigned himself to having no children of his own. And besides, he was our size, and saw the world from our perspective. He taught us how to mimic the gestures and antics of the grown-ups who towered above us, and to caricature their endless speeches. As my father used to say of him: even where he is not sown, he also manages to grow.

The fifth image is of an elderly man, balding at the temples, his beard neatly trimmed. He wears a white shirt, tie, and black jacket. The most striking family resemblance can be seen in the ears. I hated having the short-back-and-sides haircuts that were forced upon me as a child, because they exposed my big ears and made me look like a monkey. The fifth 'memorable character' in the honoured company of Yankel the Organ-Grinder, the Urchin from the Slums, Faivel Lilliput the Circus Dwarf, and the Tattooed Boy Layser, is my paternal grandfather, Bishke Zabludowski — who, as the caption informs us, was the first newsboy in Bialystok and 'disseminated culture for over forty years'.

When Bialystoker gathered at parties and concerts I would be introduced as the grandson of Bishke Zabludowski. 'We all knew him', they would say. 'A small man, with a red beard. He stood under the clock-tower, with piles of newspapers and journals. He was a familiar sight, trotting to and from his news-stand bent under the latest edition, his big ears sticking out to the sides.' And they would lean over to tweak my ears, while I squirmed and wriggled to get away from my tormentors.

Bishke Zabludowski: the bearer of news, town crier, raconteur, contact man, his big ears tuned in to gossip both local and from abroad, a familiar figure, one of the most memorable sights in the streets of Bialystok. In the grand tradition, he was a true master of the ephemeral.

In the weeks before my departure I have a recurring dream, the same fragments repeated with slight variations, each one suffused with a similar feeling of unease.

I am travelling through a town. Friends who live there have invited me to inspect the offices of the security police. When we reach the entrance of the towering grey building I become anxious, and refuse to enter with them. After they emerge from the building some time later, they tell me it has been an interesting experience and that there is nothing to fear. Since the doors are still open I cannot resist the temptation and I enter.

There appears to be no one in sight as I descend the stairs. In the basement there is a man seated behind a desk. 'You have come too late', he informs me. There is still time for me to leave as easily as I have entered, and to ascend the stairs back into daylight. Yet I linger on, my curiosity aroused.

Unexpectedly, I am approached by several burly men who exude a sense of menace and brute strength. They escort me to a lower basement in which there are a number of interrogators seated behind a long table. Opened out in front of them are files within folders.

They seem to know who I am. I realise now there is no escape; I am trapped in a cellar, hemmed in by guards. My inquisitors ask questions without a trace of feeling. They are clinical, detached. They want to know why I have come here, and it is clear they are not about to let me go.

Later I find myself in a prison cell. The guard is harsh and hostile. I envy him because, when he finishes work, he can go out into the sunlight while I will still be confined in a dark cell. I am overcome by a feeling of panic. Yet there is one saving grace. I have in my possession a large volume of stories about the Tzaddikim, the early Hasidic masters who, in the darkest of times, counselled their communities and tried to show them a way back to the light, to the source of Creation. I look forward to immersing myself in this book as a means of passing time and deriving some comfort while I am imprisoned. But on closer inspection I realise the book is moth-eaten, and that some of my fellow inmates have ripped out pages to use as cigarette paper.

I become aware that someone has smuggled themselves into the cell. It is a man who, in childhood, I used to know as the Partisan. He was a family friend who often visited us on Sunday afternoons. During the war years he had roamed the forests near Bialystok and fought in the Resistance. Many times he had narrowly escaped death and, eventually, in the wake of the Annihilation, he had made his way to Australia.

He passes me a note on which there are instructions about how to escape. But I cannot quite decipher the scribbled message.

Chapter Two

THE BEIJING-MOSCOW EXPRESS hurtles northwards across the plains of Manchuria. Villages of clay cottages give way to grasslands grazing sheep, cattle, and horses. The cities of Harbin and Shenyang loom above swamps and flooded fields; high-rise complexes emerge from barren wastelands. As we cross a river that threads through central Harbin I glimpse a solitary strip of sand, an inland beach basking under a mild sun. Hundreds of bathers cling to this patch of sand: some spill out into the shallows and others burst beyond the pack, as if freeing themselves to swim alone and undisturbed. Waves ripple back to the shores from the wake of boats, while in the distance burn the flames of industry, modern-day infernos, fuelling a city that has for centuries oscillated between rival empires.

As we move I read a photocopy of my father's life story. It is hand-written in Yiddish, a lifetime telescoped into twenty pages of fool-scap, eighty years at a glimpse, lived out in two halves, within two continents on opposite sides of the globe. Father had written it at my request, just days before my departure:

> I was born in the city of Bialystok, Poland, although at that time, December 4th, 1905, it was a part of Czarist Russia. On the Jewish calendar it was the 23rd of Kislev, the 3rd day of Channukah in the year 5666. Bialystok began as a village which stood beside a rivulet called the Biale. The village belonged to a Count Branitski, and indeed, there was a Palace Branitski set within lavish gardens enclosed behind walls of stone and gates of steel . . .

17

Bialystok is thousands of miles to the west, a journey of eight days and nights by Trans-Siberian train. I read father's manuscript carefully — not only because I am on the way to the landscapes of his youth, but also because tomorrow at dawn we are scheduled to arrive at the Soviet border. Travellers I met in Beijing had warned me of the thorough searches that take place at this border. The territory we are approaching is linked within me to a deeply rooted suspicion; only now, on the eve of arrival, do I realise how strongly ingrained it is. Word associations emerge and impose themselves on the countryside rushing towards me — exile, prison camp, pogrom, interrogation: fragments of family legends and communal remembrances. It is an ancient fear, handed down through many generations, lying dormant and liable to be triggered off unexpectedly. Perhaps the Yiddish script of father's writing will arouse the suspicions of border police.

Towards evening we move past wetlands. Herons, coots, ducks, and rowing boats glide between thick clumps of wild grass and emerge occasionally into clearings where boatmen are harvesting reeds. Horses wade through muddy streams; a boy leads a bull along a dirt track; men on horseback drive a flock of sheep.

At Zhanlitan station I have my last view of China before nightfall. On the platform there are potplants, shrubs, flowers — an oasis of greenery. Several flower beds have been sculpted into Chinese characters, with slogans that proclaim: 'Let the Trains serve the People and the Motherland'. One slogan, however, seems to have escaped the straitjacket of ideology and offers a true sense of welcome: 'Let the People's Hearts be at Ease', it advises. Several hours later, while the passengers are asleep, I tear father's manuscript to shreds and fling it into the darkness.

Dawn in no man's land: a desolate flat stretch lit up by an amber glow which has wiped out all trace of night and ushered in an eerie silence. Passengers stand in the corridors and look through windows at a slow-motion ballet. Soldiers move along the tracks with dogs on leashes. Customs officials and military police board the snail-paced train to begin their inspection. There is a bond of sorts between us, the passengers. At this moment we are united by a shared apprehension. Will we run the gauntlet successfully? Will we be allowed safe passage? Everyone seems to be under the same spell, cast by the raw face of power that confronts us at the border of a closely guarded empire.

A young officer in knee-high leather boots and a crisp khaki uniform emerges from the mist, climbs the steps into our carriage, strides down the corridor, and orders out those who have remained seated in their compartments. He is accompanied by a teenage soldier whom he sends into the emptied compartments as one would send in a dog to pick up a scent. The soldier moves quickly — poking a torch under the seats, rummaging in every possible hiding place, his eyes darting in all directions.

The preliminary search over, the officer enters my compartment and motions to me, indicating that I should come in from the corridor and place my luggage in front of him. He goes through the contents of my bags slowly, meticulously, with a cold and clinical detachment. I try to find a point of contact, a glimmer of just the slightest warmth. The officer is completely unmoved. He pays particular attention to my diaries and books. Each one is handed to an official who scans them, putting two aside for closer inspection elsewhere.

The search is relentless. The seats are littered with my clothes, toiletries, intimacies. Fellow passengers stand passively in the corridors, some glancing casually in my direction. But for the most part they are distant. We no longer share a common bond of apprehension. They are now in another category, relieved to have been spared this ordeal, their passports approved and stamped. I am now apart, a suspect, an outsider.

So this is how it is when we are placed in situations of complete powerlessness. Most of us keep quiet, it seems, lest we unnecessarily draw attention to ourselves. An instinct informs us: remain invisible, avoid eye-contact, keep out of the way. And those who hold the reins of power, they know that in their hands lies the capacity to determine the fate of others. It is a lethal pantomime that has been repeated for millennia.

And another thought occurs during this interminable search: why was I the one, out of so many, singled out for such a thorough inspection? Was it because of a deeper anxiety? Did I give off the scent of an ancestral fear, the sort of scent which induces dogs to attack?

A day which dawned in one empire, within an amber mist hovering over a black wasteland, ends seventeen hours later on a train moving west through another empire. The search is over, the threat and menace gone, at least temporarily, and I am exuberant, set free to ride the landscape of my childhood imaginings.

Night becomes day, merges with night, and becomes one endless movement across Siberia. Black-clad babushkas, their hair tucked under brightly coloured kerchiefs, line the rails as we approach stations. They sell pickled cucumbers, boiled potatoes, blueberries, and salads from an array of makeshift tables and containers — from buckets, upturned boxes, wagons, and steel drums.

In the diner we are served by a plump woman. Her greying hair is tied back in a bun; her eyes are shrewd and watchful, yet always on the brink of a bemused smile. She is a no-nonsense woman who rushes from table to table, scolding and fussing over us, while exuding a maternal benevolence that inspires a childlike trust. It is as if we are in a warm kitchen, snug and protected from the alien terrain now veiled in darkness outside our moving household. It is a time for strangers to tell their tales, to spill out life stories and dreams while babushka feeds us beetroot borscht, beef and noodles, soup swimming with vegetables, and pieces of fish laced with sour cream. There is cherry compote for dessert and vodka with which to wash down our meals. The warmth spreads and envelops us; the light appears to grow brighter, our stories more fantastic and exaggerated, while occasionally we catch sober glimpses of dark forests, mist-laden fields, and the distant twinkle of a village huddling against the Siberian night.

The waitress is our protectress, our very own babushka — so unlike the witch that stood against a dark corner in the passage of the house I grew up in. We would creep towards her, three small children chanting: '*Eins a zeiger die babushka shloft, zwei a zeiger die babushka shloft*' — one o'clock the babushka sleeps, two o'clock . . . Closer and closer we would come, our hearts pounding, our bodies tensing, daring ourselves to come within arm's length of the slumbering witch as we neared midnight; suddenly, she would turn on us from the shadows and chase us the length of the house, along the passage, through the living room, into the kitchen, and out to the backyard. We ran in fright and joy, laughing, falling over each other, sidestepping and dodging, pursued by the menacing babushka. It was one of the few times in early childhood that I clearly recall seeing the playful side of father.

The birch tree is a streak of silver flashing in and out of the journey: slender saplings maturing into slim, elegant sentinels, standing mile upon mile, reappearing the length of the empire, sometimes alone, sometimes in forests, reflecting shafts of sunlight back at us as we stand, hour upon hour, our faces peering from the carriages, alert with curiosity and mesmerised by the rhythm of the train conveying us headlong in our dash across Siberia.

The birch. The beryose. The beryoskele. It features often in mother's repertoire of Yiddish songs. She sits in front of a heater, enduring in her old age yet another Melbourne winter. Where she once lived the winters were far more severe. Here it is cold enough, nevertheless, and she bends over towards the glowing bars of a radiator and hums softly to herself. Melodies rise like wisps of smoke from a smouldering fire. The kitchen in which she sits is a jumble of chipped crockery, fading table-cloths, cracked and worn linoleum; all of which she is reluctant to replace. She feels more at home surrounded by that which is redolent of another time and place. As mother hums, the table, the stove, the refrigerator, the cupboard, and the floor all recede, and the room is suffused with evening light. The walls give way and open out onto a vast expanse of land, a continent far distant, an empire of white beryoskelech.

> Softly, softly, swaying her curly green hair,
> My white beryoskele prays on and on;
> Every single leaf of hers murmurs a quiet prayer:
> Please, little beryoskele, also pray for me.
>
> I came here alone, from distant parts.
> Alien is the God from here and alien is his speech;
> He cannot see my sadness nor understand my prayer:
> Please, little beryoskele, also pray for me.

> From the distant west a gentle breeze has come,
> And tells the tiny leaves legends without end;
> Something deep within my heart begins to yearn and pray:
> Please, little beryoskele, also pray for me.

A kingdom of white birches, swaying and murmuring: quiet witnesses weaving in and out of legends set within a far distant land
called Siberia. In Yiddish it was called 'Sibir'. The word implied dark
nights when ancestors were dragged out of bed and accused of political agitation against the Czar. Sibir meant frozen fatigued prisoners
being taken to barren snow-covered wastes, thousands of kilometres
east, in exile from family and friends. Sibir was a land of isolated
communities with inmates doing infinite time on the edge of the
horizon; a territory so raw and threatening in its vastness, yet so
familiar, embedded in childhood melodies, and so close now that
I feel I can lean over and reach into the cottages that nestle against
the railway embankments.

Tales of Sibir were first told on Sunday afternoons when we
gathered in the rooms of the Kadimah Cultural Institute, a two-
storey building which stood opposite the Melbourne cemetery. We
were the children of migrants and refugees, many of whom had
waited for years in displaced persons' camps in various parts of
Europe. Within the shadows of their recent bereavement they had
sought asylum in a New World. 'Why did you choose Australia?',
we asked. 'I looked at a map of the world and chose a place as far
as possible from Sibir', one of them had replied.

In the New World our elders had resurrected fragments of the Old:
Yiddish and Hebrew schools, synagogues and yeshivas, pre-war style
communal organisations and institutes, where they spun tales of
a past they could never forget. On those Sunday afternoons Sibir
was recreated as a luminous dream of transparent white, over which
sleds drawn by dogs had conveyed them to prisons of ice.

Beinish Michelevitz was among the many thousands exiled to Sibir.
He returned to Poland where, in later years, he founded a children's
socialist movement called Skif. Both my mother and father joined
Skif's parent bodies, the Tsukunft and Bund. This is how they had
met and become imbued with youthful visions of transforming the
world.

Their vision was shattered by a catastrophe our communal elders called the Annihilation; but stories survived, countless tales of partisans and revolutionaries, resistance fighters and firebrands, engaged in a fiery struggle for redemption and deliverance. The stories were transformed into legends forever associated with Sunday afternoons opposite the cemetery; and the tale that made the most indelible impact was of Beinish Michelevitz who, when transported to Sibir, had his hair turn from the black brilliance of youth into the white of a sage after just one night of fright. Hair can suddenly turn white in times of great fear, we were told. I marvelled at this incident and imagined it with clarity: white hair upon white ice upon the endless wastes of an ominous place called Sibir.

Yet the landscape which moves beyond dawn into a morning sun is a flying tapestry of radiant forests and fields where, seated upright in a saddle, a boy races a horse at full gallop as he swoops down upon a herd of cattle. A woman in a scarlet pullover, gold kerchief, and floral-patterned skirt picks wild flowers in a meadow between wooded mountains. There are fields of mauves, pastel blues, pale pinks, and soft yellows. Siberian summer: green upon green, multiple shades and layers of green bursting with fertility. Children play in Sibir, within forest clearings and on unpaved village streets. A man and boy, fishing rods slung over their shoulders, wade across a meandering stream as day begins to fade. A bloated crimson sun sets fire to the rails along which our train curves; the fires die back into speeding tracks blazing silver. Cottages of Siberian villages sink into darkness. Smoke curls from their chimneys into a chill evening sky; and I imagine myself inside, seated snug by my babushka, listening to tales of a Siberia I had never thought could be so beautiful.

What was it they were trying to convey, our elders, when they told us their stories? 'Kadimah' means 'future'; yet they talked endlessly about the past, sometimes lovingly, sometimes with great venom. Their stories were like the Siberian night sky as it appears now above the train, streaking starlight between spaces of darkness; and this is where their tales petered out, into an infinite darkness they called the Annihilation. They left a legacy of fragments, a jumble of jewels and ashes, and forests of severed family trees which their children now explore and try somehow to restore.

Not long after we had moved clear of the Sino-Soviet border, our train had pulled into a station where a peasant couple boarded with their teenage daughter. They escorted her to our cabin, to the seat she had been assigned, and left her, reluctantly it seemed, among strangers.

For two days she remained silent, curled up in a blanket opposite me, curious, timid, withdrawn and wrapped in a private cocoon, her shyness slowly melting. She finally accepted the food we offered to share. In return we received homemade sweet bread, yoghurt, and crisp waffles baked, I imagined, in a village of far-eastern Siberia.

On the fourth day we discover a means of conversing. We point to words in a Russian-English dictionary and slowly piece together sentences. Her name is Dorima. She is a Baryat, from a tribe in the Taiga forests that sprawl over huge areas of Siberia. Her features are Asiatic; eyes elongated, complexion dark. Her forefathers hunted and foraged, and their skins thickened into cracked leather against intense summer heat and sub-zero winters. They live now in a farming co-operative, of which her father is secretary. She had never ventured beyond her province until this journey to Moscow, where she will stay with an aunt.

We sit on opposite bunks, silent for many hours against the hypnotic swaying of the train, and seem to share a deepening understanding. We are both locked into dreamscapes by which we measure the scenes that unfold outside, shaping them according to quite different imaginings, while sharing the same relentless momentum. For Dorima, Siberia is the intimate canopy of childhood, the pungent freshness of the Taiga, and forest clearings where her father ploughs and plants. It is the world beyond Siberia that appears alien, somewhat threatening but alluring, and perhaps more accessible now, through the word-by-word descriptions we have eked out of a dictionary.

The landscape loses its raw and untamed quality as we move westwards. On the fifth day we see showers of red particles, in a storm which conveys the acrid taste of acidic rain. Layers of dust settle in our compartments. Passengers rush to close windows. Through the haze we see that we are approaching an industrial city. Massive complexes of factories and plants pump waste into the skies; gigantic motors hum and vibrate, and indicate that we are on the outskirts of Novosibirsk. Barges ferry heavy equipment across a river which flows into the city centre. A station bookshop sells manuals on mechanics and mathematics. The world is becoming functional, framed by girders and cranes: Siberian soil sealed in concrete and bitumen.

We are on the threshold of the West, the indefinite border between Asiatic and European. Mid afternoon, Dorima lies on the lower bunk asleep, a copy of *Izvestia* abandoned across her upper body, her horizontally striped red-and-white blouse peeping over the edges of the newspaper while we twist into the Ural mountains, our Siberian dream fading.

Chapter Three

THE CARRIAGES WHICH HAVE CONVEYED US thousands of kilometres, day and night for a week, stand dormant at Jaraslavl station in Moscow. Clocks on stations along the Trans-Siberian line are set according to Moscow time; so that, in the far east during summer, day has barely faded by midnight. The empire beats according to the dictates of the centre; all roads lead eventually to the palaces of the Red Square.

The momentum of the train resonates as an echo which gives way to an inner silence. Within that silence I transfer my luggage, by taxi, through the streets of Moscow. At first glance the city appears spacious, cosmopolitan, with wide avenues and grand mansions that hint at bygone imperial splendour. Yet within an instant the city appears closed, empty, a lifeless museum in which set-pieces parade like marionettes. Moscow on a mild summer day, 1986; and, as if awakening from a trance, I realise that I am viewing the city through the same fluctuating inner lens I have focussed on almost every scene that has unfolded since I set out on this journey.

Uncle Zachariah, the first child of Bishke Zabludowski and Sheine Liberman, was born in 1892, in the city of Bialystok. My father was still a child confined to cheders and Talmud Torahs, immersed in Hebraic scriptures and sacred texts, when Zachariah was already a young man, drifting among the people of the streets, increasingly removed from the protective world of religious orthodoxy.

Father idolised his eldest brother. He loomed large, and exuded the scent of side streets and forbidden fruit. Father, who is quite short, lifts up his arms to indicate how tall and robust Zachariah had been. His descriptions remind me of a time during childhood when I thought father was so enormous he could not fit into the bathtub properly, and had to sit awkwardly, his arms drooping over the sides.

Now the son towers over the father as he tells me that, on Saturday afternoons, Zachariah would visit an aunt and uncle who lived near the Bialystok fish market. Butchers by trade, on the day of rest they would lounge on the verandah, gossiping and drinking while a constant stream of visitors dropped by — hawkers, market dealers, factory hands, wagon drivers, innkeepers, and wide-eyed idealists who spoke of budding conspiracies against the Czar. The abortive revolution of 1905 had been and gone. They were lying low, those who had supported it, waiting for the next push, always seeking recruits to bolster their ranks. Most of the visitors, however, preferred a game of cards, an afternoon in the taverns, or a long snooze in hammocks that were slung over the verandah, rather than clandestine activity on their one day of relief from work.

This is how father depicts it. But beware! He retains vestiges of the Romantic. He reconstructs the past as a series of grand gestures and sweeping movements, broken occasionally by a poetic detail — such as an eccentric remembrance of Zachariah coming home from the streets and lifting him up in the air in a sudden exuberant burst of energy, hurling and catching him mid-flight and then, just as abruptly, leaving him, an irrelevant child.

In the years immediately before the First World War, Zachariah became involved in Yiddish theatre. At first he worked as an extra in the productions of provincial troupes on tour in Bialystok. He graduated to the grand position of prompter, his name featuring on programmes that father claims had been in his possession until recently, when he lent them to a prominent actor in the Melbourne Yiddish theatre. Unfortunately, he misplaced these rare jewels, as father calls the various artefacts he brought with him from the Old World. Actually, the actor went mad, according to father, and lost both his mind and his possessions. This is how it is when we talk about Bialystok. Father sidetracks, goes on many detours, and has to be coaxed back on course to describe how Zachariah would stand

beneath the stage of the renowned Palace Theatre in a halo of foot-
lights that poked from behind a trapdoor, to steer the actors above
him through memory losses. He always seemed to be carrying a script
in his hands, and became known as someone who could be relied
upon in moments of doubt.

In 1914, when the first bombs rained down upon Bialystok,
Zachariah clambered onto the roof of the building in which the
Zabludowski family lived. He stood on the tiles and watched excitedly as the city exploded around him. Sheine Liberman poked her
head out of a garret window. 'Come down, you lunatic', she screamed.
Inside, father marvelled yet again at the reckless abandon with which
his brother approached life. Zachariah was enjoying himself, apparently, from his first-class vantage point, and retreated just as fragments of shrapnel landed where he had been standing moments
earlier.

Within a year the armies of Kaiser Wilhelm occupied Bialystok.
Zachariah's love of the streets became a more perilous affair: on
several occasions he was among those rounded up by the occupying
armies to be forced into work gangs. Eventually he obtained regular
work, with a wage of sorts, as a labourer on road and railway construction projects controlled by the occupiers. And it was on these
building sites that Zachariah was drawn, along with many others,
to the whispers he had heard on an uncle's verandah in pre-war
times. He listened now with more attention and interest, for it
seemed their time had come.

The world had turned upside down. While towns and cities were
being bombarded by shrapnel and bullets, and rival armies crawled
like vermin in the trenches, a wave called Revolution was again
swelling, heaving restlessly within clandestine movements, about
to surge from under ground to sweep through a dying empire. There
was excited talk of a new order, while the old was being torn to
shreds. Political cells multiplied like countless seeds sprouting on
fertile soil. The Red Messiah was about to liberate the world from
all its woes.

The wave broke. The Bolsheviks occupied Bialystok. In their wake
there arrived the theatrical troupe of Sniegov and Dubrolov. I am
constantly surprised that father can recall such detail. He does so
only when I pin him down with specific questions. Otherwise he
continues for hours on end, when in full flight, painting vast

canvasses of life in those tumultuous times. He spells it for me: S-n-i-e-g-o-v and D-u-b-r-o-l-o-v. Zachariah was hired to work behind the scenes, prompting from the scripts of Maxim Gorky and other revolutionary writers.

The Bolshevik interlude was short-lived. They were driven from the city when the Polish nationalists regained control and reclaimed territory lost to the Czars over a century earlier. An independent republic of Poland emerged; Josef Pilsudski was the man of the hour.

Zachariah chose to go east with Sniegov and Dubrolov. They toured Russia, performing plays within the fledgling Soviet Union. At about this time Zachariah took to centre stage to act out in reality the scripts he had been prompting. He left the troupe to join the Red Army. I have not been able to gather information from our fragmented fund of family remembrances about Zachariah's involvement in the civil war between the Reds and the Whites. He lost touch with friends and relatives in Bialystok — swallowed up, it seemed, by the Revolution. Nothing was heard from him for years.

In Red Square tourists gather to watch the changing of the guard in front of Lenin's mausoleum. Three soldiers in olive uniform, with white gloves, knee-high leather boots, and bayonets held aloft, goose-step towards the two guards who have been standing rigidly to attention by the tomb for several hours. After the exchange three soldiers march away, goose-stepping first right, then left, stiff legged, like drunken puppets dancing a spastic waltz.

An empire, it seems, requires such rituals, and a figurehead who personifies its authority. That figure remains Vladimir Ilyich Lenin. His portrait appears on billboards and posters the length of the realm. There are sculptures of his bust in town squares, on railway stations, in government offices. There are institutes and museums devoted to his every move, the details of his life story, works, and pronouncements. He is the Holy Father of the Revolution, and Karl Marx the Holy Ghost, their portraits often displayed side by side.

The Communist Party completes the Trinity, officiating from the central cathedral of the Revolution, the Kremlin, which stands by Red Square. Above its spires is one of the symbols of the faith, the five-pronged star. It flashes gold in the mid-afternoon sun; nearby, crucifixes reflect gold from the spires of St Basil's Cathedral. A remnant of the old order survives, a Byzantine fantasy saved from oblivion by its bizarre shapes and gaudily painted domes and towers. From crucifix to five-pronged star: from one form of state-controlled religion to another.

In 1926 a letter arrived from the Soviet Union addressed to Sheine Liberman Zabludowski:

> My dearest Mamushka, I live now in Leningrad. I have a wife, Tzivie, a school teacher from Riga. We have been married five years and have two sons. The oldest is four years old and we have given him the name Vladimir; the other is one and is called Ilyich. Mamushka, I miss you. We have obtained a permit so you can visit us. Come and meet your grandchildren.

Sheine Liberman had always been very close to Zachariah, father claims. She often called him 'ziebendl', her 'little seven', because he had been born two months prematurely. She marvelled that Zachariah had grown up so tall and healthy despite spending only seven months in the womb.

Grandmother Sheine made her way by train to Leningrad, city of canals and palaces, the St Petersburg of her childhood dreams, an inaccessible citadel in a remote kingdom. She took a long and circuitous route. Father says she lost her way somewhere deep within the Soviet empire. For several weeks she was shunted from one train to another. She travelled through cities bedecked in red. She waited in stations plastered with revolutionary slogans. She moved through towns and cities lit up at night, recently electrified — a testimony to the greatness of the Revolution, Zachariah was to tell her.

Mamushka found her way eventually to an apartment at number twenty, Ulitza Niekrasowa, Leningrad. My father had hesitated at first, and concentrated intensely for several minutes, during which he constantly stroked his forehead. 'I've got it', he exclaimed suddenly: 'Number twenty, Ulitza Niekrasowa'. And on his face there had appeared a triumphant smile, an eighty-year-old man overjoyed that his faculties were intact, his memory so sharp.

Grandmother Sheine returned to Bialystok a few weeks later with wondrous stories and two jars of marmalade made by daughter-in-law Tzivie. Her ziebendl had become an important man, she claimed.

He had studied, become an engineer as well as a singer, his baritone trained and refined at the Leningrad conservatorium. His job was to divide spacious apartments and redistribute them, 'according to need', he had told mamushka with pride.

It was the springtime of Revolution. When Zachariah arrived home from work he would ask his elder son to step forward and stand to attention. Zachariah would salute and command: 'Ready?' Vladimir would return the salute and reply: 'Always ready. Always ready to serve the people.' Grandmother Sheine, however, had a few tricks of her own, rituals far more ancient. She told Vladimir to close his eyes, after which she massaged the sockets with fresh eggs, to protect him from the evil eye. Comrade Lenin may well have turned in his fresh grave at this sacrilege.

Sheine Liberman's stories of her ziebendl and her glimpse at what was taking place on the other side of the border stirred my father's curiosity. Perhaps it was indeed the Paradise so many dreamed of at that time, especially in a Poland immured in poverty and stagnation. Perhaps there were better prospects in the young Red Empire. Father wrote to Zachariah. He poured out his ideas, his longings, his feelings to the brother he had idolized; page after page, revealing himself as if kneeling at a confessional. It was a novella that Zachariah received in the mail, father has told me.

Zachariah's reply was acidic, and littered with slogans and labels:

> With your present orientation and outlook, you are unsuitable for a revolutionary society. You are too much a Romantic, an individualist, a Tolstoyovich with petit-bourgeois fantasies of peaceful reform. You don't understand reality. You dwell too much upon the beauty of nature rather than focussing on class struggle. Study the works of Lenin and Marx rather than your bourgeois poets. Identify with the workers, share their fate, and perhaps then there will be a place for you here.

Father comes to me with revelations. It is as if he hoards secrets which he will release only at the appropriate time. Whenever we had talked of Zachariah there was never a hint that something tangible of his presence existed in the house — until the day father reached beneath his bed and pulled out a cardboard box in which he had stored a number of documents. He extracted a manilla envelope which he had labelled, "Sentimental". 'Beware of sentimentality', the old man has often warned me. He maintains a tight rein on his feelings, and reveals them only when pressured. 'That is why I have lived so long', he claims.

Within the larger envelope there is a smaller one, postmarked in Russian, dated May 25, 1926. The letter is short, written in pencil on both sides of a single sheet of unlined paper. Scrawled in Yiddish, it is far softer in tone than I had imagined from stories about Zachariah. He informs Sheine that her grandchildren often think of the babushka who had recently visited them:

> At the dinner table there are disputes over the utensils you left behind. Vladimir has appropriated babushka's spoon, but the knife and fork have been put aside for Ilyich. The plate however, they have to share. In this way their babushka is with us at every meal.

This was one of the last letters between the two households. It had become apparent that they were being intercepted on both sides of the border. Police agents raided the Zabludowski home in Bialystok and searched for incriminating documents. Father was detained overnight at police headquarters, interrogated, and accused of having links with the Bolsheviks. Letters from Leningrad were cited as evidence. On Zachariah's part it was increasingly dangerous to write to Bialystok, for fear of being accused of having connections with 'reactionaries' and 'foreign spies'. Correspondence ceased. Nothing has been heard of Zachariah or his family since.

All afternoon newly married couples arrive in Red Square with their wedding entourages, to lay wreaths at Lenin's mausoleum and to be photographed against St Basil's Cathedral or the Kremlin. Groups of schoolchildren in navy-blue skirts and trousers, white shirts, and red neckties tour the square, their teachers fussing over them. Muscovites approach me in the streets to whisper, 'Have you anything for sale?' They are hungry for perfume, a copy of *Vogue* or *Playboy*, American cigarettes, a pair of blue jeans — any forbidden fruit. Long queues snake from shops and restaurants. People wait stoically, resigned, with an occasional flicker of discontent. In the subways thousands of fatigued commuters sway against each other in crowded carriages. The dominant expression seems to be an ironic smile.

It can be felt at the edges, a faint breeze, a patient expectation;

something is stirring in Moscow, in the summer of 1986. Yet the city remains at arm's length, not quite accessible, a veil between me and the descendants of Uncle Zachariah. After all, I am in transit for just two days. My mind is on other destinations and a time far removed, when an ancestor arrived with the theatrical troupe Sniegov and Dubrolov to tour the provinces proclaiming the birth of a new order; and on a continent far distant, where under a bed there lies a frayed letter detailing the means of the distribution of grandmother Sheine's cutlery and plate between two children called Vladimir and Ilyich.

'Beware of sentimentality', the old man has often warned. 'That is why I have lived so long.'

Chapter Four

A TRAIN MOVES across the Soviet-Polish border. Flat fields extend
to the edge of a flat universe. Haystacks criss-cross rectangular fields.
Isolated homesteads shelter under clusters of pine: solid mansions
that exude a sense of solitude, and thatched cottages that hint at
warmth and intimacy. A car moves just below the horizon harmonising with the movement of the train. The Bialystoku region
extends north for several hundred kilometres. A summer Sunday
welcomes me quietly to the land of ancestral presences.

The train pulls into a provincial station. Booths aflame with
bunches of flowers line the platforms. Customers make their last-
moment purchases which they present, soon after, to a friend or
relative who has just disembarked. Scouts carrying knapsacks file
by. There is little regimentation; rather, a sense of ease on a casual
Sunday of open-necked shirts, unhurried conversation, cotton skirts,
and flowers.

The journey has become one flowing movement that now conveys
me across the Vistula and down into underground tubes which curve
beneath a sprawling metropolis. Warsaw Centralny Station. I walk
from the station with a rucksack on my shoulders. The heart of the
city is deserted and silent. I am within that still point which rests
between breaths. There is no longer the sense of urgency I have felt
so often since I first planned this journey, no longer any need to hurry.

Everyone seems to have a different estimate. Some claim there are
several thousand, scattered throughout the metropolis in isolated

pockets. Others say, with annoyance, 'Don't listen to such grand-mothers' tales; there are no more than a few hundred, and most of them are old, receding into the shadows you are pursuing. The one place you can be certain, well, almost certain, of finding more than a quorum assembled at any one time, is within the newly restored Warsaw synagogue, on the Sabbath. Postpone your journey until the weekend. Bialystok can wait a few days. And besides, what do you think you will discover there? The Messiah? Here at least there are some Jews; there you will need a miracle to find just one.'

Warsaw synagogue, mid morning. Of the fifty or so in attendance, about half are immersed in prayer. The others seem restless. They pray on the move, circling the hall from one huddle of friends to the next, grabbing a quick chat here and there. A steady murmur of voices conveys the discordant tones of a Sabbath service in which Hebrew prayers mingle with a babble of conversations in Polish, Russian, Yiddish, English, and a smattering of other tongues. At times the chatter ascends above the prayers and provokes an angry rebuke from an irate member of the congregation: 'Enough already! Have you forgotten what we are here for?'

Newcomers are instantly noticed and greeted warmly. 'Shalom-aleichem. Where are you from? Australia? So far away? How goes it for a Jew over there? You can speak a word of Yiddish? Step up to the pulpit and read for us a portion of the Torah. Can you give us a donation? A little something for our shul? It never hurts to give. Come. Meet our friends. Nathan! What do you know? A Jew from Melbourne.'

Nathan Berman shakes my hand vigorously. He greets me with a booming voice which issues from somewhere deep within his con-siderable frame, as if driven by a bellows that pumps forth an enveloping warmth. His words resonate through the prayer hall. 'Sshhh. Be quiet! Have you forgotten what we are here for?', comes the voice of admonition from the bowels of the chamber.

Nathan is a large man spread wide and tall. His luxuriant eye-brows arch in perfect symmetry and add a touch of the aristocratic to his weathered face. Tufts of hair spring from an otherwise glistening pate; reddish clumps which, like the eyebrows, are tinged with grey. He is about sixty, but robust, exhaling rapid-fire talk with an urgency that hints at a fear of boredom and lonely nights.

'A man must enjoy life and keep moving', he exclaims, his body heaving and sweating as we climb the wooden staircase which spirals from an inconspicuous back entrance to the synagogue. I have gathered from him, so far, that he is a professor of mathematics, retired. He was born in Warsaw, stumbled in adolescence through the war years, emigrated to Palestine, and has lived for decades in New York. But his heart gravitates here, he tells me more than once, and he comes every year now, for several months. 'It's a madness. Yet somehow, in Poland I feel most at ease. It has the smell of my childhood and a distant remembrance of the womb. I have a flat in Warsaw, and a girlfriend. She's a Poilishe. She knows how to look after me: a true sweetheart. Sometimes, mind you, she gets cold feet and runs to the priest. So let her confess! It does no harm. At such times I have many friends to spend time with. We take trips to the Tatras mountains, to Zakopane, Krakow, Gdansk, the Baltic Sea resorts, as I did during my youth. What more is there to say? This wilderness is for me a home, a habit I cannot break.'

We emerge from the stairs into a crowded dining room with a dozen tables scattered over exposed floorboards. Nathan has donated a Kiddush, a little something to eat and drink for the Sabbath. We are served bread rolls and gefilte fish — imported from Hungary, Nathan informs me. On each table he places several bottles of vodka which are quickly consumed.

The room sways with conversation. Guests circulate from table to table. A man seats himself beside me and announces, without introduction, that he has two brothers, both of whom are rabbis. 'One lives in Brooklyn, the other in Buenos Aires. And I, may the devil have such luck, live in Warsaw, where there is no one you could call a rabbi.'

Holding court at the same table is a visitor from New York. His face is set in a permanently sour expression. He is wearing a pink suit, mauve shirt, and a crimson tie which dangles over the gefilte fish as he proclaims: 'My son is an adviser to the President. You've never heard of him? Of course not! How could you? He is no boaster. He maintains low profile.' My newly acquired friend throws his well-worn refrain at Pink Suit: 'I have two brothers. Both rabbis. One in Buenos Aires, the other in Brooklyn. Mermelstein is the name. Perhaps you know him?' Pink Suit, annoyed at the interruption to his monologue, shoots back: 'Know him? Why should I? You think I should know every Jew in New York?'

A gaunt stalk of a man paces around the room, his eyes aflame as he mutters to any unsuspecting guest whom he ensnares with his relentless gaze. He is wrapped in a shabby suit, and his face has the corrugated tan of a tramp who sleeps by highways and in barns. He stutters angrily, in a monotone of broken English: 'I have put my case to the chief rabbi of Israel. I wrote him a long letter. I sent also a copy to Gorbachev. Neither of them has replied.' He strides away before he can be engaged in dialogue, and from time to time I hear his voice rise above the tumult with the same fierce lament. 'What is his case?' I ask Nathan. 'Ah! Here everyone has a case', he says. 'They cling to their cases for fear of opening them and seeing, with finality, that they are empty, and were in fact emptied one lost generation ago.'

Nathan waltzes back into the chaos. He is the attentive host, pouring a glass of vodka here, serving a slice of honey cake there, dispensing gusts of laughter and humorous remarks for dessert. The room dances with increasing abandon, a whirlpool of drink and talk at the centre of which sits Reb Greenbaum. A fertile beard flows from his cheeks, and he strokes it while he observes the revelry with a bemused smile. His eyes are a sheepish green, slightly moist, somewhat remote. He seems always to be hovering on the verge of a sigh. Nathan had pointed him out in the hall, totally absorbed in prayer: 'He's the only one in this shul that I can guarantee is one hundred per cent pious. The others come to talk, to do business, to pass the time. They are as pious as cats', claims Nathan. 'Only Greenbaum I can guarantee. He walks all the way from Praga, on the other side of the river, refusing any form of transport on Shabbes. The genuine article, one hundred per cent.'

Everyone seems to be talking at the tops of their lungs, although at close range I realize many of them are actually whispering with an urgency which lifts their voices into stabs that punctuate the air. At the height of the storm a scream arises. A spasm of fear shudders through the room. An uneasy silence stretches the seconds, broken only by the sounds of a woman sobbing. 'This is a cursed place', she says repeatedly. But Greenbaum remains undaunted. He reaches out and touches her on the back: a gentle pat, a knowing smile. The woman dissolves into laughter. As her mirth increases, the spell she has cast is abruptly broken. The room spins back into the storm. The remnants of Warsaw Jewry, or at least a proportion of them, dance frenzied conversations on a naked timber floor in the garret of a synagogue. And the next moment they are gone, the room deserted, except for a woman who alternately weeps and laughs, and an exhausted Nathan Berman who stands among the abandoned chairs like an actor deprived of an audience.

As we make our way down the spiral staircase we stumble across the last departing guests. They toil slowly, an odd couple, leaning often against the wall to grab another breath of air. The woman is wafer thin except for a leg, swathed in bandages, bulging out to elephantine proportions. Her eyes, in spite of their vein-ridden whites, are kindly and girlish. Her face tapers to a sharp chin that sprouts grey bristles. Her hair has withered to strands of decaying straw. A worn cardigan and cotton dress hang from a body that has barely enough substance to keep clothes afloat. Her companion hunches beneath his shoulders. He looks up just occasionally to glance at us timidly as we edge by. He wears a limp grey suit and huddles against the frail elf as he steers her down the stairs. They both carry plastic bags full of leftover food from the Kiddush.

As we are squeezing past we are stalled, involuntarily, by a barely audible monologue that issues from the lips of the elf. Her lilting Yiddish takes us on a stroll to a cemetery in a village near Krakow, forty-five years ago. We are caught in her labyrinth, the four of us balanced on three stairs, Nathan's massive frame swaying nervously, as a girl called Chanele Fefferberg hides for two years in a burial ground. She witnesses mass executions as she darts from stone to stone. One day her mother, father, brothers, and sisters are among those the SS drag to the cemetery. Chanele maintains her girlish smile, a set grin in eyes that are far distant. I realise this is her permanent tale, which she weaves without beginning or end. There is no need to intervene, or to do anything but gently disengage ourselves from her universe, and unwind out of the creaking folds of the synagogue into the fresh air.

I accompany Nathan in search of a coffee shop. On Saturday afternoons central Warsaw is lifeless. The people are at home in their private domains or in the countryside to absorb the final few weeks of summer. Within the weekend emptiness the heart of the city is exposed as a curious mixture of boutiques with modern facades, supermarkets with emptied shelves, boarded-up foodstalls, and run-down buildings surrounding vacant lots given over to silence and the occasional solitary pedestrian.

Nathan guides me through this wilderness to the Samantha coffee shop. Single men sit at laminated tables sipping drinks. Elvis Presley sings, 'Come with me to Blue Hawaii'. When at last the caffeine stirs in his veins, Nathan winks at the waitress behind the counter and comes back to life with tales of Polish girlfriends, disapproving priests, and escapades to holiday resorts. 'I come to Poland to have a good time, not to fall prey to the gloomy past. Life here is cheap. The dollar goes very far, especially on the black market. Time passes smoothly.'

Like an apparition, the odd couple appear, struggling along the pavement, turtle-paced, in full view of the Samantha. Chanele drags her swollen appendage, inching her way through the street. Her escort pauses occasionally to examine objects lying in the gutter.

Nathan registers their presence uneasily. Fatigue and sadness skitter beneath his surface gaiety. We watch their progress in silence, until they are fully out of sight. Nathan orders a second cup of coffee, stirs in three, perhaps four teaspoons of sugar, and remarks with a touch of defiance: 'As far as I'm concerned Reb Greenbaum is the only kosher Jew left in Warsaw. The rest are battlers and shnorrers. They live in the past and can barely deal with the present. But Greenbaum I can guarantee you. A pious man. There were tens of thousands like him, before the Annihilation. Now there is just Greenbaum. But him I can guarantee. A true Tzaddik. The genuine article. One hundred per cent!'

Marszalkowska Avenue winds for many miles through central Warsaw. It is so bloated that the opposite sides seem lost to each other. But in some sections it narrows to a more intimate scale, enclosed by buildings whose shadows touch in the early mornings and evenings. In pre-war times the display windows of department stores lining the avenue drew thousands of passers-by. Among them there wandered my father during one of his rare visits to Warsaw. Marszalkowska was a thoroughfare of the future, an avenue of dreams that challenged the provincial outlook of a man from the flatlands of White Russia. Dummies clothed in the latest fashions from the

West glittered reflections of legendary cities: Paris, London, Berlin, Rome.

Warsaw overwhelmed father. He preferred the moderate scale and familiarity of his native Bialystok. Yet he was irresistibly drawn to wander the streets of the city which had become, by the 1920s, the vibrant centre of Polish Jewry. He would lose himself in its maze of courtyards and neighbourhoods, its self-contained kingdoms of stone-clad tenements teeming with feverish activity. Within the courtyards grandmothers sold potato latkes, hawkers peddled a wide array of household needs, artisans sat in cramped workshops to ply their trades; while mothers tended their hordes of children, who seemed to split the seams of their crammed apartments and spill out into the passageways, into the open air, like plants reaching desperately for light.

Street musicians and jesters would spread their blankets and make their frantic bid for a living. Crowds quickly surrounded them, while from the upper reaches faces peered down from windows and balconies where drying clothes fluttered in the breeze. The cries of new-born babies mingled with the relentless clatter and chatter of commerce, as the performers strained to be heard above the din. And, on days when their coffers were empty, they would mutter, 'You may as well go beat your head against the wall'.

Father recalls sprawling markets where life was endlessly recycled until there was hardly a thread left on a garment or barely a leg for a table to stand on. There were goods for sale that nowadays you would find only in rubbish dumps. Father is at pains not to romanticise Warsaw, yet his growing excitement in describing it betrays his efforts. Images tumble out in a rush: of side-streets where yeshiva boys and talmudic scholars swayed in houses of worship; of homes which were merely a room in a garret or basement; of makeshift timber shacks that had somehow found a place between the brick and mortar. Every square centimetre of space was used by the devout or profane — for business or prayer, scriptural studies or a game of cards.

But the Vistula River, that was a different matter altogether. Here, father's voice slows down, and his hands stroke the air gently. The Vistula was a retreat from the tumult, a comfort, full of stillness, such a contrast to what was happening in the bowels of the city. Ferries and barges steamed by, and the vast expanse of water hinted at broad estuaries that meandered into oceans he would one day cross to gain access to a new life.

From the river banks the streets climb as steeply today as they did then, when father trudged back towards the boulevards, the beckoning display-windows, the avenues crowded with trolleys, horse-drawn coaches, and omnibuses. Pedestrians chewed bagels on the run. Bearded Hasidim hurried to and from prayer averting their eyes from the temptations of modernity; and the sons and daughters of wealthy bankers and financiers flocked to the Bar Central nightclub to hear Rosenbaum's jazz band play music of the New World.

Again the images are racing, father's hands are dancing, and Warsaw whirls into a frenzy of activity as the hub, the headquarters of political movements left, right, and indifferent. Bundists, Zionists, assimilationists, the orthodox, and freethinkers fought each other for communal control and allegiance. Their many factions and splinter groups seemed to rain down upon the city like confetti at a never-ending society wedding. Yiddish theatre groups played to full houses every night; provincial circuses pitched their tents in vacant lots; and news vendors sold Yiddish dailies, Hebrew periodicals, Polish tabloids, and cheap paperback romances. Circles of aspiring artists and writers gathered in cafés and meeting rooms to argue, exchange ideas, and feel the ebb and flow of what they believed to be a wave forever rolling towards an inevitable redemption. Warsaw was the vortex that absorbed the creative energies of a people who had honed their survival skills on the piercing edges of wildly fluctuating fortunes and centuries of impending disaster. And in the final years of the 1930s it stood poised, a community of 350 000 Jews, teetering on the brink of annihilation.

I turn off Marszalkowska into Ulitza Litewska, a street shaded by trees and medium-rise flats clad in greystone. Pre-war Warsaw endures in these cool shadows, its fading elegance intact. An arched entrance draws me into a courtyard presided over by hanging gardens suspended from balconies. Craning my neck I see them rising upwards, seven storeys of subdued greys interspersed with splashes of colour sprouting from miniature jungles of potplants. Each entrance — from street to courtyard, from courtyard into dark foyer, from stairs onto a third-floor landing — brings me closer to the familiarity I crave.

Szymon Datner, historian of Bialystok, is a frail man in his seventies. He walks with difficulty, each step an act of will as he guides me into his study. It is lined with books from floor to ceiling, numerous volumes with titles in English, Polish, Russian, French, Hebrew, and Yiddish. Among the books there are spaces in which stand wooden statuettes carved by folk artists: figures of klesmorim, the families of musicians who played at shtetl festivals and weddings. Wooden parrots daubed in purple, scarlet, and turquoise perch on antique cabinets. On every spare area of wall space hang paintings and photos: family friends, historical figures, and scenes of pre-war Bialystok. In the centre of the room there is an oak table, reassuringly bulky. Nearby stands a desk cluttered with papers, manuscripts, dictionaries, writing pads: a work in progress.

The room is saturated with learning: that ambience of cultured and humane fellowship which led me at an early age to identify with a continent I had never seen. Europe meant a sense of warmth and scholarship, love of family and tradition. It had the scent of yellowing manuscripts which evoked and spoke of bygone centuries hidden in mist-laden valleys. It was only in later years that the child began to be aware of cracks which undermined the fragile romance. Beneath the surface there hovered a different Europe of tribal brutality, where books were piled onto bonfires around which armies of the night danced in a frightening frenzy.

In Szymon Datner's study, Europe-the-haven prevails, in a room watched over by a wise guardian. Potplants are scattered throughout, their leaves spilling over with vitality. They reach towards rays of light that filter through double doors opening out onto a balcony. Books and plants, heart and mind, the Europe of my primal imaginings is concentrated in this one room hidden within the centre of 1980s Warsaw.

Szymon Datner lives out his remaining years in Warsaw, an internal exile, documenting the history of Bialystok in books and articles I have read on the other side of the globe. He is puzzled as to why I am so intent on exploring a city which he sees as one massive tomb. '*A Yid derkent nisht zein Bialystok*', he tells me — a Jew cannot recognise his Bialystok. In common with others I have met in this past week, he too has a refrain that ripples through his reminiscences.

As we converse, Datner's initial wariness fades and gives way to a fatherly warmth. I am, after all, the grandson of Bishke Zab-ludowski. Datner's eyes light up with the remembrance . . . Bishke, standing beneath the town clock behind a pile of newspapers, the transmitter of local news and gossip, the town crier who reduced momentous historical changes to a succession of headlines. He was the constant, a reassuring presence when time still had meaning, and when the young Datner, then a teacher of physical education at a Hebrew College, could still count on a future.

Bialystok is burning, and an old man in Warsaw is telling me that he is circling the flames, trying desperately to get through from the surrounding forests where he roams as a partisan and courier, moving in and out of the ghetto, delivering messages, smuggling food and arms, helping to foster and co-ordinate the Resistance, as he has been for many months, until this day when the ghetto is burning, and he cannot get through; and he knows that his wife and chil-dren are somewhere within, but all he can do is circle the flames. And over forty years later it seems as though he is still circling the flames, daring himself to come closer, then withdrawing, scorched, to pen the details of his vision as he retreats into his endless refrain: 'A Jew cannot recognize his Bialystok'.

Datner fetches a large pre-war map of Bialystok which he spreads across the oak table. It is a detailed directory of streets, many of which have changed names or no longer exist. 'The city you will see tomorrow', he tells me, 'will be, at best, a distorted reflection of what once was.' It is as if, slowly and deliberately, he is wiping out any false expectations I may have, just as I am about to see Bialystok with my own eyes.

Chapter Five

SOON AFTER DAWN the Bialystok express emerges out of the subways of central Warsaw. A mist rises from the Vistula, unveiling a metropolis stirring into life. Just beyond the city limits a heron perches, motionless, on the banks of a stream. A woman dressed in pink sits astride a motorcycle at a level crossing. A farmer milks a cow on an embankment by the rail tracks; behind him, in the fields, rows of haystacks perspire vapours of gold-dust. Warmth spreads as the carriages are heated by an ascending sun. A moving landscape eases me into stillness. It is as if I have always been here, watching from a mobile window, tracing a path along the periphery of ancestral lands.

Open countryside gives way to the fringes of a city. On the outskirts loom high-rise housing estates. The rays of a midday sun mingle with the fumes of industry. The train slows down through a gauntlet of factories and emerges against a long platform drawing into Bialystok station.

A hand touches me gently on the shoulder, an unexpected greeting. I had met Witold's wife in Warsaw and she had offered me a room in their Bialystok flat. Witold welcomes me and we drive immediately to the centre of the city. A sudden halt, and we are in front of the clock-tower. 'Give my regards to the town clock', were the last words my father had said to me when I left Melbourne. But he doubted whether it was still standing. And in a sense he was right. The clock-tower that overlooks the central square is a replica, erected after the War on the site where the celebrated original had stood. In fact the entire central enclave is a replica, recreated brick by brick in a land where memories cling tenaciously and demand to be honoured. Flowers in full bloom pour from balconies. Wooden cottages adjoin tenements that match pre-war appearances. Bialystok is far more ancient and beautiful than I had expected; at least, this is how it appears at first sight.

Witold leads me to a plaque inconspicuously attached to a building facing the pavement. It indicates that here once stood the Great Synagogue of Bialystok. 'I was over there, on Friday morning, June 27th, 1941', Witold tells me, as he points to the corner diagonally opposite. The soldiers were annoyed at the nine-year-old Polish boy roaming the streets, hindering their work. They pushed him aside but he stayed, transfixed, as grenades exploded in nearby Jewish neighbourhoods, sending smoke billowing skywards. Menfolk were being dragged from their homes and driven to the house of worship. They were crammed inside, the doors locked and barred, the building doused with petrol and set alight. The intensity of the fumes drove Witold back. He saw windows broken and figures trying desperately to escape, only to be gunned down by the cordon of soldiers surrounding the inferno. The synagogue burned for twenty-four hours. Over fifteen hundred perished in the fire. This was the first Aktion; the day the Nazis entered Bialystok.

The tone has been set for my stay in Bialystok; an inevitable pattern, in fact, determined long before my arrival. Romance and terror, light and shadow, replicas and originals, hover side by side, seeking reconciliation, while within me there is a sense of awe and a silent refrain: I am here, at last I am here; and it is far more beautiful than I had imagined. And far more devastating. Yet, somehow, never have I felt so much at peace.

In 1320 a village is founded on the banks of the Biale by a Lithuanian nobleman, Count Gedimin. When my father tells the story he loves to separate the syllables. Any chance to dissect a word, any chance to take it back to its origins, he seizes upon with relish; for in words, he claims, lies the essence of things. Biale means white. Stok is a Slavic word for river. The kingdom of the White River is where we come from, says father, with one of his Romantic flourishes.

The village of Bialystok is handed down through generations of Lithuanian families until 1542, when the Polish King Zygmund August marries the widowed and childless Lithuanian Princess Varvara, and the lands of the White River become his private fiefdom. Six years later the first Jews settle in the village.

We leap through the centuries. Bialystok becomes entrenched Polish territory and the property of the Branitski family. In 1703 Count Stefan Branitski erects a wooden palace by the White River. Under Branitski patronage a house of worship is built in 1718 and evolves into a synagogue court around which Jewish settlement expands.

Count Jan Klemens Branitski the Second inherits the village from Stefan. As a child I would often gaze at his portrait in the Bialystok photo album, fascinated by his globular head. The Count's face is a fat full moon. A black toupee forms a perfect crescent on the uppermost rim. A formidable forehead descends beneath the crescent to thick but neatly trimmed brows arching over fiery black eyes. A handlebar moustache extends well past the extremities of the mouth, placed high above an enormous chin that collapses into several folds, rolling in waves across a bullish neck. A velvet cape is draped across a white blouse buttoned high onto the lower rim of the moon. The Count glows with the proud confidence of born rulers. The eyes, however, speak of something deeper, of cosmic visions and universes far beyond a mere village.

Jan Klemens propels Bialystok into the future. Anxious to expand, the Count invites Jews from nearby hamlets to settle and help build a town. In 1745 they are granted equal rights, and in the same year a wooden tower is erected over a municipal hall to be used as a prison for criminals on remand. Under the tower eighty shops are built and divided among Jewish families. Each family is given a key for which they must pay three gold coins — at least, this is how the story is told. We are in territory in which the boundaries between history and legend are thin.

In 1750 the entire settlement is destroyed by fire. Undaunted, the Count supervises the reconstruction of Bialystok. A more solid core of brick and stone emerges, with a new clock-tower — which is destined to become the first sight my father registers, as a two-year-old, dressed in a sailor suit, running beside his mother through the town square.

Count Jan Klemens Branitski dies in 1771 and bequeaths Bialystok to his third wife, Isabella, a sister of Stanislaw Poniatowski, the last of the Polish kings. Towards the end of the eighteenth century, Bialystok's fate is increasingly determined not so much by local nobility, as by decisions taken in distant palaces, in the courts of contending empires eager to feed their voracious appetites for more territory. The ancient Polish-Lithuanian kingdom is dismembered in a series of partitions. Austro-Hungary, Prussia, and czarist Russia scurry off like hungry wolves clutching their share of the spoils.

The pace is fast; the game played for high stakes. Prussia grabs control of Bialystok in the partition of 1795. Napoleonic armies on the march eastwards take over the city for a year. In 1807 it falls into Russian hands. Napoleon recaptures White River territory in 1812. Three years later Czar Alexander the First regains jurisdiction and, for the time being, the ferocious game comes to an end; during the next one hundred years Bialystok is firmly under Russian control.

An invasion of a different kind takes place. The Industrial Revolution finds its way to Bialystok. In 1850 Nachum Minc and Sender Bloch establish the first silk factories, and the city is spun into orbit around steam-driven machines churning out textiles that are exported throughout Eurasia. Bialystok is harnessed to the assembly line, with both Jewish and German entrepreneurs directing operations. A new class of workers emerge, their schedules dictated by machines that permeate the tempo of their lives. Soon after dawn, sirens shriek the start of another working day, a typical day which will last for decades, throughout the latter part of the nineteenth century. 'And thereafter', adds father, 'the Biale River was no longer white, but a dirty ribbon polluted by industrial waste.'

In the surrounding countryside there are hamlets and towns where the hand-loom, the craftsman, the peasant, and the shtetl community move at a slower pace. In these settlements there live the families Zabludowski, Probutski, Liberman, and Malamud. Aron Yankev Probutski of Orla marries Chane Esther of Grodek; Bishke Zabludowski of Orla marries Sheine Liberman of Bransk. They are drawn, like so many others of their generation, into an industrial vortex called Bialystok. The lure of the factory, of an expanding city, can no longer be resisted. A young family needs bread, work, prospects for a better life.

Bialystok bursts beyond its boundaries, its outer limits trailing off into wooden cottages. In the city centre, three- and four-storey buildings shoot up in a housing boom during the last decade of the nineteenth century. By 1900 there is a population of 70 000: communities of White Russians, Tartars, Ukrainians, Germans, Lithuanians, Cossacks, Gypsies, Poles, and 40 000 Jews.

Steam power is replaced by electricity. The machines spin faster. Boom is followed by economic bust. Bialystok is on the roller-coaster again. My father is born in the year of the first Russian Revolution. The czarist empire is shaken to its foundations, and in the aftermath there stream shock waves of reaction, pogroms, confusion, and false Messiahs. Floundering empires are again on the prowl, and Bialystok is yet again prey to the wolves. The Great War erupts. The armies of Kaiser Wilhelm capture a city set adrift in a no man's land between past and future. There is fighting in the streets. Regimes come and go overnight. Europe is frantically sorting itself out. Red Army fights White Army. Poles, Tartars, Ukrainians, and Lithuanians flex their nationalist muscles. Each tribe wants its own territory, while Jews and Gypsies look on perplexed, not quite sure which way the wind is blowing. Mother and father run errands for their families in streets where armies sweep past them running east and west. At night they shelter at home to the sound of sporadic gunfire and artillery.

'March, march Pilsudski', is the cry of the hour. In the 1920s the veteran nationalist triumphs and consolidates a reborn Poland. For two decades the infant republic remains poised in an uneasy truce between wars. Bialystok appears to flourish. Schools, secular and religious; houses of worship and study; cinemas and theatres; cafés, choirs, orchestras, and political parties all overflow with patrons, supporters, and fellow travellers. And years later group photos will appear in the albums of a vanished city, portraits frozen into still lives within which, if one looks closely enough, it is possible to discern the tiny face of my mother as a member of the Morning Star gymnastics troupe, or my father on an outing in the forests, with comrades of a youth movement called Future.

It could be said that these are good years: the harvests quite abundant; communal life intimate; love affairs permeated by the scent of forests; couples strolling arm in arm along tree-lined Sienkiewicza Avenue. And yet there are those who are boarding trains for distant ports, slipping away to faraway corners of the earth with a healthy sense of premonition, or just plain luck in having received a visa moments before the city gates are closed. To the west, armies are again assembling, with a ferocious hunger for conquest and territory, and a calculating madman at the helm.

As I wander the streets of Bialystok for the first time I follow primitive maps drawn by my parents, indicating the various neighbourhoods they had lived in. A light rain falls incessantly. A damp veil hangs over the city and keeps me at a distance. A cat sits inside a cottage window in front of a white lace curtain. Pedestrians scurry by under umbrellas and newspapers. More than ever Bialystok seems ethereal, a dream whose texture eludes me.

A fair-haired boy appears at the window and edges in beside the cat. He stares at me with cold suspicion, until I realise that I am confronting him with my sense of disorientation. When I smile, the boy instantly reflects my change of mood. He is joined by a girl of about three, a sister perhaps, and we are drawn, the four of us, into a sort of complicity, a bond of recognition between stranger, boy, girl, and cat. Someone calls from within the house. The children withdraw. The welcoming committee has retreated; but the veil has lifted, and I find myself in Ulitza Kievska, the street where my mother lived in the years immediately after World War 1.

The cobblestones of Kievska glisten under fresh coats of rain. The moisture has subdued their colours into sombre ochres and burgundies. Kievska is a mere hundred metres long, wedged between Ulitzas Grunwaldzka and Mlynowa. Mother had placed her house at number 14, perhaps 13. Number 13 is an abandoned weatherboard. The shutters are closed, except for one which swings in and out with the breeze. Through it I can see rooms scattered with debris, loose floorboards, and broken bottles. Directly opposite is a three-storey greystone building with an arched entrance: number 10. It fits mother's description, but not the address. Numbers 12 to 16 are non existent. In their place a stone wall encloses a yard piled high with used tyres and car parts. Adjoining the yard is an unkempt garden in which vegetable patches merge with wild flowers, shrubs, and trees. Two Alsatians bark ferociously as I peer over the wall.

A horse-drawn cart turns into Kievska and pulls aside to make

way for a car. An elderly couple walk along the pavement, where
tufts of grass spring from gaps between the cobblestones. Kievska
on this rain-soaked day seems so familiar; yet so downtrodden and
desolate, empty of the souls it once housed. *Judenrein*. A gust of
wind catches the shutter on number 13 and slams it back to a
close.

Twenty-four hours later the sun soars above the city. The shutters
on the cottages of Kievska are flung wide open. The windows frame
displays of potplants. Several windowsills are a jungle of ferns and
flowers which nestle together, vying like a crowd of eager spectators
for a view of the street, where cobblestones smoulder under the sun,
a muted blaze of faded reds and light browns.

Kievska is within the Chanaykes, a neighbourhood where impoverished Jewish families were concentrated in a whirl of alleys, narrow
streets, and back lanes which still continue to snake and curve into
each other like dancing dervishes. I am surprised at how intact it
appears, as if history had somehow overlooked this forgotten corner
of the world. On days like this, I imagine, the Probutski children,
the six sisters and three brothers, would spill into the streets to play
in vacant lots strewn with weeds and rubbish. Or perhaps it wasn't
like that at all, and I am merely imposing such a scene on empty
sites scattered throughout the neighbourhood like gaps in rows of
rotting teeth.

Ulitza Zolta is a dirt path which squeezes off Kievska between
several cottages before opening out into a large clearing that resembles
an abandoned town square. The Probutski family shifted house in
1920, from Kievska to somewhere in this vicinity; perhaps to the
two-storey building which stands apart, overlooking the clearing.

As I enter, I catch the scent of dust and rotting timber. A flight
of stairs leads to a balcony which overlooks the square, but I cannot
climb up to the attic that I believe my mother may have lived in.
The way is barred by an old man who sits in an armchair on the
first-floor landing. When I try to speak to him he does not respond.
I hand him a note which Witold has written in Polish, explaining
that my parents and their families may have once lived here. I am
from Australia, the note adds, and I am searching for their former
homes. The old man stares blankly into the distance. His head

occasionally falls limply to his chest and rolls from side to side while he mumbles incoherently to himself.

As I turn to leave I see a grey-haired lady clutching a shopping bag. She eyes me with suspicion as we pass each other on the stairs. I hand her the note, which she quickly scans. The old lady is unimpressed. I am an intruder.

His apartment is on the second floor of a six-storey tenement; one of several drab grey blocks built up from the ghetto ruins in the immediate post-war years. It is now run-down, cracking at the seams, joints wracked by arthritis. The stairs smell of fried onions and neglect. I am ushered into a sparsely furnished living-room with a single bed, table, and television set on a linoleum-covered floor.

He is rotund and squat, his substantial paunch offset by muscular shoulders that barely contain an outrageous energy which seems always on the verge of bursting beyond the confines of his tight body. He speaks to me with a conspiratorial air, while his hawk-like eyes, full of an ancient suspicion, dart from side to side, always alert, distracted. Buklinski, one of the very last of the Bialystoker Jews, has burst into my life.

Buklinski disappears into the kitchen and dashes back with plates of stewed potatoes and gefilte fish. 'Imported from Hungary', he announces triumphantly, jabbing his fingers at the fish. He runs back and forth from the kitchen, and soon the table is laden with bowls of herring, pickled onions, loaves of bread, cheeses, and several bottles of vodka. Buklinski seats himself opposite and commands, in a voice strewn with gravel, 'Nu? Eat! Is anyone stopping you? Who are you waiting for? The Messiah?' He speaks a rich colloquial Yiddish laced with earth, fire, and black humour. Looking at me, he muses: 'A miracle! Our Bialystoker have wandered off to the very ends of the earth in all their dark years, and yet their sons speak Yiddish. A miracle! Nu? What are you waiting for? Eat!'

The vodka flows. Buklinski's monologue accelerates. He weaves tall stories in a frenzy. 'I was born on Krakowska, in the Chanaykes, in that very same neighbourhood your mother lived in. We were crammed on top of each other; slept three, four, sometimes more to a bed. We froze in winter, baked in summer, and roamed the streets in gangs of little scoundrels who hunted in packs, seeing with our own eyes everything the heart desired — swindlers and saints, devoted mothers and beggars, prostitutes and yeshiva boys scurrying home, their eyes glued to their sacred books as they bumped into lamp posts. Ah, what a treasure it was to live in Bialystok! Well, my friend, what else could we do but love it? You think we had a choice? Well? What are you waiting for? Eat! Drink! Don't be shy!'

Whenever one dish is empty, Buklinski dashes back into the kitchen and emerges with reinforcements, plates piled high with cheese blintzes.

'This is my specialty, which you must eat.'

'You are like a Yiddishe mama', I protest.

'I'm better than a Yiddishe mama. No Yiddishe mama makes blintzes like mine.'

'But I'm full. I can hold no more.'

'Full. Shmul. There is always room for more. Eat! I cannot rest until I see you eat.'

Buklinski hovers around the table, restless, imploring, prodding, scolding: 'Eat! I won't sit down until you eat!'

Where have I heard these familiar words, the same pleas, this same script? Where have I seen that same intensity, and felt that same tinge of menace in the voice? I have known other Buklinskis. They stood in Melbourne homes, by tables overflowing with food and drink, and talked of hunger and mud.

'In two things I am an expert', Zalman would say. Zalman, the family friend, the Bialystoker, the survivor who had brought us tales from the kingdom of night. 'About two things I know all there is to know. In these things I am a scholar, an expert, a professor. In all other things I may be an ignoramus, but on two subjects I can lecture for days on end and never come to the end of it: mud and hunger. We lived in mud. For six years we were soaked in it. We came to know its subtle changes in texture, from day to day, hour to hour, depending on the amount of rain, the number of wagons and dragging feet that churned it up, the number of work battalions that laboured through it. The ghetto was an empire of mud. And hunger. Hunger had so many nuances, so many symptoms. Sometimes you felt so light, so empty, you could fly. But always it was an infernal ache, a relentless yearning, a search for any possible thing that could be chewed and swallowed. And now I know that a kitchen must be full, and a man is a fool who does not seize a chance to eat . . .'

But this is no time to philosophize. Buklinski has opened a second bottle of vodka. He is up on his feet, dancing around the table like a boxer between rounds. I try to break into his monologue from time to time, but Buklinski is a bulldozer who flattens me with his manic, domineering, frenzied, suspicious, yet affectionate energy. One moment he has his arms around me, and is kissing my cheeks with joy while exclaiming how good it is to have such a guest, a son of Bialystoker come half-way around the planet, the grandson of Bishke Zabludowski, no less, whom we all knew, and who didn't know him as he stood under the town clock selling newspapers, telling us what was going on in this twisted world, and now, can you believe it, his grandson has come to us from the very ends of the earth, like manna falling from the heavens. A miracle!

And the next moment he is wheeling and dealing, and claiming all foreigners have a dollar to spare and that money grows on trees over there, while we are stuck here, in this black hole, our friends old or dead, the clever ones gone, scattered over lands of milk and honey, while we, may the devil have such luck, we languish here where there aren't even enough Jews left for a quorum. So? What would it hurt to spare us a dollar? What harm would it do to give us a little something? And just as I think Buklinski has got me against the ropes he is suddenly off and running again, propelled into the kitchen by a burst of obsessive generosity to fetch a third bottle of vodka, another plate of pickled herring. *Nu?* What are you waiting for? Drink! Eat!

The room is bursting with heat and words. Buklinski jerks off his jacket. I see tattoos on both arms: a mermaid curls around one forearm, and on the other a muddy-blue clumsily applied number sprawls through a scattering of grey hair. 'Two years', he says quietly when he catches me looking. 'For two years I was in Auschwitz.' All words grind to an abrupt halt. Buklinski sits at the table, his head propped up on his elbows, his gaze extending beyond me, far beyond the confines of the apartment. Tears, just one or two, replace his torrent of words. They travel crookedly along paths that weave across a face engraved with furrows and troughs, the face of a member of an almost extinct tribe, one of the last Jews of Bialystok.

Buklinski is running ahead, dragging me by the arm. 'No one knows Bialystok as well as I do', he repeats for at least the fifth time this morning. In motion Buklinski is a tubby dynamo, fuelled by nervous energy and raw suspicion, trotting on his stout little legs. His stomach, the receptacle for a thousand-and-one meals of gefilte fish washed down by vodka, protrudes and bounces as he drives himself along. Head held high, hooded eyes squinting in the sun, nose sniffing the air, Buklinski nears the streets of the Chanaykes.

'This is my territory, Ulitza Krakowska. Here I was born. In 1919.' His words tumble out, breathless, between gulps of air. His fingers stab at the empty space where his house once stood. The Chanaykes is an amalgam of weed-strewn clearings, cobblestoned streets, and rheumatic timber cottages. We are on home turf, and Buklinski is a weather vane registering every slight shift in the atmosphere. His arms swing in one direction, then in another, a stream of anecdotes flowing from his fingers. 'That was a bordello', he exclaims. 'The boss lived upstairs, there, in the garret. I often saw his face poking out of that window, eyeing the customers who used to sneak in through that wooden gate. Fifty groshen it cost for doing it standing up, and one whole zloty for doing it lying down.'

Buklinski is unable to keep still. It is as if the streets are pursuing him and that, if he were to stop for long enough, they could lure him into a web of memories that would soon suffocate him. So he keeps running ahead, with short steps, while conducting a feverish commentary: 'This was once a prayer-house; that building housed a kibbutz where young pioneers prepared for the Promised Land. Over there stood a Hebrew college; here a Yiddish trade school.' Occasionally I register a deeper response, jolted by a sudden shock of recognition. The trade school features in my mother's repertoire of recollections; in this school she had learned to make dresses. 'Ah! You see? I know where to take you', Buklinski proclaims triumphantly. 'I know my Bialystok.'

On Ulitza Slonimska flocks of pigeons swoop down to perch on the window-sills of pre-war buildings. Their grey facades are a patchwork of exposed brick blotches coated with rust. We veer sharply into a narrow alley, to a timber shop-front painted clumsily in a pale blue wash. It leans askew, like a dilapidated shed on an abandoned farm. Inside the workshop Yankel the shoe repairer stands bent over a bench, cutting strips of leather. I am also introduced to Bunim, who is seated by the counter, his shoulders slumped, his head swaying as if in perpetual prayer.

'Bunim! Get us a bottle of schnapps!', Buklinski orders. 'Here! Take these zlotys and fetch us something to drink, something to bite.' Half an hour later the compliant Bunim shuffles back with a bottle of spirits. We tear chunks from a loaf of freshly baked bread, slice pieces of garlic and sausage, drink glass after glass of spirits, and the room blazes.

'Aron! Welcome to Bialystok!', Yankel exclaims after each toast. The room spins about us, a blur of shelves piled high with shoes, pieces of leather, soles and heels, tacks and nails, and workbenches crowded with an array of primitive tools with which to cut and glue, hammer and sew, brush and polish, while Yankel is drinking, working, and proclaiming: 'Aron! You cannot imagine what it was like!'. This is the refrain to which he constantly returns, as his story unfolds in a workshop saturated with the smell of garlic and sweat. 'You cannot imagine! We were hunted like animals, swatted like flies. Wives in front of husbands. Children in front of mothers. Aron! You cannot imagine what it was like!'

Yankel's eyes are sunk deep in their sockets, and nestle behind cheekbones that protrude, stretching taut the layer of beaten skin that clings to its skeletal frame. 'We ran like frightened hares into the countryside and burrowed under the ground. For two years I hid in my warren. At night I emerged to scavenge. Lice made a home in my flesh. We had a contract: I lived in a hole; they lived on me. Aron! You cannot imagine what it was like!'

This is what it is always like, I am beginning to see, when the last few Yidn of Bialystok gather, as they often do, since they crave each other's company; together they wax and wane like candles that flicker for a moment into glorious light, and then almost die out, as the flames shrink back into themselves, into indelible memories that will accompany them to the grave. 'When I came out of my warren for the final time, on a July day in 1944, I saw four Russian soldiers on horseback. The lice were crawling around me, going on family visits. I addressed the captain in Yiddish. He looked at me in astonishment and replied in the same mother tongue: "A living corpse! A survivor! A miracle!" He escorted me to the nearest village where he organised a banquet. I ate until I was sick.'

Several hours later I walk with Bunim, Bialystok's most dishevelled son. He shuffles, chin sunk into his chest. Occasionally he glances warily over his shoulders. 'Someone is always watching, always taking note', he warns. The Sabbath is approaching, creeping in along deserted streets that have retired for the weekend. The sky is streaked with wafer-thin clouds of mauve and crimson; Bunim is, as usual, close to tears. This is what Buklinski had warned me about: 'Watch out for him. Just give him a chance and he'll cry. Ah! Can he cry!'. He was the butt of many jokes that winked between Yankel and Buklinski. 'Look! It's coming! The storm is gathering. Bunim is about to cry. Ah! Can he cry!'

'Don't make such a noise', a perpetually anxious Bunim had said when our revelry had begun to shake the floorboards of Yankel's workshop. 'It's not wise for us to attract attention. You must always remember who we are and who they are', he had added, while motioning towards the window. 'Bunim is going to cry. It's coming! Ah! Can he cry!', replied the merciless duo, dancing arm-in-arm around the work benches.

Bunim's apartment is lean and bare, and mother Mary peers down at us, a babe with golden locks in her arms. The last shafts of light from a dying day poke into the kitchen, illuminating layers of peeling paint and cracks that thread through the walls like erratic blood vessels.

Bunim slumps into a chair and leans back against the wall. 'Bialystok is a stranger to me now, the streets are my enemies. I have wanted to leave for many years. One by one my friends have gone. But I must stay because she saved my life. For three years she hid me, fed me, and gave me warmth. So after the war I married her. She prays to an alien God. Christ is her saviour. And I'm not even worth her piss. You see my friend, she saved my life and I must stay with her.'

When Bunim speaks, the words are barely audible. He is almost a non presence, mumbling in the background, as if afraid to register his imprint upon the earth. The permanent red blotches on his cheeks deepen to beetroot in the evening shadows. The silence within the apartment seems to offer solace and relief, and for the first time there is a hint of ease on Bunim's unshaven face. 'I knew your grandfather', he says unexpectedly. 'Everyone knew your grandfather. A small man. With red hair, a red beard, he ran here and there under the clock-tower, always excited, always darting about like a rabbit. *Heint! Moment! Express!* Always shouting, selling, waving his arms, earning a few groshen from his newspapers. *Heint! Moment! Express!*'

Bunim rises from the chair, a sudden flicker of animation in his leaden body, his bloodshot eyes aflame, the words tumbling out rapid fire, his voice reaching above whispers: '*Heint! Moment! Express!* He stood on the corner of Geldowa and Kupietzka, just a block from here. Everyone knew your grandfather. *Heint! Moment! Express!*'

And, just as abruptly as it has risen, Bunim's voice trails off into a confused monologue, and his body slumps back into a chair: 'My father wanted me to be a talmudic scholar. I studied in yeshivas with great interpreters of the scriptures. But she saved my life, and I'm not even worth her piss. Children we could not have. That would have been a terrible transgression, an insult to my ancestors. And Bialystok I could not leave. That would have been a betrayal. After all, she saved my life . . .'

Everyone has his story; everyone his refrain. Aron! You cannot imagine what it was like! Aron! Do you know what a treasure it was to live in Bialystok? Aron! She saved my life and I'm not worth her piss. Aron! Eat. Drink. What are you waiting for? The Messiah? Aron! Do you know how wonderful it was to live in Bialystok? Aron! Please stay with us a little longer. Aron! Help us leave this God-forsaken hole. Take us with you to the land of milk and honey. Aron! I cannot leave. She saved my life. Aron! Spare us a dollar. What would it hurt to give? Aron! Eat! Drink! What are you waiting for? The Messiah? Aron! You can never imagine what it was like.

Chapter Six

HER EARLY CHILDHOOD was of palaces and weddings, mother has told me. The central palace was inaccessible. It loomed behind guarded gates and a high fence that could be seen from the street in which she lived. Sometimes she was taken on strolls around the perimeter of the palace grounds. She would peer through gaps in the fence at the imposing edifice set far back within lush gardens. Nowadays the gates are always open, the buildings used as an academy of medicine. A path stretches several hundred metres to the palace doors. A framework of scaffolding grips the walls, and workmen stand on platforms from which they restore the crippled facades.

Count Jan Klemens Branitski had the palace built in 1763. At that time Polish nobility tended to look west for models to emulate. They aspired to the grandeur of its monarchies; the palace was designed in the style of Versailles, complete with gardens laid out in perfect symmetry. But whereas the West may have inspired dreams of imperial splendour, the East emanated the threat of imperial might and the brute strength of the descendants of Peter the Great. The eastern empire triumphed in 1815. The Bialystok coat of arms — a knight on a rearing horse, shield grasped in one hand, sword brandished high above the head in the other — was removed, and Branitski's Versailles became known as the Czar's palace. A succession of Romanovs stayed there with their entourages en route to hunting expeditions in the Bielowieza forests.

The weddings were somewhat more accessible. The Probutski

family moved to Bialystok from the shtetl of Grodek in 1910. Mother was three years old at the time. Her new home was a timber cottage that stood in the grounds of the landlord's solid brick mansion. Directly opposite was a reception hall where weddings were held day and night, a perpetual simche, a seemingly endless celebration. Bands of klesmorim played for hours at a time, and the melodies of their violins and flutes hovered over neighbouring streets and lanes. While the guests danced within, the Probutski children stood on tiptoe outside, to catch a glimpse of the bride and groom through the windows. We are talking of events that took place over eighty years ago. At such a distance memories streak like fireflies that flash brightly for a moment in the mind of my mother, before receding back into the darkness. The son is hungry for information, for any spark that might illuminate the beginning of things.

In a wooden shack next to the Probutski home, within the grounds of the landlord's house on Ulitza Palacovej, there lives an elderly couple, Layser and Polina. When a buzzing sound is heard in the heavens on a midsummer's day in 1914, Layser and Polina rush out into the yard to join the crowd that has rapidly assembled, not so much out of alarm as out of curiosity. Layser, a devout Hasid who sees the hand of God at work in everything, jumps with joy as he points up at the sky: 'Look! A messenger from heaven! Could it be that the Messiah has come at long last?' He embraces Polina while the Probutski children run wild, circling the crowd, squealing and laughing as they point to the iron eagles winging above. This is a grand spectacle, a commotion, a miracle, a riddle. And as the crowd gazes the eagles release their droppings, and the first bombs rain down on Bialystok.

Layser is lost in the smoke and confusion. 'God is angry', he cries. 'We are not yet worthy of the Messiah.' Polina takes hold of him by the ears and drags him from the yard. 'Run, you old madman! This is no time for useless sermons!'

Everyone is running. The landlord has flung open the doors of his mansion; the crowd tumbles inside and descends to the cellar. Little Hershel, two years old, the last born of the nine Probutski children, sits on the cellar floor. With each explosion he claps his hands and exclaims: 'Another bomb! Another bomb!' This is a circus!

A carnival! Bialystok has become a wild fairground, alight with fires and collapsing buildings.

A bomb grazes the Great Synagogue. A fragment streaks towards the roof where Zachariah, my father's eldest brother, is leaping with excitement. Such a fireworks display demands the best of vantage points. Sheine Liberman has rounded up the younger children and shields them from the smoke and debris as they huddle against a wall. The buildings of Bialystok are swaying precariously. My father recalls to this day how the walls trembled while he hid behind his mother's skirts, and he retains the clear image of a clock rattling and shaking above Sheine Liberman's head, yet somehow remaining intact and secure.

The noise subsides; the iron eagles become a distant murmur. Sheine Liberman surveys her brood, and realises that her youngest daughter, Feigele, is missing. Bishke Zabludowski, who has been out on the streets by his news-stand under the town clock, is running homewards. As he nears the three-storey block of apartments he sees smoke billowing from the upper floor. The area has been cordoned off; the wounded and dead are being ferried away. A policeman stops the anxious Bishke. 'My wife! My children!', he remonstrates. 'They are gone. All dead', the policeman replies matter-of-factly. 'There is nothing you can do.'

In later years, Bishke would often claim that, as a result of this incident, he knew what it would feel like to face a firing squad and live through a mock execution. It was several hours before he was able to determine that his family had survived. After a frantic search, Sheine Liberman had found Feigele on a lower floor, cowering in a corner, injured. Father recalls the name of the doctor, Rosenthal; when Feigele was taken to him for treatment, he greeted her with a warm smile and the remark, 'Congratulations! You are the youngest among the wounded!'

For almost a year troops loyal to Czar Nicholas fought rearguard actions against the armies of Kaiser Wilhelm; between them, caught in the crossfire, were the 60 000 Jews and 20 000 Poles of Bialystok. Those who favoured the Russkis argued it was better to live with the devil one knew. Others preferred a German régime. After all, they had gotten on well enough with the German manufacturers who ran many of the larger textile plants. At least their language was similar to Yiddish, said the jokers: we would still know that a table is a table, and a chair a chair.

A growing number viewed the fierce battles as the death throes of the old order. Taking up the cry of 1905, they looked forward to an uprising of the proletariat and an end to all empires. The resurgent Polish nationalists put their faith in the legendary Pilsudski. The Orthodox gazed at the fiery heavens exploding with shrapnel, and proclaimed that the end of days was at hand and the prophesies of the ancient scriptures were about to be realised. But most of the populace scavenged for something to eat, and cast quick glances at the skies before ducking down into their primitive shelters. And with every explosion, little Hershel clapped his hands and exclaimed: 'Another bomb! Another bomb!'

Entire factories were packed away: machines, tools, materials, were crated and sent by rail towards the east. Those who could afford it piled their belongings into droshkes that conveyed them to the Bialystok station where they joined their travelling factories. As the Germans advanced, White Russian and Ukrainian peasants abandoned their fields and they too fled east, to seek refuge deep within the belly of their Czar's ailing empire.

Field Marshal Hindenberg's armies laid siege to Bialystok. The city was abandoned by the Russians and left in the hands of a Cossack army led by General Orlov. Leaders of the Jewish community hastily collected 4 000 roubles and delivered them to the General, for fear that otherwise he would allow his men to run wild on a pogrom and last-minute looting. Orlov took his troops out of the city on a Wednesday evening, in July 1915. Artillery continued to pound the outskirts of Bialystok. The station caught fire and burned, while the populace hid behind locked doors.

For a night Bialystok remained suspended between régimes, in a vacuum within which the echoes of incessant bombardment gradually subsided until, just before dawn, the shelling petered out into an uneasy silence. A restless populace waited and watched. 'So, what's new?', the town jesters murmured. And, as was their custom, they composed a couplet for the occasion, the same one they had chanted throughout the ages, changing only the names of the leading actors:

One season leaves with the fire, another begins.
The Czar marches out, and the Kaiser moves in.

The first to arrive are the advance scouts, on motorcycles. They move cautiously along deserted streets to the clock-tower. Soon after, the infantry appear, bayonets fixed as they stride out in regiment upon regiment, led by commanders in armoured cars, cavalry on horseback, and artillery divisions wheeling cannons and tanks: a parade of thousands. Above them floats a massive Zeppelin, preceding a formation of aeroplanes. In the Zeppelin are Kaiser Wilhelm and Field Marshall Hindenberg — or so the rumour spreads, racing through the streets, filtering into cellars, garrets, and obscure courtyards, as slowly the besieged inhabitants emerge, blinking in the midmorning sun. They stare in awe at the great ship hovering above the clock-tower. Could it be? The Kaiser, no less? Looking down upon us?

The victorious troops hold aloft flags and regimental banners as they march to the rhythm of military bands. They seem benevolent in the first flush of triumph. Doors and gates are swung open with increasing confidence; the inhabitants of Bialystok swarm onto the streets, unleashed from their self-imposed exile. 'Who knows? Perhaps this lot will be better than the last one that ruled us', some of the more optimistic are saying. 'A plague on all their houses', mutter those whose memories are more ancient, and they spit on the ground.

But for the children this is a picnic. My father, then a boy of ten, runs with hordes of children after the soldiers, scuffling for the sweets they are throwing into the crowds. And mother, whenever I ask her to recall the day the Kaiser's troops entered Bialystok, searches for a tune; it comes first as a humming, then glides into the words of a German marching song which resounded through the streets of the city on that July day:

> When the soldiers into town come marching in
> Girls open doors and windows to let them in.

Marching songs, sweets, flags and banners: the initial flush of a new order. But all too soon the reality of occupation was apparent. Even as the Kaiser's war machine was being paraded through the streets, Field Marshall Von Galvitz was issuing the first orders. He sent for the chief rabbi, the head priest of the Russian Orthodox church, and the Catholic archbishop of Bialystok, and imposed a fine of three hundred thousand roubles on their congregations, for 'bad conduct'. The city was cordoned off, movement strictly controlled, and special passes and identity cards introduced.

> When the soldiers into town come marching in
> Girls open doors and windows to let them in.

My father, the arch realist when it comes to talk of war, asks me, 'What else could one do?' When the soldiers came marching in, either you fled, assuming there was somewhere to flee to, or you opened up. The girls who opened up were called 'sugar boxes', he tells me. They were sent by pimps, go-betweens, even families who were desperate for something to eat. In return for sexual favours they received flour, salt, and sacks full of sugar. The pimps organised it well, father claims. It was a polite, well-run business. My father, a prince in the art of survival, rarely speaks of heroism when he discusses times of great upheaval. Instead, he focusses on the back alleys, the side-streets, the small-time wheeler-dealers who saw their families and friends through with a dash of cunning, a willingness to bend the knee, and much more than an ounce of luck. As for me, the deeper I journey into the terrain of his youth, the less judgemental I become, the less inclined to argue with him. And the arguments between us had been, at times, quite ferocious.

While a few may have profited, the bulk of the populace was consumed by hunger. Bishke Zabludowski could no longer sell newspapers. Reb Aron Yankev could only find occasional work in textile factories requisitioned to make uniforms for the occupying army. The family matriarchs quickly saw what was what, and took charge.

Sheine Liberman made regular trips to Polish villages in the surrounding countryside to barter safety-pins, needles, buttons, and salted herring for peas, potatoes, corn, and cucumbers. Father often accompanied her on these missions. For him they were great adventures. When he tells these stories he creates images of a small boy running beside his mother on errands of survival, through an autumnal countryside bathed in gold, through field and forest into villages with ramshackle peasant cottages.

'Come in, come in', the old widow beckoned. 'You are welcome.

Stay overnight. It's getting dark. You can start back in the morning.' She fed them borscht and toffee apples, and made up the beds. Sheine Liberman and her Meierke slept in the one big room with the old widow, her son, and daughter-in-law; and, late at night, father heard for the first time the sounds of love-making. He could just make out the movements of the bodies in the darkness, against the faintest outline of wooden crucifixes, dangling from the walls, in mute submission to the instinctive ways of the world.

Sometimes, however, their trips could end on a bitter note. Gangs of bandits roamed the forests. They would attack and, with a few deft kicks and punches, seize Sheine's food and trinkets, and run off with the loot. And even though many of Sheine's missions were fruitful, gold turned eventually to snow, cool breezes to biting winds, and autumnal romances to the brute reality of desperate winters.

As for Chane Esther Probutski, she surveyed the ice-laden streets of the city and decided upon a more radical course of action. With her customary precision she packed a wagon with bedding and furniture, and set out with her children, under the cover of a stormy night, towards the east, to a shtetl called Grodek.

Chapter Seven

A COUNTRY ROAD stretches between open fields interspersed with groves of pine trees. A cock crows, a town clock strikes ten and, as if awoken from a dream, I find myself approaching a small town. It appears in the midmorning sun like a mirage of shimmering jewels. The onion-shaped domes of a church rise above the mirage to dominate the skyline with silver spires that catch fire in the sun. On the outskirts of the town, clay paths peter out into fields where isolated cottages and shacks slant as if caught and frozen in the middle of a dance. Grodek, birthplace of my mother, stands motionless before me in one of those rare moments that hover on the edge of revelation.

Nikolai Tomasewitz cycles along a road that leads away from the town. I wave to him, and when he dismounts I introduce myself and try to explain why I have come to Grodek. He is wearing a weathered black cap, a threadbare navy blue jacket, baggy grey trousers held up by braces, and a flannel shirt: clothes which match a worn and creased face. There is a softness in his features, however, an expression of childlike awe and wonder, which offsets the jagged edges. We communicate awkwardly at first, as I extend my Polish beyond its narrow limits; it is more effective when we give way to a language of signs and gestures.

Nikolai reaches into his trouser pockets and extracts identity cards that indicate he was born in 1915. A glance through these tattered cards reveals that each one coincides with a different régime which had at one time or another ruled over these parts. It is as if he carries his various guises with him, just in case the pendulum swings

yet again. For this is border country, where rival empires have fought
ferociously over every centimetre of territory. Yet they do not seem,
these contending armies, to have made a lasting impression on this
rural backwater. Grodek, on this mild summer morning, lies outside history, a town that has managed to remain camouflaged by
its pastoral quietude.

And this is what Chane Esther may have thought and hoped
for as she fled towards Grodek from war-torn and impoverished
Bialystok in the year Nikolai Tomasewitz was born. Children, furniture, roosters, pots and pans swayed and rattled on a wagon drawn
by two horses. For thirty kilometres they had trotted along ice-laden
roads, beneath a canopy of falling snow, back towards the shtetl
where for generations the Malamuds had been a prominent family.
They travelled under cover of night to avoid patrols of the occupying
army. As they neared the Jewish cemetery of Grodek the wheels
slipped on ice, the horses reared high, and the wagon overturned.
'*Loift kinderlech, loift*', Chane Esther urged. 'Run children, run!'

Nikolai leads me away from the town along a dirt path through
fallow fields that give way to a forest of pines. The old man indicates that somewhere within is the place I am looking for. We part
company as I set out in search of an ancient burial ground. Recent
rains have induced a strong aroma of resin. Thick layers of pine
needles carpet the forest floor. What seem like stones from a distance are revealed, on closer sight, as tree stumps or the charcoaled
remains of campsites strewn with empty vodka bottles.

I move in circles for an hour before coming across the first stone,
on a rise, where the forest thins into a clearing of brambles and
wild flowers. Soon I have located about a dozen, slung between
shrubs and long grass. There are no headstones, not a single Hebraic
letter, merely body-length slabs: some uprooted from where they
had covered corpses for many years, others lying like solidified slugs
glistening in the sun. Lizards dash frantically into the undergrowth,
disturbed by the unexpected intruder. Fungi and moss grow from
layers of earth encrusted on the stones. Clusters of ferns are dying
at the edges with the approach of autumn. A crow squawks, cicadas
shriek and, from the distance, where the town stands hidden from
view, bells chime midday.

'Run children, run', Chane Esther calls out in the night. 'Don't
let the cold take hold of you!' The children dart between wet graves

and slippery paths. The snow is thick and soft, and it is hard to lift feet that sink deep with every step. 'Master of the Universe, help!', Chane Esther pleads; and just beyond the muffled thud of falling snow can be heard the cling, cling, cling of a sleigh. This is how mother has told the story many times: with the vision of a seven-year-old girl who will never forget the cling, cling, cling of a sleigh driven by two peasants towards an overturned wagon, and a horde of children running in circles among tombstones, shattered furniture, panicking roosters, and horses struggling to regain their footing on snow and ice. They were like messengers from heaven, mother tells me. With their timely help the wagon was set back on its wheels. Soon after, it trundled through the familiar streets of Grodek as the first light of day was beginning to dissolve the darkness.

Mid afternoon I stroll through the streets of a town which never quite leaves the countryside. Fields eat into the very heart of Grodek; market gardens extend from the backyards of many houses, and a stream moves in and out of side alleys. On the main street a turkey sits on a wooden bench, sunning itself; rows of upturned buckets and porcelain jugs lie side by side, impaled on the pickets of a cottage fence. Nearby, a bucket dangles from a rusting chain over a water well . . . And over a century ago, great-grandfather Vigdor Malamud and his wife Freidel set out from these quiet streets to journey to the town of Slonim for an urgent meeting with the Rebbe of the Slonimer Hasidic dynasty, the one his disciples claimed was a saint who could work miracles.

All his life Vigdor had been a Misnagged and had looked upon the Hasidim with disdain. An ancient quarrel still simmered in towns and hamlets of the Pale. In the 1700s, the Misnagdim, led by Elijah ben Solomon Zalman, the Sage of Vilna, the renowned scholar of his era, had condemned as heresy the practices of the newly emergent Hasidic movement. A man requires years of study, a sober and pious life, strict observance of the Laws, the Sage had argued, with the desperation of an outraged prophet fearful that his people were about to sink into apostasy. The Hasidim had chosen a dangerous path, he claimed, with their emphasis on devotion, dance, and wonder-workers. There were no short cuts to the Creator, no cheap miracles, he warned.

The quarrel had split communities apart and cut deep schisms in shtetl life. There had been bans, book burnings, and family feuds.

Denunciations to the czarist authorities had resulted in imprisonment. Rival houses of worship had ordered Hasidim to leave their congregations. They were not to be given even one night of lodging; and it was forbidden to marry them or assist at their burials.

Vigdor Malamud seems to have inherited the stern outlook and attitudes of the Misnagdim. From the few anecdotes that have filtered down through the generations, he is depicted as a disciplinarian and a strict patriarch, in the mould of the legendary forefathers. At least, this is how I liked to picture him in those childhood years when my obsession with the family tree first began. I needed an ancestral elder. I had dreams of a patriarch with a long white beard around whom angels and seraphim whirled and floated. For many months I tried to redream him, night after night, until he faded and became impossible to recreate. When I heard talk of a great-grandfather who had been venerated in a shtetl called Grodek, I adopted him as the patriarch I could no longer bring to my dreams.

Vigdor's avid piety and stern adherence to his faith had not, however, averted a great misfortune: one by one, his first five children had died, each succumbing to illness in infancy. Vigdor and Freidel's efforts to have new offspring, as they approached middle age, had failed. In Grodek there lived followers of the Slonimer Rebbe. They constantly sang the praises of the Tzaddik, their wonderworker. 'Go to him', they urged the despairing Vigdor and Freidel, and finally the couple relented. There was, after all, nothing to lose. Vigdor and Freidel returned from Slonim with the Rebbe's blessing. Within a decade there were seven healthy children, and Vigdor had become the most fervent of Hasidim.

Chane Esther was the fifth child born in the time of the miracles. She was raised in Grodek, and as a teenager she was betrothed, in the usual way, to Aron Yankev Probutski from the shtetl of Orla. What was the usual way? According to father, who certainly loves to embroider a story, the usual way was for a shadchen, a matchmaker, to be hired. In his notebook he kept lists of potential brides and grooms. 'Ah', muses the shadchen, 'it is obvious!' In Orla there is an Aron Yankev, son of Isaac Probutski and Rachel the Rebbetzin, pious God-fearing Jews and fervent devotees of the Slonimer Rebbe. The fast-talking matchmaker shuttles between the two families — quite a demanding task, if one considers that Grodek and Orla are many kilometres apart.

Preliminary discussions over, Reb Isaac, Aron Yankev, and Rachel the Rebbetzin travel to Grodek to meet their potential in-laws. They are served afternoon tea by Chane Esther, and thereby the teenage Aron Yankev has a chance to observe his prospective bride: her appearance, her demeanour, how she performs domestic duties. He must decide at a glance. 'And did the bride have a choice?', I ask father. 'It wasn't for her to make such decisions', he replies. 'And judging by the number of failed marriages these days', he adds, 'perhaps this method was as good as any.'

There is another possibility. Vigdor Malamud and Isaac Probutski may have become acquainted in Slonim during one of their pilgrimages to the Rebbe's court. Perhaps they had arranged the marriage there on behalf of their children, without intermediaries and matchmakers. Years later my mother would see Aron Yankev depart on such pilgrimages. He would make his way to the Bialystok station to meet up with fellow devotees. As they travelled east, on a journey of several hundred kilometres, their numbers were swelled by groups of Slonimer Hasidim who clambered aboard at stations on the way.

The whisky began to flow long before they reached their destination. If the Hasidim had a whole carriage to themselves and felt safe enough to let go, they would sing nigunim, songs of praise to their Rebbe, their link to the heavens, their passport to a kingdom of joy.

A devotee could seek the advice or blessings of the Rebbe at any time. There were also special occasions when Hasidim came en masse, particularly for the Yomim Naroim, the ten Days of Awe between the New Year and the Day of Atonement. Throughout Eastern Europe pilgrims would be on the move at this time, converging upon the many shtetlech where courts of Hasidic dynasties flourished. They came on the miraculous trains that had recently been introduced, or by horse-drawn coach to more remote destinations. They travelled through forests and mountain passes, along highways and country roads, across rivers and streams. They journeyed together in large convoys with friends they had known all their lives; others moved alone, preferring the company of their own heartbeat. Many of them were men who had left families in the hands of wives and mothers to become wanderers again, released, for a while, from their worldly concerns. Chane Esther would stay at home with the children, while Aron Yankev, free of the textile mills

of Bialystok, journeyed with his Hasidic brothers in a dream of God
and Tzaddik.

Disembarking at the Slonim station, they trudged into town
carrying bundles of bedding, prayer books, and phylacteries. They
crammed into taverns and inns, or boarded with local followers of
the Rebbe. They slept on straw mats, in narrow cots and hammocks,
in garrets, attics, barns, or houses of study, huddled against stoves
for warmth during long nights that stretched towards winter. The
town's fortunes would leap overnight. Butchers, bakers, grocers, fish-
mongers, saloon-keepers, and blacksmiths scurried about all day to
reap the whirlwind that had swept into their midst.

Houses of worship were full to the limits. Some crowded into the
tiny wooden prayer houses that could be found in almost every street
and alley, while others prayed in the magnificent stone synagogue
which had stood in Slonim since the 1600s. Pilgrims exchanged
greetings, renewed friendships, accompanied each other to the ritual
baths. They argued politics, gossiped about intrigues between rival
Rebbes, and arranged marriages between their children.

Late at night, long after the evening prayers were over, they
gathered at the Rebbe's court, to share a meal, to hear a few words
of wisdom from their Tzaddik, and to dance until perhaps they did
indeed draw out the divine sparks they believed resided in every
object, in all beings and things, animate or inert. There were many
who claimed that just a glance from a Tzaddik could fan the sparks
into a blaze of all-consuming fervour that provided solace and release
from all sorrows and struggles. And mother, as she tells the story,
finds her way back to the nigunim she heard Reb Aron Yankev hum,
wordless melodies that took flight, ascending slowly at first, occasionally dropping back and reascending, spinning a spiral of notes
that urged themselves on to even greater heights, towards complete
immersion in God and total forgetfulness.

Whether arranged in the court of the Slonimer Rebbe, or by a matchmaker shuttling between Orla and Grodek, it is known that, after
the marriage, Aron Yankev went to live with his in-laws. Vigdor
Malamud took him on as an apprentice weaver and taught him to
use the handloom. The first seven of Reb Aron Yankev's and Chane

Esther's children were born in Grodek, before Reb Aron moved to Bialystok in search of work at looms now powered by steam.

When Chane Esther and the children embarked on their flight to Grodek, Aron Yankev had remained in Bialystok. What was there for him to do in a shtetl? Vigdor had died a decade earlier. The weavers' workshops had closed down when the armies of Kaiser Wilhelm had cut off markets in Russia. In Bialystok there was the possibility of an occasional job in factories which had been commandeered by German troops. Above all, there was a fine company of Slonimer Hasidim with whom to spend the idle hours. Indeed, Reb Aron Yankev moved into the cramped prayer-house of the Slonimer Hasidim, and lived there for a time with his companions, while Chane Esther and her brood fended for themselves elsewhere.

It was almost entirely a clan of women that had assembled in Grodek to see through the war years, a matriarchy skilled in the arts of survival. They were firmly grounded in a way that many of their men, who had spent their youth bent over holy books in cheders and yeshivas, were not. In orthodox families the woman's domain was the household, and often they controlled the purse strings and ran small businesses.

At the head of the Malamud clan was the grand matriarch, Freidel Shapiro Malamud. Since the death of Vigdor she had expanded the dairy she ran from home. She also dealt in poultry. She would purchase fowl from local peasants and take them to the ritual slaughterer. Mother often accompanied her on such errands. While the shochet performed his task, Freidel talked to him about this and that. Mother can recall snatches of conversation about battles that were raging nearby, abductions of menfolk for enforced labour, occasional raids on local homes; yet life still went on, praised be the One Above. Freidel would carve the kosher chickens into pieces that she sold and bartered. But to those who could not afford it, Jews and gentiles alike, she lent money, or gave away chicken and cheeses. For such deeds she had acquired the name, Freidel the Angel.

As she ages, mother's memory of distant times grows sharper, and that of more recent events vaguer. Memory has a momentum of its own. As mother advances deeper into herself, time dissolves into details, and she can see it clearly — the timber cottage she descended upon with her sisters and brothers, as they balanced precariously on an overloaded wagon in the early hours of a winter's day in 1915. She enters a room in which a solitary kerosene lamp is burning. In a corner there rises a mountain of potatoes, beside a smaller one of corn, gathered from the abandoned fields of White Russian peasants who had fled east with the advance of the Kaiser's armies. The walls are whitewashed with lime. Twice a year a fresh coat would be applied: on the eve of Passover, when houses were thoroughly cleaned and every crumb of unleavened bread removed; and before the New Year, in preparation for the Days of Awe and the annual cleansing of the soul.

At night mother sleeps in a small room outside which stands a solitary oak. In winter, full moons hover above a river of ice upon which children skate and drive their makeshift sleds. Distant sounds of peasants singing drift over the ice; nearby, Malka the goat bleats, Sheva the cow yawns, and Freidel's gaggle of geese punctuate the night with an occasional chorus of shrieks.

Freidel had also given each goose a personal name, and they certainly earned their keep. Mother would help her aunt Rivke pluck the feathers. Peasant women brought jobs to Rivke, and they wandered around the house gossiping while she sewed their sheets, pillowslips, and quilts, which she stuffed with goose feathers.

Apart from one or two small rooms, the cottage consisted of a larger room that was part sewing-workshop, dairy, grocery, nursery, bakery, kitchen, sleeping quarters, and dining area. Fresh milk from the udders of Malka and Sheva glistened in clay jugs. Freidel had taught her daughters and grand-daughters how to churn cream into butter and make cheese from sour milk. The corn was picked off the cob and ground between two stones. Chane Esther was expert at mixing and shaping the corn flour into loaves which she placed in a deep oven. For a treat she would sometimes bake sweet chalahs.

As the war dragged on the townsfolk had to scavenge for food. The younger Probutski children, Hershel and Tzivie, would be left at home in the care of their eldest sister Liebe; Chane Esther, aunts Rivke and Tsore, mother, and her sisters Sheindel and Chaie, would take to the forests to gather blackberries, gooseberries, mushrooms, and leaves that were used as a salad or mashed with potatoes into a stew. 'Mmmm. The stew was delicious', mother tells me. They would leave at dawn, the residents of Grodek, in large groups, throughout spring, summer, and well into autumn. They wandered forever further afield, so that at times they became lost in forests they had never seen before. For lunch they gathered in clearings to eat blackberry jam, and they returned well after dark, lighting their way with kerosene lamps as the streets of Grodek came back into view.

Another sister, Feigl, worked as a cleaner and cook for German officers at the Grodek station. Yoshua and Motl, the older brothers, the two men among a company of women, were forced to labour for the occupying army. They cut down trees for lumber, and extracted resin from conifers to be stored in barrels and transported to Germany. When they returned late at night Yoshua and Motl would slump down, and that was it; there they would remain, exhausted, to be fed and allowed to fall asleep. The scent of resin and fresh wood they exuded was sweet, says mother. She was a girl of eight, nine. She does not recall these as hard times. She loved the expeditions to the forests. Everyone worked, everyone contributed. The years have softened the memory, so that what remains is the sweet smell of resin and the enticing aroma of potatoes and leaves simmering on a stove.

Among the German soldiers were Jewish officers who paid visits to the women and courted the older girls of Grodek. One officer declared his love for Tsore, the youngest daughter of Vigdor and Freidel. He would come for her after the war was over, he claimed. There was another officer who would ride into town to inspect the houses. He had a particular fetish for clean windows. Just one speck of dust on a window, he warned, could result in severe punishment.

War years in a town called Grodek: the soldiers strutted, the women were wary, the food was in short supply, homes could be raided at any time, an officer could be bribed, another might rail at a speck of dust — while just beyond the horizon the fighting continued with unabated fury. And as I recreate the story, I must make do with snippets of information gathered from kitchen conversations in which the silences grow longer, and mother seems increasingly lost in an inaccessible world of her own.

A sandy side street comes to a dead end at a ramshackle two-storey dwelling, its weathered boards flaking like fish scales. 'Probutski?

Malamud?' replies an old man, who sits beside a child asleep in a pram. He shakes his head as he rocks the pram. These names are unfamiliar, but his face brightens when he recalls: 'Ah yes! A doctor Zimmerman once lived in this house. He was taken away with his wife and daughter. They were shot in the forests, not far from here. It must have been about 1941. A son of his survived. He lives now in America. He also came to Grodek several years ago. Like you he wanted to see the place he was born in.'

While the old man talks I am overcome by an uncanny feeling that there are many of us at this moment — sons, daughters, nieces, nephews, grandchildren — wandering country roads and city streets, or picking our way through forest undergrowth to uncover mould-encrusted tombstones. Perhaps this is how it has always been for descendants of lost families: we search within a tangle of aborted memories, while stumbling towards a mythical home which seems to elude us as it recedes into false turns and dead ends.

In the centre of town there is a park with flower beds, paths that weave between expanses of well-kept lawns, and a monument honouring 'Polish martyrs'. It could be for any one of the many conflicts that have erupted over the centuries in this part of the world. A young man wearing jeans and a leather jacket approaches me. He asks for my name, and I am pleased to have come across someone I can converse with in English. It takes me a while to register that the card he has uncovered in the palm of his hand bears his photo and the word, 'Police'.

He is joined by a middle-aged man in a drab blue suit. 'Just routine questions', they say. 'Why have you been taking so many photographs this afternoon?' The tone is neutral, almost friendly. They are obviously aware of every place I have been to since I arrived in Grodek.

They seem to accept my explanations, and leave me after writing the details in a notebook. Yet with this incident the scales have tipped. I had planned to stay in Grodek overnight, or perhaps for several days. But I am, after all, a stranger here, and there are eyes on the alert, watching my every move.

Within the hour I am on a bus returning to Bialystok. An evening chill has settled as we move into the countryside, and I recall the warnings of my parents and family friends of their generation who now live in Melbourne. 'Why embark on such a journey?', they had asked. 'What do you think you will find?'

Chapter Eight

'AFTER THE GREAT WAR a higher truth should have been born', father exclaims. He is racing full-steam ahead on one of his extended monologues. One question of mine is enough to set him in motion. Anecdotes, memories, philosophical asides fly from his lips. The locomotive hisses and gathers speed. It stops unexpectedly at unknown stations, or jumps tracks to charge off in a new direction. Occasionally a signal is required to gently steer him back to the main track: 'After the Great War a higher truth should have been born'.

Summer, 1917. In Bialystok wild rumours are circulating, embellished with exaggerations and fantasies. Revolution has broken out in Russia. Palaces are burning. Soldiers are shooting their officers and deserting the front. The rumours grow more fantastic. The Czar's crown is rolling in the gutters. Rasputin has been found strangled in the Czarina's boudoir. In the streets of St Petersburg people are dancing for joy. Towns and cities are being decked out in red. A new order is being created to the east, beyond the borders. Centuries of oppression are going to vanish overnight.

When the Zabludowski home was bombed at the outset of the Great War, reporters who came to survey the damage were able to note the exact time the shrapnel had struck, from clocks that had stopped at the moment of impact. The Zabludowskis moved to Nieronies Lane, within a neighbourhood of derelict cottages and tenements near the Bialystok fish market. Father depicts it as a world of snarling cats, skirmishes between rival gangs over control of territory, police raids, and nightly gatherings of unemployed youths who sang bawdy ditties and traded jokes and insults. It was a great spectacle, a theatre of poverty. The young rascals had talent. They were artists in their own fashion, says father, and their songs had rhyme and rhythm, a poetry of sorts; they were bards of the Jewish underworld in a time of hunger and desperation.

Father has now warmed to the subject. He draws me with him to Nieronies Lane. Just several doors away lived the prostitute Feigele. She would receive her clients at home, rather than on the streets as did those lower on the social ladder. Not so far distant, in the Chanaykes, the widow Zlatke presided over a brothel which included girls of White Russian, Polish, Ukrainian, and Jewish origin. 'But they all spoke a common language of caresses and sighs', father emphasizes. There was always a light shining at Zlatke's, regardless of the wars, pogroms, revolutions, and rebellions that regularly swept by.

Apart from small-time crooks, there were chronically unemployed weavers, factory workers, and artisans who continued to eke out a living from their crammed workshops. Ah yes, father recalls. Next door lived Zeidel, the master wood-carver. He had bloodshot eyes, and a wry smile that seemed to mock the absurdity of existence. For hours on end he would engrave flowers, biblical scenes, geometrical shapes, and folk symbols on building ornaments and furniture. His workshop was littered with timber shavings and a fantastic array of carving implements.

An assortment of characters wandered the neighbourhood. They strutted their obsessions in full view and left themselves open to taunts and barbs. In a world gone mad, says father, it was difficult to know the boundaries between 'normal' and 'insane'. Take, for instance, Moishe Shloimele. He would dress as a woman, and walk unsteadily and bow-legged on high-heeled shoes so worn down on the sides that his ankles seemed to be forever falling flat on the pavement. He looked like a crippled chicken, and bands of children followed him shouting obscenities while imitating his awkward movements. Yet he was a harmless soul, gentle in manner and bearing, always drawn towards the domain of women. He made a meagre living by cleaning kitchens, and had become expert in removing stains from pots and pans, and putting larders in order.

The neighbourhood prostitutes were far gentler towards him than were the hoodlums. He loved to be treated like a lady; and they obliged by taking him into their houses of pleasure, where they sat drinking tea and gossiping between stints with clients.

Father makes a distinction between born crazies and those who became so due to the circumstances of their lives. Whereas Moishe Shloimele was a 'geborene', of those who had been born to their peculiar fate, Chane Yolkeshe was a 'gevorene'. Little rhymes pepper father's monologues, and he recites them with the delight of a child, repeating them over and over as if reluctant to let go of their simple musicality:

> Moishe Shloimele was a geborene;
> Chane Yolkeshe, a gevorene.

Chane Yolkeshe came from a family of porters and wagon drivers. She had a brother, a murderer, who was nicknamed 'Yolke'. Since she also displayed wayward tendencies, she was called 'Yolkeshe'. She would roam the streets and approach women to demand a few coins. If they refused she lifted their dresses to shame them. This was her technique, and it often proved successful. She had a masculine build, a deep voice, and there were those who claimed she had been possessed by an evil spirit, a dybbuk. Thereafter it was common in Bialystok to call an aggressive woman a 'Chane Yolkeshe'. 'But I never made fun of her', father claims. 'To this day I can clearly see the desperation that lurked on her face with increasing intensity as the Great War dragged on.'

Yet, through it all, communal life continued. When he wasn't scavenging for food, father attended a succession of cheders and Talmud Torahs, where he was initiated into the mysteries of orthodox Jewish life. It had begun several years before the War. His first tutor was Reb Eli, a tall man with a long black beard who would threaten his five-year-old pupils with a kanchik, a whip of dangling leather strips with a calf's-bone handle. Reb Eli's task was to teach the alphabet, and the most basic of prayers. '*Baruch ato adonai aluheinu*, Blessed be thee oh Lord', he intoned with the toddlers in his charge. One way or another, by stealth, smiles, threats, and bribes, he beat this knowledge into their young heads.

When Reb Eli had accomplished his task, father attended Lubelski's cheder where he learned to read prayer books; and since the cheder had reformist tendencies, he was also taught some Russian and Hebrew. Lubelski was a thin man with an emaciated face from which there sprouted a blond goatee. He had developed a unique method of teaching languages to youngsters. He would stroll by the desks, and confiscate toys and playthings — pen knives, slingshots, chestnut marbles, whistles made of plum stones — which were added to those he had stored in a large wooden trunk. He would take some of them out daily and ask the class: 'Well, my friends, what have we here?' And his pupils would have to describe the objects in Hebrew or Russian. They quickly came to know, of course, that it was unwise to take any toys with them to cheder. But soon enough they moved on, and a fresh batch of youngsters would contribute their toys to Lubelski's growing collection.

Whereas Lubelski had been mild mannered, with a perpetual grin on his face, even as he snatched away toys, father's next teacher, Kabatchnik, was perpetually angry. He not only threatened pupils with his kanchik, but he used it, especially on such carefree and undisciplined students as father. 'To tell the truth', he confides, 'I wasn't very interested in my studies. I preferred to be outside, on the streets or roaming the forests.'

When the Zabludowski family moved to Nieronies Lane, elementary school assumed an entirely different appeal. In time of war it was a relief to get out of home for any reason, including school. In even the poorest neighbourhoods there were Talmud Torahs and cheders, sponsored by rich philanthropists for the children of unemployed workers and artisans.

Reb Mendel from Orly was a melancholy man who spoke in a monotone, as if to himself, while he introduced his students to the five books of Moses, the Pentateuch. There was no place for discussion in his classroom. Everything was dictated, copied, learned by heart, while Reb Mendel paced around and lectured to the walls and ceiling. But he would suddenly come to life, pounce upon a student, tweak him by the ear, and ask the stunned boy to recite a portion of Torah or answer an obscure question on a text. 'Ignoramus!', Reb Mendel would exclaim in mock despair when the wrong answer was stuttered nervously; then he would resume his pacing and his colourless explication of the scriptures.

By 1917 father had graduated to the classes of Reb Chaim, who taught Gemara — the commentaries — and the finer points of biblical interpretation. Reb Chaim was a learned man, with a huge reservoir of traditional knowledge. He taught in the ancient manner, in a sing-song voice, while swaying at the pulpit. He laced his sermons with parables, anecdotes, digressions, and sharp insights. He initiated his pupils into a private universe of Jewish lore that had survived two thousand years of exile, to be recreated again and again, even in mud-splattered alleys such as Nieronies Lane. There was virtually no street without a synagogue or house of study, where devotees prayed three times a day and studied in their spare time — regardless of the upheavals taking place in the outside world.

Late night was the time to penetrate the mysteries. Study groups gathered to contemplate the scriptures. They sat around tables, eyes riveted on their Gemaras, and kept themselves awake until dawn with sweet tea and cigarettes. There were those, father tells me, who awoke at midnight to chant the psalms of King Solomon, or to delve into the Kabbala and the Zohar, the Book of Splendour — the writings of mystics who had sought to experience the very core of Creation.

On Simchas Torah the many houses of prayer in Bialystok came to life with celebration. The Torah scrolls were taken from the Ark of the Law and paraded around the bima, the pulpit where the last chapter of the annual cycle of readings had just been completed. Groups of congregants filed from house to house, where they were treated to delicacies such as cabbage soaked in honey and butter. Father tagged along with the boys of Nieronies Lane, even though, during the Great War, the feasts had been reduced to a pittance.

Father's memory unravels like the scrolls that were paraded on Simchas Torah. He recalls the monthly sanctification of the moon, when orthodox Jews gathered outside, on the first Sabbath night after the New Moon, to bless the renewal of its light. The Hasidim of Nieronies Lane prayed with such fervour that, whenever they came to the 'amens', their voices resounded throughout the neighbourhood with an emotional force which seemed to spring from the depths of the earth.

1918. Europe is falling apart. Bialystok is a battleground for rival armies. Father would make his way from Nieronies Lane to the cottage of his grandfather Reb Moishe Beinish Liberman and his grandmother Breine. She was a small, plump woman, with a creased forehead poking out from under her wig; and she was extremely pious, alert to the most minute transgression of ritual law. As soon as father entered the house she would ask: 'Nu? Have you said your prayers?' In contrast, Moshe Beinish was far softer; a kindly man, straight backed, with a long beard. He was always dressed in a black caftan, with a peaked cap beneath which his eyes were constantly downcast. Yet, no matter how hard times were, he maintained his dignified bearing and would urge: 'Have faith. Always maintain faith and all troubles will be overcome.'

Moishe Beinish had taken on the task of preparing father for his bar mitzvah. For three months they would meet weekly and walk together to the nearby house of prayer, of which grandfather was the caretaker. They sat in the empty prayer-hall, where Moishe Beinish showed his grandson how to wind on phylacteries and pronounce the portion of Torah he was to recite on the day of initiation.

Yet it was at this time, as Moishe Beinish was inducting him into the basic procedures of adult religious life, that father was being drawn towards a quite different God. This religion too had its many sects and factions, rival schools of thought and preachers, each proclaiming the greatness of their particular brand of socialism. Since the news of the Czar's overthrow had swept Bialystok, the streets had been alight with longing for a new form of redemption. A higher truth was about to be born out of the wreckage of the old order. Father's elder brother Zachariah had become a convert to Bolshevism and, with his furtive comings and goings, the dilapidated cottage on Nieronies Lane became, like so many others, permeated by a sense of conspiracy and agitation.

According to father's freehand maps, this is where Nieronies Lane was located, more or less. At any rate it fits the description, a neighbourhood of narrow alleys that I follow randomly until I meander into a cul-de-sac of cottages which look as though they have stood here since well before the turn of the century.

An elderly woman pokes her head out of a doorway. She is stout, with fully-rounded hips, thick muscular arms softened by a cushion of fat, and a jovial moon face above which arctic white hair sweeps up into a bun. She exudes the raw health of a peasant, and she gazes at me with a curiosity that gives way to an invitation issued with the wave of a hand. I follow her through the front entrance, which leads directly into a cramped kitchen dominated by a wood stove cluttered with kettles, pots, and pans, some of which sizzle and jump among others which remain mute beneath their charcoal coats.

She ushers me into an adjacent room. Rarely have I seen so much crammed into such a confined space. There are two large beds, a circular table, and an old Singer sewing machine, all of which are strewn with clothes and materials. Everywhere there are dolls: some sit on the window-sill, others lie naked on the floor, while a large company lie huddled on pillows. Clay pots sprout jungles of ferns; a television set squats on the floor beneath carvings of herons and ducks, and the walls are covered with pictures of kittens, ancestors, saints, and dogs. Several live cats lie curled up on piles of material. Dominating all else is an altar crammed with framed photographs of the Pope, an army of Christs adorned with crowns of thorns, the Virgin Mother in various guises, and mountains of flowers: plastic flowers, fresh flowers in vases and jars, paintings and posters of flowers. 'A wonderful mess', the babushka says cheerfully, as she catches me scanning the room. She serves cups of tea, and biscuits on stained and cracked plates which she places on the table, after clearing it with one sweep of the hand.

A second elderly woman enters, carrying a plate of stale bread rolls. Her face is thin, her complexion waxen, and her smile fixed but kindly. 'My dearest comrade', she murmurs, pointing towards my hostess. She is her partner in a sewing business , and the companion with whom she shares this room.

As we sip tea an agile dwarf of a man darts into the cottage. His face glows a drinker's scarlet, his bloodshot eyes shift nervously from person to person. The old ladies wink at me. Watch your bag, they indicate in sign language, this man has nimble fingers. Within ten minutes, with a deft hop and a skip, he is gone. We remain in the darkening room in silence, two babushkas munching bread rolls with their unexpected guest from abroad, in a disintegrating house, within a neighbourhood that was once childhood home to my father. They take delight in feeding me, continually bringing more food to the circular table, as if they wish to welcome back a son who has returned after an absence of many years.

The German war effort is on the brink of collapse. The commandant of Bialystok, a celebrated general, shoots himself, unable to bear the humiliation of defeat. Posters circulate with the news that workers' and soldiers' councils have been formed in Berlin. After over a century of oppression, Polish nationalists seize the opportunity to declare an independent republic. They set fire to German-controlled warehouses and grab ammunition, clothes, and food. Polish youths with guns slung over their shoulders organise themselves into legions to drive out the remaining troops of the Kaiser's army. In the streets of Bialystok, German soldiers are thrown to the ground. Their coats and boots are torn off, and the soldiers sent on their way. In December 1918 the Poles take over the city. Resurgent Polish nationalism has, however, a darker aspect. There are those, especially among the troops of General Haller's 'Blue Army', who drag Jews from trains on the Bialystok-Warsaw line, to beat and rob them, and shear off their beards.

Red Army, White Army, Blue Army — armies and ideas of all colours and persuasions are running rampant in 1918, 1919, and 1920. Europe is sorting itself out. Bialystok becomes a key railroad depot for unloading and maintaining arms. Its factories churn out uniforms and blankets for Polish troops. Reb Aron Yankev is again able to support his family from work in the textile industry. Chane Esther and her children return from Grodek. As for Bishke Zabludowski, he is back on the streets near the clock-tower, selling Polish and Yiddish newspapers; while to the east, the Bolsheviks are on the march.

On July 20, 1920, with the Polish authorities having deserted the city, the Bolsheviks entered a Bialystok decked out in red banners and flags. The Revolution had arrived in town. A rag-tag army of Russians, Cossacks, Ukrainians, Jews, and Tartars, accompanied by Polish communists released from Siberian exile, marched through the streets. 'We thought our liberators had arrived at long last', father recalls. 'After all, among the soldiers in this hybrid army there were some who spoke Yiddish!'

Yet these Red Messiahs were a worn-out and somewhat frayed band of saviours. They struggled by on emaciated nags and rickety wagons. They wore torn boots and ragged uniforms. Their faces were unshaven and caked with dust; their artillery held together with pieces of string. It was an army reduced to skin and bones, craving water and bread: 'The heroes of a pauper's Republic', the town wags sneered.

Soon the picnic began in earnest. Bialystok sprang to life with revolutionary fervour; and, at first, even the traders thought their liberators had come. Red Army soldiers crowded shops and stores, their pockets stuffed with crisp, newly printed Bolshevik roubles. Sales of shirts, silks, socks, and leather goods soared. Never mind that the money was useless, or that the liberators had confiscated sacks of flour and sugar stored in cellars and back-rooms. 'You must expect excesses', defenders of the Revolution argued. And besides, the news had spread, through the alleys of Chanaykes and Piaskes: 'The Bolsheviks have opened the palace gates! Come and take what you like! Branitski's palace belongs to the people!'

Mother tagged along with her brothers and sisters as they streamed with the crowds towards the abandoned palace. The hordes surged through the unguarded entrance, along broad asphalt paths that wound between flower beds, towards the three-storey replica of Versailles, with its hundreds of windows, balconies, and arched doorways. They swept up a flight of steps flanked by stone sculptures: on one side, a naked bearded Prince holding a bow, with the arrow aimed at the heart of a naked woman posed on the opposite side. For the first time, the people of Bialystok laid eyes upon details they had barely glimpsed through holes in fences set several hundred metres back from the buildings.

The crowds burst through the doors into a grand hall supported by six fat marble columns. They swarmed all over the palace, through ornately decorated rooms, penetrating every corner, from the cellars to the garrets, looting everything that could be detached, in a frenzy that was contagious. Like an army of ants they emerged back out onto the paths, lugging their booty: chairs, mirrors, household utensils, tables, royal robes, and servants' boots. One group pushed and dragged a grand piano; another carried a double bed on which, it was said, Czar Nicholas himself had slept.

The Probutski children had grabbed their share of the spoils — a white porcelain bowl which glows with a pristine freshness in the dreams of an elderly woman in a Melbourne house many years later. 'What did you dream about last night?', I ask mother. 'My brothers and sisters,' she answers. 'They were waving goodbye at the Bialystok station, and they were holding aloft the white porcelain bowl we carried through the palace gates on the day the Bolsheviks came to town.'

The new authorities set up headquarters in the Hotel Ritz, opposite the gates of Branitski's palace. Commissars of the Red Army strolled around the city in knee-high boots, three-quarter-length jackets, and with revolvers tucked into holsters. Factory workers seized the opportunity to settle accounts with bosses who had underpaid them for years. The most hated were denounced and imprisoned in the infamous remand centre on Nikolaievska Street. The palace gardens were converted into a Red fairground, where thousands thronged to hear the fiery speeches of revolutionary orators. They stood on the grand balcony of the palace, surrounded by red flags, and proclaimed a new order. Land would be handed over to the peasants, they thundered. The workers would overthrow their blood-sucking employers; and children would be eternally well-fed, clothed, and educated. Bolshevik armies were marching triumphantly forward, the speakers declared. Already they were on the outskirts of Warsaw. Red flags would soon be hanging in Paris, Berlin, and London, they prophesied. Poland, Germany, and Russia were to be united in a grand Bolshevik federation.

All over Bialystok mass meetings were taking place. Father ran from gathering to gathering — from the palace grounds to the town square; from the clock-tower to circus tents that stood on the banks of the Biale. Everywhere speakers were mounting soap boxes to add their interpretations and predictions. The Poles were trying to decide between Moscow and Warsaw. Jewish speakers argued and debated: some supported the Reds; others claimed that only in mass migration to Palestine would they finally obtain redemption. Zachariah and his comrades commandeered the Great Synagogue for their meetings. It was rumoured that he had profaned the sacred Ark of the Laws. Religion was the opiate of the masses, he claimed, with a passion that shook cobwebs beneath the synagogue dome. No place was immune from the fever burning in Bialystok.

For father it was the poetry of the speeches that mattered, far more than the content, and I suspect it has remained like that ever since. 'When poetry disappears from a movement, the evil of the demagogue triumphs', he has often asserted. Inspired by the fiery debates, he would gather with his teenage friends in the abandoned rooms of a factory where they would play at oratory. They formed their own groups, elected leaders, read each other books on socialist theory, recited Bundist and Zionist tracts, and aped their older brothers and sisters. As for Bishke Zabludowski, he now sold Yiddish and Russian newspapers produced by Bolshevik sympathisers, and wondered how long it would be before he sold newspapers of another persuasion.

For one long month the Red interlude lasted. And just as suddenly as it had erupted, it fizzled out. Towards the end of August artillery fire could again be heard on the outskirts of Bialystok. The tide had turned in Warsaw, at a battle that would long be remembered as the 'Miracle of the Vistula'. The independent Polish Republic was again on the ascendancy, driving out the Red Army from town after town as it swept towards Bialystok. There were rumours that hundreds of Jews, accused of collaboration, had been beaten and imprisoned, or left hanging from trees by mobs on the rampage.

The road to Minsk was crowded with soldiers, party cadres, and townsfolk who had decided to make a run for the east. In the city gardens young Jews were assembled, issued with guns and ammunition, and told to fight a rearguard action as they fled. On the streets the fighting was fierce. My mother stood by the third-floor window in a tenement on Ulitza Kievska, with a bird's-eye view of the skirmishes. She recalls the panic, the screams of neighbours as their homes were attacked and looted. Another of mother's recurring stories emerges: she had descended the stairs and ventured onto the streets, having volunteered to acquire food for the Probutski family as they sheltered from the battles raging below.

From Kievska she turned into Ulitza Grunwaldzka; she recalls the name of the street, and indeed I have now traced the route, a distance of about fifty metres from where she lived. As she rounded the corner she saw, at first, a rifle abandoned against a fence; then she saw the body, its head split open, brains exposed on the pavement. Whether it was a Russian or Pole, Bolshevik or Republican,

Jew or Gentile, Red or White, she would never know. But the image was to remain embedded in her psyche. And in years to come she would describe it many times, with a weary and quiet detachment.

Father stood on the pavement in Ulitza Kupietzka, in front of the apartment block to which his family had recently shifted from Niero-nies Lane. He listened intently to the sound of sporadic gunfire that resounded throughout Bialystok. A soldier of the Red Army dashed around a nearby corner. When he saw father he begged him for a place where he could hide. Father led the fugitive inside: 'He was a rebel, a hero from a world of idealists and revolutionaries whom I had so admired and envied.'

Bishke and Sheine were frightened and angry. 'Don't meddle in such affairs. It always ends badly for Jews. We will be caught in the crossfire.' But father was insistent. 'Let him stay for a few hours', he said. And besides, he was already firmly inside.

The soldier washed, shaved, tore into the food that was set in front of him, impatient to alleviate his burning hunger. After the meal he fell immediately into a deep sleep. In the evening father accompanied his hero to the door. The soldier was refreshed, his senses fully revived. As he stepped outside with his adolescent saviour, he asked him the way to the establishment of Zlatke the widow. This was the last father saw of his Red Messiah — disappearing into the maze of lanes over which Zlatke reigned supreme. And whenever he tells me this story, father adds his familiar words of advice: 'Do not be overly idealistic. Revolutions and wars come and go, but our inner drives and obsessions remain forever the same.'

Father's monologue seems endless. Stories beget more stories and multiply late into the night. A fourteen-year-old boy wanders through battle-torn streets and comes across a funeral procession. It is led by a band of musicians: fiddlers, flautists, drummers. A coffin sits upon a wagon drawn by a team of horses. Behind the wagon there stretches a long line of mourners, among whom there are weeping prostitutes veiled in black. Father imitates them as he tells the story, shaking his head in mock mourning from side to side, and swaying vigorously like a penitent at prayer.

The Bialystok Jewish underworld had turned out in force for the last journey of their Yanketchke, their small-time crime boss, pimp, and card sharp. He had been a ruffian, no doubt, a larrikin with a grim sense of humour and a cunning that befitted the times. A man of frenetic energy, he had darted about town for decades, doing deals with a succession of occupying armies while keeping firm control over his troops of 'sugar boxes' and the houses of pleasure in which they plied their trade. Yanketchke's associates and dependants accompanied him to the grave in style. After all he had, in his fashion, helped them survive.

Father is a survivor. Initially he was rescued by his wife, who had preceded him to the New World. That was not so long before the news began to filter through. The Old World was burning. Bialystok was in flames. And then, silence; an ominous silence, broken just occasionally by a rumour, a garbled report, a fragment of news, nothing ever quite definite. Something inconceivable was taking place, 'over there', in that distant city that had once been home.

Names began to appear in newspapers: lists compiled by the Red Cross and welfare agencies. There were survivors; people seeking to make contact from refugee camps. Displaced persons, they were called. And the realisation seeped through that what had taken place was a Shoah, an annihilation. Of the Zabludowski family, there were no survivors. Mother too had lost all those she had left behind over a decade earlier. 'After the Great War a higher truth should have been born', father repeats. 'And at the end of the second War there emerged the annihilation of all that had been near and dear.'

As I retreat from the cul-de-sac I glimpse behind me the two babushkas out for a walk. In the open they seem so much smaller, more stooped. They cling to each other and support themselves with walking sticks. They move very slowly, followed by a gang of cats that glide alongside a row of crumbling cottages.

It is a shadow play that I am engaged in, on this journey in pursuit of ancestral myths. Only when I stop do the shadows become still. And from that stillness there emerges the refrain of an ageing sceptic warning his offspring: Beware of being overly idealistic. Revolutions and wars come and go, but man's inner drives and obsessions remain forever the same.

Chapter Nine

YEARS LATER, WHEN MOTHER FELL on a Melbourne street, the memory of another fall, in a time and place far removed, came flooding back. Rivke Malamud had been her favourite aunt. When the Probutski family first moved to Bialystok, soon after the turn of the century, Aunt Rivke often made the journey from Grodek to visit her sister Chane Esther. She would always bring sweets and the latest dolls she had sewed to distribute among her nieces and nephews.

Soon after the Great War, Aunt Rivke married Chaim Berel Chilke. She left Grodek and moved to live with her husband on the few hectares of land he farmed on the outskirts of the provincial town Bielsk. Mother was with her at the time, picking cucumbers, when Rivke tripped and fell; and, as a result, Aunt Rivke miscarried.

Mother lies curled up in bed, in a foetal position, as she recuperates from her own fall. 'What are you thinking about?', I ask her in the darkened room at the back of the house.

'Nothing', she replies, with a tinge of defiance.

Her eyes are blackened, her nose bruised, perhaps broken; and she shields herself from any suggestion of pity. I have known her as a tough person at most times, hiding any sign of pain. She seemed always buried in work, as she brought up three sons in the New World. Memories of that other world she had known in her childhood were restricted; while those more painful were kept at bay, and only revealed themselves unexpectedly, triggered by something that would throw her off guard. Such as this sudden fall; or the disturbing dreams from which she would awaken, shouting, 'Mama! Mama!', unaware that I could hear her from the room next door where her cries had awoken me. In the moments that followed I would creep along the passage to my parents' bedroom door, to gather snatches of whispered conversations between them as mother recounted her dream of towns on fire, and of her mother, father, brothers, and sisters running from the flames. In time, such dreams also became dreams of my own.

She would take the night train from Bialystok station, for she loved watching the lights of villages emerging from the darkness. She looked forward to this journey every year, for she would spend the summer months with Aunt Rivke and Uncle Chaim Berel Chilke. On a day of incessant drizzle I set out on the same route, for the sixty kilometres south to Bielsk. The train moves slowly, stopping often in hamlets or isolated stations in the middle of open country-side. Passengers scurry out in the gloom, and make their way towards solitary homesteads or clusters of cottages.

It is evening when I alight and make my way along the main street of Bielsk. The rain has stopped, the sky cleared. A pale full moon has begun its ascent over a forest of television antennae jutting from the red-tiled roofs of pre-war apartments. In the centre of town, as in Bialystok, there is a clock-tower. It rises above a row of poplars and, at the apex of the spire above the clock, a wind vane shifts erratically in the evening breezes.

This is the terrain of the shtetl, where market gardens and farms clutch at the hems of townlets and villages. On the following after-noon, a Friday, I stroll through Bielsk along dirt roads lined with weatherboard cottages. In this neighbourhood there lives, I have been told, a coal dealer by the name of Kaminski. On the way I am drawn by the sound of chanting to a Russian Orthodox church, overflowing with townsfolk at prayer. Women in kerchiefs kneel outside the arched entrance, while others crowd in the vestibule and church hall. The air is thick with incense, the walls lined with icons of gold haloed saints, tapestries of biblical scenes, and portraits of Christ in his mar-tyrdom. A bearded priest leads the chant, and a chorus of women echoes his resonant voice with a harmonising refrain.

A cottage: its timber slabs recently painted light brown; the front garden in full bloom with chrysanthemums, daisies, marigolds, sunflowers — gold upon gold. The drive beside the cottage opens out into a back yard. Used tyres lie scattered among piles of wood. A battered truck, without wheels, its underbelly buried in dirt, sprawls behind an empty cart. A horse stands in a shed, quietly munching oats. A scrawny terrier leaps from a kennel and yelps furiously at the stranger in the yard.

I knock on the front door; there is no response. Through an open window I can hear the drone of voices which seem to be coming from a television. I persist and, after ten minutes or so, the door is opened by an old man who has obviously just been aroused from sleep. He moves out onto the verandah with measured steps. His cheeks are sunbaked crimson, his hair a dishevelled mass of greys, while his shoulders emanate a strength that reflects a lifetime of physical labour. He speaks slowly, in a Yiddish that has retained its melodious softness. It is obviously mama loshen, his mother tongue, spoken with ease and fluency. I detect a similar cadence in the Polish as he calls on his wife, who has been visiting a next-door neighbour, to prepare a meal for this unexpected visitor from abroad.

Kaminski the coal dealer: at dawn he harnesses his horse to a cart laden with coal, and plods through the streets of Bielsk selling fuel to householders. At night, on the verandah, Kaminski tells me his story in a Yiddish drawl that lapses occasionally into a reflective silence.

He was born in the nearby shtetl of Orla. 'My grandfathers, Bishke Zabludowski and Reb Aron Yankev, were born and raised in Orla', I tell him. 'There are no more Jews left in Orla, not a single one', he replies.

Kaminski had been raised in Orla, and had worked in his father's bakery. At the outbreak of war, when Orla was occupied by the Soviets, he had joined the Red Army. In 1945 he had returned to a shtetl that was Judenrein. It was as if all those he had known had vanished overnight.

Kaminski moved to Bielsk, married a Polish woman, and became wedded also to the streets of the town. Decade upon decade he had followed a familiar route, in horse and cart, delivering coal to a daily rhythm, to the turning of the seasons, to the unfolding of the years. Meanwhile, one by one, the few remaining Jews had left to begin life anew, in lands far removed.

His two grown-up daughters had also moved. Their portraits stand on a mantelpiece in the dining room where we eat kasha and chicken. Our hastily assembled Shabbes meal continually expands as Zoshia, Kaminski's wife, delivers yet another dish from the kitchen. One daughter lives in Israel, another in West Germany. Between them they have eight children. On the wall there hangs a painting of a young couple gazing over Jerusalem, 'city of gold'. Nearby there is a framed portrait of a rabbi, prayer shawl draped around his shoulders, at worship in front of Torah scrolls.

Shabbes in Bielsk: Kaminski plays Yiddish records, and one song in particular, which he plays over and over again. When it ends he lifts the needle, places it back on the same track, and settles in his chair. He listens with a bemused smile to the 'Ballad of the Miller', for whom the turning of the wheel, the grinding of yet another batch of grain, marks the passage of time in a shtetl of fading dreams.

As we eat, Kaminski's son Marek arrives. At first he seems distant, a touch wary, an awkward giant who towers over us with little trace of his father's shtetl warmth and spontaneity. Marek has inherited the fairer features of Zoshia. His Yiddish is clumsy, unpractised. He relaxes only much later, as he drives us to the apartment of Moshe Berman, the one other pre-war Jew who still lives in Bielsk.

Moshe is not at home. Marek suggests we look for him on the patch of land he farms just out of town. A dirt road leads us several kilometres from the lights of Bielsk, to a huddle of sheds. It is nine-thirty on a Friday night, long after the stars have ushered in the Sabbath, and Moshe is at work. The land around us appears barren and desolate under a shroud of darkness.

Moshe seems surprised and bewildered to see us, although I soon realise that this sense of distraction is always with him. He is short and stout. When he laughs, his forehead splits across the centre and his eyebrows lift like the hoods of twin cobras. And his mind: it never ceases to twist and shift from thought to thought, abruptly changing direction midstream as he rushes from chore to chore.

'The cows must be locked up for the night', Moshe mutters. 'They must be fed properly, made warm, comfortable, content. Only then can I allow myself to go home.'

He dashes towards the cowshed, suddenly stops, turns, and veers back to greet me again while apologising for not having welcomed his guest properly. This is, after all, a rare occasion, to have a compatriot visit from so far away. Moshe waves an arm in an arc to indicate the extent of his land.

'My ten hectares, my cows, my wheat fields, my life. Do you know what it is for a Jew in Poland to own land? All my life, this was my dream. Who would have believed that in old age it would happen? And has it brought me happiness? Peace of mind? Prosperity? Look for yourself. A Shabbes night, and still I am working. I am a servant to this land, bound to the needs of animals, may my enemies have such luck.'

Again Moshe runs off to round up a stray cow. He returns gasping for breath. 'A man of seventy, working on Shabbes. I always thought that to have land was to be secure, a man of substance. Instead I am a peasant, a slave, a fool.'

Moshe dances from shed to shed, runs nervously here and there to attend to his duties, dashes back to tell me anecdotes, beams, frowns, blows his cheeks up into bloated balloons as he heaves in the night air, urges his cows homewards, berates his luck, and veers erratically from self mockery to vigorous handshakes. The last prewar Jews living in Bielsk stand in an open field on a Shabbes night, a full moon on the decline, as a chill descends. Both of them are captive to a land that has yielded a bitter harvest. And yet it is obvious that this terrain was their first, as it will be their last great love.

Sometimes on a journey there is an unexpected symmetry to things, a moment in which all seems to be balanced on a fine point of harmony and stillness. Bielsk stands equidistant between the townlets of Bransk and Orla, which are about ten kilometres away on either side. Late on a Shabbes night, two ageing men are standing in an open field within sight of the lights of Bielsk. Kaminski the coal dealer is the last Jew from Orla; Moshe Berman the peasant is the last Jew from Bransk. Both of them returned to their beloved shtetlech in the wake of the Annihilation to find them razed, their loved ones gone. Both decided to move away, but did not have the heart to completely forsake the province of their childhood. So they settled in Bielsk, where a visitor from afar now stands between them, equidistant from Bransk, where his paternal grandmother Sheine

Liberman was born, and Orla, where his grandfathers Reb Aron Yankev Probutski and Bishke Zabludowski were raised.

This is a tale of three shtetlech, two old Jews, and a traveller in search of family lineages that have almost faded from existence. And at this moment, under a waning full moon, there is a touch of perfection and a hint that somewhere, very close, there hovers another realm in which can be found an understanding and acceptance of things that goes far beyond mere words.

At 4 a.m. on summer days, throughout the 1920s, Chaim Berel Chilke, accompanied by a niece from Bialystok, would harness a pair of horses to a wagon loaded with cucumbers, beetroot, cabbages, and potatoes. In the pungent pre-dawn air they trotted through the streets of Bielsk onto the road to Bransk, past a necklace of villages lit up by lanterns that could be glimpsed through windows and doorways as peasants prepared for another day of harvest. The wagon would come to a halt in the town square of Bransk, where the market was teeming with early buyers hurrying between stalls to take their pick of the best vegetables. So many times I have heard the story of this journey, the most joyous of mother's remembrances; and each time she tells it, she smiles with the reliving of it.

On a summer morning in 1986 a bus ploughs through pools of water which are spreading under a persistent rain. The road is lined with poplars that have begun to shed their leaves. Every few kilometres there is a settlement: Kolnica, Grobowiez, Lubin, each a collection of cottages dripping rain. Just a few villagers can be seen scurrying by, rugged up in thick overcoats. Scarecrows lean at precarious angles over crops that bend under the storm. Cows stand against each other under solitary trees. Waterfowl forage in soggy swamps, and a man leads a horse across farmland.

In these swamps and fields, they sought a place to hide — in barns, between reeds and long grass, or dug in beneath the ground. They crept towards the houses of Polish peasants and acquaintances, pleading for refuge — if not for themselves, for their children. Those that succumbed to hunger became fodder for foxes. To harbour a Jew was to risk execution. Eyes glanced furtively over shoulders. This was the season of hunter and hunted; the bonds of civility had been cut asunder and left to rot in the summer of 1942.

Among the hunted was Moshe Berman. In the summer of 1942 he lived under the land, in a shelter burrowed deep into the earth. From time to time, under cover of night, the Polish farmer who had allowed him to stay in his fields would deliver food. And among the many Jews of Bransk who had remained trapped within the town were relatives of my father: uncles, aunts, cousins from the Liberman family; while in the towns of Bielsk and Orla dwelled Chaim Berel Chilke, Aunt Rivke, their daughter Freda, and Probutskis, and Zabludowskis. In the summer of 1942 they awaited their fate, within crowded ghettos, increasingly aware of what loomed ahead. Couriers and partisans had conveyed the rumours: not so far distant was a forest clearing called Treblinka, a journey by train of just a few hours . . .

The bus lurches through the streets of Bransk to avoid flooded gutters. On arrival at the bus depot I set out immediately on a familiar errand, with always the same question to get things started: 'Where is the Jewish cemetery?' A drunkard points the way. A horse-drawn cart splashes past, sending up a spray of muddied water.

The road leads out of town across a stream swollen by the rains. Floodwaters swirl beneath a bridge and spread across harvested fields. Everyone I meet seems to know where the burial ground lies. 'Take the road until the grove of oaks. Turn left, and walk along the overgrown path until it peters out in the long grass.' I find the headstones, hidden beneath shrubs, and wedded to roots of trees. The Hebraic characters are, as usual, almost indecipherable. A word here, a name there. No Libermans. And hardly any stones. This cemetery has long been abandoned; yet everyone in Bransk seems to know where it is, this gathering of stones just beyond the town limits.

Moshe Berman sits at the table perplexed, his forehead split by deep furrows that ripple to the sides in smaller troughs. Gradually, as the night proceeds, the creases loosen, and his breath flows more easily. Occasionally, now, there is a flash of radiance, a look of triumph: Moshe Berman has recognised a nigun. He gropes for the words, drawing them from deep reserves of his memory, where they have lain dormant for years:

> Yidl with his fiddle,
> Berel keeping beat.
> Sing me a melody
> In the middle of the street.

The hours of the night are being consumed one by one, gulped down with vodka and food. The spirits flow freely in the apartment of Zirel the widow. A table bulges with roast duck and potatoes, slices of beetroot soaked in oil, carrot stew, gefilte fish, salted herring, poppy-seed cake, apple compote, borscht, wine, and whisky.

'My stomach is exploding', gasps Kaminski, as he whirls around the room to refill glasses that are eagerly stretched out towards him. This is a special occasion, a celebration; and I comprehend, fully now, how it was in Yiddish shtetlech that stood defenceless on the flatlands of East Poland, wedged between imminent perils, dodging disasters, keeping heart and soul together with evenings such as this.

Moshe hums snatches of melodies. He dredges up random verses like fragments of lost parchment, and flings them across the room:

> There's a well in my garden with a bucket dangling
> And my lover comes to drink there every evening.

'Moshe! Now you have many wells on your land!', exclaims Kaminski.

'But no lovers; just water for the cows', laments Moshe. 'Who would have thought it possible,' he adds, 'that in my old age I'd be an owner of fields and beasts, a man of property.' Moshe Berman thumps the table with his fists: 'Aron! A Jew must have a bit of land and a sword in his hand to defend it!'

'The sword won't do us any good', retorts Kaminski. 'No matter what we do, there will always be a black plague upon us sooner or later. What we need is a nigun and a glass of schnapps!'

Tonight we have a rare quorum, almost, for there are nine of us in all; just one short of the required number. Let me introduce the company that has gathered in the apartment of Zirel the widow. Besides Moshe Berman and Kaminski there is Zoshia, Kaminski's wife, ruddy faced, her shock of auburn hair beginning to grey at the edges. On marrying Kaminski she had converted to the Jewish faith. Their son, Marek, the fair-haired giant, had begun the evening with that same awkwardness he had displayed when we first met several days ago; but as the night progresses he loses his reserve and, for a time at least, relaxes in our company. Our hostess, Zirel, was born a daughter of Jews; but before her childhood was over her parents had said, 'Enough of this curse; it brings us nothing but miseries!'. They had ripped the mezuzah off their door, and had never again mentioned their origins. Zirel's young son and daughter have watched tonight's antics with astonishment — shocked to see their mother find her way back to a tongue they had never heard her speak, and join in melodies they had never heard her sing. As the room spins with increasing abandon, the children give way and join us in our wild attempts to reawaken ancestral dreams.

Towards midnight, Moshe's son Romek arrives. He is a chubby man with a pale pink complexion and a large forehead which extends back to a receding hairline. His eyes, however, betray an enduring anxiety. Romek, it soon becomes apparent, is driven by a single obsession: how to find a way out of this provincial town. He clings to me with increasing tenacity. I am the one who possesses a foreign passport.

'Can you obtain a permit, a visa? This country is no place for me. I am a fish out of water here.'

Moshe comes to his aid: 'He is right. I don't mind if I die here. I've lived long enough. But for him it is different. Maybe you can find him a sponsor? A job? A wife?'

'Why not Zirel the widow?' says Marek.

'One husband was enough', laughs Zirel. 'That is, unless you can find me a robot, someone who would never talk back.'

'Oh, God in heaven,' sings Kaminski: 'Where does one find such a husband, a golem? So meek and so mild, a man who doesn't ask any questions; a man who does everything he's told; such a man is a piece of gold.'

Romek descends to the downstairs apartment he shares with his father, and returns with a pile of letters. He pushes them into my hands. As I sort through them I see that they are from various countries.

'I have many penfriends', says Romek. 'I am always asking them to send me a permit. None of them seems able or willing to do so.'

'Enough! Leave our guest alone!', interjects Kaminski. 'If you want to leave so badly, find your own way to escape. As for me, I'm here to stay. This is where I'll be buried. Let me enjoy my simche in peace!'

Kaminski heaves himself onto a chair. He sways unsteadily as his hands extend upwards. The chair groans beneath his considerable weight as he reaches out for the chandelier and pushes it into motion. The chandelier sweeps shadows and patterns onto the walls, and we clutch each successive hour until the night finally runs out of its allotted time.

At dawn Kaminski, Zoshia, Moshe, and Zirel accompany me out onto streets which glisten with freshly fallen rain. We stumble forward together, humming fragments of Moshe's long-lost song:

> There's a well in my garden with a bucket hanging
> And my lover comes to drink there every morning.

And behind us, oblivious to our singing and joking, Romek, driven by his obsession, sticks to me like a shadow, tugging and whispering: 'Aron! A permit! A visa! Please help me leave this black hole.'

Over a century ago, great-grandfather Shmuel David Zabludowski regularly walked the road between Bielsk and Orla, delivering mail to remote hamlets at a time when Yiddish shtetl life was at its zenith. Great-grandfather Reb Isaac Probutski was then the sexton of a small prayer house. Of him it was said that, when he prayed, his fervour was so great all the townsfolk could hear him. 'Ah! Reb Isaac has taken leave of his senses again', they observed in admiration.

Reb Isaac's wife, Rachel the Rebbetzin, more than matched him in piety. Rachel ran a cheder for girls, where she taught the rules of orthodox conduct and the basic prayers as practised by the Slonimer Hasidim. Rachel observed every letter of the law. Mother has an enduring memory, from one of her childhood visits to Orla, of Rachel crawling under the kitchen table to remove her wig and comb her natural hair, out of sight of the menfolk, as orthodox law required.

Generations of Probutskis and Zabludowskis lived in Orla. Where they had come from before they settled there, and exactly when they did so, I can only speculate. As for when I became aware that there existed such a place, of that too I have little idea. It seems to have always been with me, the knowledge that somewhere on this planet there was an ancestral village called Orla where, centuries ago, my forebears had emerged after years of wandering to begin life anew.

A storm is fermenting as I set out for Orla on the back of a motorcycle. I nestle behind the driver's leather jacket to shield myself from the gravel and clay that gush from the wheels as we ride through flash floods. My first taste of the road to Orla is of grit, hailstones, and a biting wind that penetrates to the marrow of my bones.

We come to a halt in front of the Great Synagogue. Random blotches of peeling plaster infest raw brickwork. A pair of fat columns guard an arched doorway boarded by thick slabs of oak. The synagogue towers forty metres above me, deformed by years of neglect.

A burst of violent wind sends me scurrying up a steep stairway ascending from a side entrance, to a room littered with bird droppings and feathers. A dozen dead pigeons lie scattered over the floorboards. Gusts of wind rip through gaps in timber panels nailed clumsily over what was once a slender arched window. Birds fly in from the storm. Feathers are sent swirling and chaos prevails.

I make my way to the cavernous main hall. Four massive pillars arch into ceilings that rise into vaults far above. On the walls and pillars can be seen the remains of frescoes: faint bunches of grapes clinging to vines. The building, both inside and out, is clad in scaffolding: planks, beams, and platforms scale the walls and trail across the ceiling. The voices of workmen can be heard discussing the restoration. A notice outside the synagogue proclaims that this is now a protected relic. It is a crime punishable by law to deface the property. The synagogue is to become a museum.

And the Jewish cemetery? This is different from others I have seen; it stands fully exposed, on a rise which overlooks undulating fields. Sheep graze among the twenty corroded stones. The wind is in a frenzy; flocks of ravens veer out of control, caught in spiralling air currents. On this first visit to Orla all seems in disarray, as if the primal elements are hell-bent on tearing to pieces the last decaying remains of the past.

The next day I set out for Orla by bicycle. Several kilometres out of Bielsk the road meanders through Parcewo, a hamlet of farmers' dwellings, sheds, and stables. The arms of an abandoned windmill stand motionless, silhouetted against a sun that has forced its way through the clouds for the first time in many days. A pair of horses drag a wooden plough: the horses snort and pant; the farmer pushes and curses. Man and beast beat the land and each other into submission, and thereby extract yet another crop from worn and weary soils.

In the hamlet of Wolka a young farmer invites me into a yard where he keeps bees, poultry, and carrier pigeons enclosed in cages of wire mesh. Janek shows me his collection of magazines on the art of pigeon rearing, and claims he can train one to deliver messages to me in Australia. A massive Alsatian rages and strains at the leash, while a fragile kitten wanders aimlessly around the yard. Janek's mother limps from the house and scolds him for his lack of hospitality. Together they stuff my shoulder bag with jars of honey, fresh apples, corn, and home-baked bread rolls. As I cycle back onto the road I encounter the postman. A century after Shmuel David walked this route with the mail, it is delivered by moped.

By the time I ride into the cobbled streets of Orla the sky has cleared completely. A gaggle of geese waddle along the main street and hiss menacingly whenever I come close. The leader of the pack steps forward, eyeing me like a bull about to charge. Hens totter on their ungainly legs, sunflowers glow in back lanes, a chainsaw whirs, punk rock shrieks from yards where youths in tattered jeans are tinkering with motorbikes, while elderly men and women sit on wooden benches quietly gossiping.

I approach a cottage where an old woman is attending to an array of potplants scattered about the verandah. Ivies and creepers crawl over the weatherboards and cling tenaciously to a fence that encircles the cottage. Long grass, piles of firewood, and shrubs nuzzle against fruit trees. As I draw up to the front gate the old woman stares at me intently.

'Mmm. Yes . . . Gypsy', she mutters eventually.

I tell her that my grandparents and several aunts and uncles once lived in Orla; they were Jews.

'Ah . . . Jews!', she exclaims. 'Probutski? Zabludowski? Yes, I did know a Zabludowski once . .' But the memory eludes her; she cannot quite place it. 'No. There are no more Jews here', she adds. 'Gone. All gone. Gone a long time ago. Vanished . .'

She invites me inside. The living room is cosy, exuding the scent of musty wallpaper and worn sofas. A stuffed eagle, a masterpiece of taxidermy, leaps out from the wall over the doorway. It glares at me ferociously, wings fully extended, frozen in full flight. In a corner there stands a grandfather clock, and on the walls hang a wooden crucifix, a portrait of a Polish nobleman on horseback, and a montage of photos of the Pope.

'Yes. I knew a Zabludowski once', the old woman mutters. Again she clutches at a vague remembrance, and again she appears to have lost it. 'Perhaps; perhaps I knew a Zabludowski once . . .'

Orla recedes as I cycle towards Bielsk at dusk. A woman sits upon a stool in the middle of a paddock and milks a cow. Farmsteads and tottering barns lean against the horizon. Green pastures yielding a late harvest fade into the night. Constellations and galaxies come to light beneath a vast turquoise dome. Yes, Probutskis and Zabludowskis did live here once; and on such a landscape, on such a night, against fields such as these, over a century ago, great-grandfather Shmuel David, mailbag slung over his shoulders, came trudging home to a Yiddishe shtetl called Orla.

Early morning, as I am about to leave for Bielsk station, Marek arrives unexpectedly. 'You need not go by train', he tells me. 'You are our guest. We will drive you to Bialowieza forest.'

He cannot understand why I prefer to travel alone. He becomes insistent. My refusals are a slight on his offer of hospitality.

Marek's car is waiting downstairs, with two companions in the back seat. The drinking has been in progress for quite a while; the floor of the car is littered with empty bottles. Whereas on previous nights the spirits had flowed with a sense of family and trust, the feeling today is very different. The protection and restraints of elders, children, and community are gone. There is an edge of frustration and raw menace in the drinking. As we speed along country roads the car almost veers out of control on several occasions. The men laugh. They have their arms around each other. They curse their small-town life. Today they are on release from prison, free to fly over the countryside and dare themselves to the brink of the abyss.

In their eyes red rivulets are spreading, criss-crossing, flowing in circles. The men have become a mob, a herd. Join us, they are beckoning to me, and together we will rampage. The rivulets are paper thin, as too is the border between love and hatred, between their desire to overwhelm me with declarations of friendship and their desperate need to give vent to an inner rage. Welcome to the brotherhood. Together we can be a force, invincible, triumphant.

The day crumbles into an aimless stupor, a series of taverns, liquor stores, roadside pauses to relieve ourselves in fields before again resuming our relentless pursuit of oblivion. The journey is slipping away from me. I am becoming a mere cipher in a furious charge towards an endlessly receding landscape. It is time to insist, to get out. Marek refuses; he cannot comprehend.

'You want to desert the brotherhood? You want to break our oaths of loyalty? We have just begun', he tells me. 'The hours of the night are yet to come. You cannot leave us now.'

It is then that I realise confrontation cannot be avoided. He must be faced directly; and when I do, I am drawn into an ocean of confusion. There are wild waves of anger, dull blotches of hopelessness, a glint of obsession. Yet there are also specks of light sparkling with the last promise of love, the barest sign that Marek can still be reached. To look away now would mean defeat, but to continue to look much longer would overwhelm me.

Suddenly Marek awakens from his trance. He changes direction abruptly, with a look of contempt, and skids towards Bialowieza forest. The game is up; the brotherhood dissolving. Two men lie sprawled across the back seat. Marek seems broken. 'It could have been such a great night', he stutters, as we pull up by the Bialowieza Inn.

Now I understand that there have been many such nights: some led by well-organised brotherhoods who have calculated their assaults before priming themselves with spirits to spur on their rage; and others, which have begun as ours today, with a show of love, an intent to create intimate bonds, and yet they too have ended with a blind charge towards darkness. And as a result the earth is soaked with blood.

Bialowieza forest straddles the border between Poland and the Soviet Union. It comprises 58 000 hectares on the Polish side alone, within which are bison, elk, wolves, foxes, beaver, lynxes, and many species of birds and beasts on the verge of extinction. Late afternoon, and there emerges from the forest an isolated bird call, an insect's soft shriek, a rustle and flash of reptile scurrying by, petrified at the intruder. Fungus, moss, lichens, and wild herbs cling to each other; vines, foliage, and a dense undergrowth of living and dead matter give way to meadows of wild flowers illuminated by the last light. Paths thread through groves of spruce, lindens, and maples, deep into the forest; and even here, in the remotest recesses, I come across a primitive crucifix made of oak. Beneath it is a stone and, upon the stone, figures indicating how many were executed here, in the cold shade, beneath the forest canopy.

The country is littered with reminders: stones, plaques, monuments; in forest clearings, within open fields, on busy city streets, in village squares, by roadside shrines, and in provincial museums. In all seasons, on anniversaries that crowd the calendar from one year's end to the other, there are candles to be lit, silent vigils to be held, and pilgrimages from abroad to be undertaken in a land stalked by smouldering sorrows. And beyond the physical borders, the echoes of what happened just one generation ago, on this soil, reverberate in the dreams of survivors scattered throughout the world; and the children of the survivors, they also have been drawn into this landscape of darkness with its aborted stories and its collective memory of suffering.

There must be a way beyond this grim inheritance. It is as if, having come this far, I have no choice but to continue the journey, completing tales half told and half imagined, as I follow my forebears on their final trek, wherever it may have taken them, and beyond, far beyond, so that I will never have to return.

Part Two

Part Two

Chapter Ten

I MAKE MY WAY at dawn to the Palatz station, so called because here once stood the summer palace of Count Branitski. It overlooked the Bialowieza settlement, and became a hunting retreat for a succession of kings and czars. They would ride into the forest on horseback, accompanied by large retinues of cavalry and soldiers, with hunting dogs scurrying about their feet. Palaces loomed large in the Yiddish novels I consumed as a child. They would be situated on hills overlooking a shtetl in which life revolved around a synagogue, a marketplace, and a ritual bath-house. At least, this is how father describes it. 'Take these three ingredients', he tells me, 'and you have a shtetl: a place to pray, a place to trade, and a place to bathe; while above, stood the world of Polish and Russian aristocracy — remote and inaccessible.'

It was a fragile romance, my dream of the shtetl. And it was vague. I skimmed the many books father had brought with him from Poland. They exuded a scent of decay and a comforting feeling of warmth and solidity. Occasionally I came across flowers my father had pressed between pages. The Yiddish texts, in Hebraic script, revealed their meaning only in fleeting glimpses. I did not have mastery over the language. English had submerged the mother tongue; and as a child I was not seeking detail. I was content with the skimming, as a skier is more than content with a landscape that whirls past in a brilliant flash of colour.

The romance can be felt on this cool dawn as I wait for a train back to Bialystok. On the station roof two herons perch in a nest, outlined against a pale blue sky. The moon is still visible, descending towards the upper reaches of the forest. Throughout the Bialystoku region, mists are rising and, in provincial stations, groups of peasants sit upon their luggage as sleepy station-masters signal the arrival of the first train.

When Dorota received a blue dress on her fourth birthday, she recalled the blue hat she had recently noticed in a shop window. She crept into her mother's bedroom, removed some money from a handbag, and ran back to the shop to purchase the blue hat. Her mother's anger was softened by pride in Dorota's sense of good taste. She chided her about the stolen money, but was more than pleased to allow her to keep the hat.

Several days later, Dorota wore the blue dress for the first time. Her mother pinned a pink flower to the hat. They walked together: mother, father, two sisters, under a clear blue sky; blue upon blue with shades of pink on an autumnal landscape in a town somewhere in the vicinity of Bialystok.

Dorota tells me the story forty-seven years later in a chance encounter, on a train travelling between Palatz station and Bialystok. There are countless such stories lying dormant in remote Polish towns and hamlets, always about to be told yet again, variations on a common theme, memories which refuse to fade.

They were on the way to church. She was overjoyed with the new dress, the hat, the presence of her parents and sister. Life was an infinity of blue in which there hovered a ball of gold; and as Dorota gazed up at this expanse she noticed that, from the halo surrounding the golden ball, a silver streak had materialised and was diving towards her. The first bomb was falling; the girl was being pushed by her parents, screaming frantic instructions: 'Run! Jump! Stay down!' The infinity of blue was now blotted by a swarm of machines spitting fire, and Dorota's blue dress was stained by mud as she lay on the ground in a town consumed by flames: September 1, 1939. Another war had begun. Never again would the family be together.

Father isn't sure when he received his last letter from Bialystok. Despite the many hours he has spent sorting out journals and letters from a past life, there never seems to be an end to it. 'At first I lose a valued document', he explains. 'Then I find it again, unexpect-edly, when looking for something else. So I put it in a new place, which I am sure I can easily locate. But then I forget where it is and I have to start searching again.' It is as if the past refuses to allow itself to be put in order, and is always intruding into the present with disturbing hints of a world of irredeemable chaos, forever spin-ning out of control.

Yet, as usual, when I press him hard enough, something seems to turn up, and father finds a letter from his brother, Isaac, dated August 1938. 'Isaac was down to earth', says father, 'family oriented, ready to lend a helping hand in the toughest of times.' He had joined Bishke as a partner in the family business, making deliveries to local subscribers. Eventually he branched out on his own, to work as an administrator in the offices of Yiddish newspapers.

Isaac writes of family matters and confesses to having become a simple 'Yidl', preoccupied with his son's teething problems and bowel movements, immersed in 'my little corner of existence where all yesterdays are the same as tomorrows'. His infant son is a rascal, a cheeky boy who leaves behind him a train of torn and broken objects. 'But when he gazes at you with his wide-open eyes it is impos-sible to get angry, no matter how much damage he has caused.'

Father's eyes light up as he reads me Isaac's letter, and is reminded of friends he has not seen for over fifty years. Each one referred to by Isaac he expands upon, with eccentric accounts of their var-ious deeds as young men about town.

'Ran into Godel Perelstein the other day', writes Isaac. 'He carries your last letter around with him as if it were a precious treasure and apologises for not having replied. He claims he can only com-pose letters when he is in an appropriate mood.'

'Godel was a great reciter of Yiddish poetry', father adds. 'He would perform in front of packed audiences in the Palace theatre, declaiming the works of my favourite writers.'

'Moishe Poznanski sends his regards', reports Isaac. 'He was a hand-some man', says father. 'A leather-worker by trade. For many years we dreamed of setting up our own business with the name "Ever-lasting Shoes". When at last we managed to scrape together the money, the business lasted for about a month before our creditors realised how hopeless we were and dismantled our fantasies.'

As for Zundel Mandelbroit, father needs little prompting. He was his best friend. 'We used to go out into the fields on summer nights and camp under the stars. We wanted to penetrate the mysteries of the night. But if even a few mosquitoes attacked, we quickly forgot our resolve, broke off our philosophising, and ran back home.'

And as he reminisces father recalls that, yes, there had been another letter after Isaac's, written by Zundel, sometime towards the end of 1939. It had disappeared. 'Perhaps it is lying somewhere around the house', father speculates. 'But what he wrote I can never forget. "Help us get out", he had pleaded. "We need visas, permits, a means of escape. The ground is beginning to burn beneath our feet! Help us get out!" '

He moves fast. Time is slipping through his clutches. Yet he holds on. He often breaks into a run, a little trot, as he careers around the house. He paints the peeling kitchen walls in pinks and blues, bright colours. But only in patches. Father is far too impatient to remain still for long. His spritely body scampers up and down ladders.

'You're a growing boy', I tell him when he reaches the top rung.

Never at a loss for words, he replies: 'Yes, growing down into the ground, towards the everlasting, a meal for the worms.'

He trips through the ninth decade of his life, a joke here, a comment there, forever rushing, as if pursued by ghosts that have never quite caught up with him. And I begin to suspect that, for him also, the ground is burning beneath his feet, and has been for many years. As for mother, she has become increasingly withdrawn, her arms folded hard against her chest, her glance directed elsewhere, far removed. She sits still, resigned, hunched within herself, allowing the ghostly dance of memory to have its way.

Chaimke, Uncle Joshua Probutski's first child, seems to have been everyone's favourite. When he was a baby the six Probutski sisters would argue over who would have him sleeping next to them. He was the first of their nephews, their first opportunity for mothering.

Mother last saw Chaimke in December 1932, on the day she left Bialystok to join her sister Feigl in Melbourne. A third sister, Chaie, left soon after for Argentina where she was reunited with her husband. Liebe, Sheindl, and Tzivie remained in Bialystok, and Chaimke continued to enjoy the devoted attention of just three aunts.

In contrast to father, mother spends little time sorting out old documents. Instead she has selected the few she seems to regard as essentials, and assembled them in one compact bundle held together by a rubber band. Included are several photos taken in happier pre-war New Zealand days; letters she had received from her three sons during their various journeys abroad; and a postcard I had sent from Milan after attending a concert in the renowned La Scala opera house. Of all the cards I have written over the years, this is the one she has retained — touched, it appears, by my references to her as a singer.

The postcard lies wedged between a number of letters, extracted from the many sent by her husband between 1932 and 1936, during their three-and-a-half years of enforced separation. As a child I had often come across the letters, tied neatly together, in a dining room cupboard which I would explore when mother and father were both out at work. Father scolded me for tampering with such important documents; but he had allowed us, the three brothers, to remove stamps from the envelopes. They became the pride of our collection. Not one of our friends had seen such ancient Polish stamps, and they were worth a fortune in exchanges.

The few letters that mother has retained appear to have been chosen with some deliberation. Within one of them, among father's usual ten pages or more of Bialystok gossip and poetic declarations of love, he had included a note written by Chaimke. It is short and to the point:

> My dear Aunty Hoddes,
>
> I am going up to fifth grade. At the moment we are on holidays. We've already had two months and only two weeks remain. Now I'll tell you how I spend my day. I wash myself, eat and pray. Then I go out into the street. Now I want to tell you that I'm collecting stamps. You always send me a yellow and a green one. Send me other colours also. I'm ending my letter. I give my regards to everyone. Goodnight. I am going to sleep.

Sometime towards mid 1939, mother received a letter from Bialystok written by her sister Sheindl. 'Is it possible to obtain visas for our parents?', she had asked. 'Or for a brother? A sister? And if not, at least for Chaimke? Forgive us for asking, but things are looking bleak.'

Whenever mother talks about Chaimke, as she often has over the years, she lapses into a voice tinged with weariness and regret. She had tried to obtain a visa for him. She had hounded immigration officials in Wellington, knocked on doors, pleaded on Chaimke's behalf, turned this way and that — all to no avail. Doors to the New World were not easily prised open. Mother had to make do with sending money; and she was never to find out whether the family received it or not.

Through provincial stations westwards, from the Bialowieza forest via Bielsk, before turning north, the train conveys me back towards Bialystok. Although it is barely a month since I entered Poland, Bialystok has become a home of sorts, a focal point around which the journey revolves. Yet I continue to approach it with wariness. Faint traces of forgotten dreams are reawakened by the hypnotic pulse of trains moving across Polish landscapes; and no matter how evocative the scenery, I invariably turn to a more compelling inner world, churning with fragments that for a moment seem accessible, alight with magic and promise, before they fade into a disturbing sense of suffocation and dread.

One dream in particular, which had threaded through my childhood, resurfaces as a conscious memory. I am on a picnic with mother and father. Holding my elder brother's hand, I begin to stray into a nearby forest. Our parents' faces fade behind us; their comforting presence vanishes. We are alone, lost, wandering. Trees and bushes seem like shadowy creatures. In the distance a light appears. It draws us to the edge of a clearing where a massive fire is blazing. We remain hidden among bushes, and gaze upon figures darting with bodies which they hurl into the flames. As I turn to look at my brother, I realise he is clearly visible in the firelight. We are both fully exposed. There is no hope of escape. The figures are advancing towards us. I force myself to awake and, as always, I come out of the dream choking.

Friday, September 15, 1939. The second day of Rosh Hashonah. Midmorning. In crowded synagogues and houses of prayer, the New Year is being ushered in when townsfolk dash by, waving their arms in alarm, their voices straining with terror as they shout: 'The Nazis are on the outskirts of Bialystok. *Loift! Untloift! Farbalt zich!'* — the age-old cry which precedes a pogrom. 'Run! Flee! Hide yourselves!'

At noon the first Wehrmacht divisions appear on the deserted streets, firing flame-throwers through windows into homes and stores. Hundreds are wounded or killed in the assault. Raids, robberies, and arbitrary beatings become the order of the day. Women are shot for not giving up the rings on their fingers. The populace cowers indoors, sustained by one desperate hope fuelled by broadcasts on Moscow radio: Red Army troops have crossed the eastern borders and are heading in the direction of Bialystok.

On Thursday, September 21, three planes swoop in low to release pamphlets proclaiming the imminent arrival of Soviet forces. On Friday, Yom Kippur eve, German soldiers can be seen packing and taking to roads bound for Warsaw and the East Prussian border. The last retreating divisions are pelted with rocks hurled by embittered youths.

Towards evening the Red Army marches into a city decorated with red flags. Communal delegations greet them with flowers and speeches of welcome. Thousands of elated Bialystoker throng the streets. Jewish youths embrace Russian soldiers with great enthusiasm. On this, the holiest of nights, the culmination of the Days of Awe, orthodox Jews pack the synagogues and pray with renewed fervour. It is as if a miracle has taken place. Bialystok had been granted a reprieve.

On the Day of Atonement the town clock is reset to Moscow time. My grandfather, Bishke Zabludowski, stands again on the streets below, now selling the Soviet-backed Yiddish newspaper, the *Bialystoker Shtern*. The Nazi-Soviet pact, signed before the outbreak of war, has enabled the two empires to repartition Poland after a mere twenty-one years of independence. History has again turned full circle before Bishke's eyes, while he seems to have remained the one constant, the observer of yet another spin in Bialystok's fluctuating fortunes.

To this day, when Bialystoker refer to the winter of 1939-40, they shake their heads and exclaim: 'You have no idea! Such frosts! So relentlessly cold! We were buried in snow. Water froze in the pipes.

Field rats abandoned the countryside and sought shelter in the city. They scurried about our houses in hordes and fought over crumbs. Long queues would form soon after midnight as we vied for a meagre ration of bread. By the time the shops were within reach, the shelves were often already empty.'

But a haven it was, nevertheless, for refugees who stole across the nearby border, in flight from Nazi-occupied Poland. Within months the population had doubled to over two hundred thousand. The community responded with an open heart. Public kitchens were opened. Accommodation was provided in houses of study and private homes. And in Melbourne a decade later, a newly arrived immigrant, Pinchas Albert, told my father that he had been one of the many Warsaw Jews who had found temporary refuge in Bialystok, and that Bishke Zabludowski would regularly send him a loaf of bread, fresh from his daughter Etel's bakery. That bread became the key to Pinchas' survival. He had retained an image of it in the ensuing years — for there came a time when even the memory of a slice of bread was like manna from heaven.

Thereafter, whenever Pinchas saw father, he would remind him of Bishke's deed; while for father, this occasional reminder became one of the last treasured fragments of information about his own father.

In the 'Red Paradise' as the town wags called it, there evolved an active and frantic night life. Yiddish and Russian drama ensembles, bolstered by actors and writers who had fled Hitler's pogroms, played to packed audiences in the Palace theatre. Eddie Rosner's renowned Warsaw jazz band had also shifted base to Bialystok. Guest singers, musicians, and the Yiddish vaudeville company of Zhigan and Schumacher toured the provinces. Cinemas were refurbished and their seating capacity increased in response to enthusiastic demand. The black market thrived, and illicit gambling houses found eager patrons in a city moving towards a degree of prosperity. Soviet occupation had opened up markets to the east. The textile industry was rejuvenated, and grandfather Reb Aron Yankev could again make his way to a factory job, soon after dawn, as the familiar wail of sirens signalled the start of another working day in Bialystok.

Reb Aron Yankev never allowed himself to be photographed. Not a single portrait exists. He regarded the camera as an 'evil eye', an instrument of the devil. It could rob a man of his soul, erode him of the divine presence. So I picture him trudging to work, as my mother has described him, a small Yidl, averting his eyes from worldly distractions, locked tightly in a private dream of God and his Tzaddik, the Slonimer Rabbi. Reb Aron lived for his brother Hasidim, and for the lean wooden shtibl, the Slonimer prayer-house, where they would gather on Shabbes and holy days. It always seemed, says mother, that he was never quite in the world of the living, except when he was with his beloved Hasidim.

As a child, mother would sometimes deliver Reb Aron Yankev's lunch, and she had noticed that he often stood apart from the other workers. He ate alone, since they were unbelievers. He wrapped himself in a cocoon which thickened as he became older. By then his own children had become unbelievers, or as good as such in his eyes, since they flirted with modernity, shunned arranged marriages, joined leftist political groups, or had left Bialystok altogether to move thousands of miles to the ends of the earth, where they lived, surely, among pagans and apostates.

We can merely speculate about Reb Aron Yankev's thoughts in the factories of the Red Paradise, for he never wrote to his three daughters in the New World; besides, we have reached that point where mother cuts her stories short. Her eyes are lowered, her head slowly nodding. It is as if, so many years later, long after the Event, she still cannot understand how it could have taken place.

Despite the renewed prosperity, the night life, and the large Soviet department stores, all was not well in the Red Paradise. In the shadows there glided the keepers of the city. It was a time for compiling files — intelligence records about suspect ideas and the individuals who held them. The New Order thrived on denunciations, stool pigeons, and informers. Many an old score was settled by a discreet visit to the offices of the secret police.

There are Bialystoker, survivors, who still recall precise details of the first raid, the sound of banging on doors at 3.30 a.m. in mid-April 1940, and the order: 'You have half-an-hour to be ready!' Factory owners and merchants, rabbis and priests, refugees and Polish officers, an assortment of souls labelled as 'untrustworthy elements' were led to the Bialystok station and crammed into freight wagons. 'On the sides of the wagon was written "capacity eight horses". Or was it twelve?' Memory is slippery at such a distance in the living rooms of suburban Melbourne. But there is agreement that about sixty people were conveyed in each wagon and that, many days later, after a suffocating journey across mountain ranges and through vast tracts of forest, they arrived in 'The Land of the White Bears': Siberia.

After subsequent raids many more men were jailed in Bialystok prisons, and their wives and children banished to the Soviet interior. Yet, for all this, Bialystok remained a place of refuge, and the populace was fully aware of it. Despite the news censorship, the refugee grapevine had kept them informed of the terror raging on the other side of the border. The Jews of Bialystok clung to their reprieve.

The air is pungent, the streets dancing with afternoon light. It rebounds from pavements and reflects a golden glow on the windows of ageing tenements. I make my way from the station towards Witold's flat, my Bialystok address. From Kosciuszki Square, the cobblestoned heart of the city, past the clock-tower, I skirt the city gardens before turning, like a homing pigeon, into the narrow streets of the Chanaykes.

Weekend delirium permeates alleys and lanes. Children clamber over an abandoned car and stomp on the roof in a frenzy. Dogs leap excitedly at their feet, yelping and howling. Factories are at rest. The week's work is over. Shabbes is approaching. And in the fading light I can imagine them, as they stream from the Great Synagogue and smaller houses of worship.

Among them walks Reb Aron Yankev, from the Slonimer shtibl towards the Chanaykes. Even though mother had strayed from the ways of her elders, she refers to Shabbes in Bialystok as the most magic of times, and she has always maintained the ritual of blessing the Shabbes-licht. Every Friday evening, throughout my childhood, she would place two candlesticks upon a newly washed white cloth over the kitchen table, and light the candles as it grew dark.

The candles have burnt low. Wax pours down the sides and swells in a heap at the base. Reb Aron sits by the table after the meal, overcome by fatigue. His entire body is enveloped in warmth. He surrenders to dreams, his face resting upon his arms. The Queen of Shabbes now reigns supreme.

He awakens several hours later, stretches, runs cold water over his face, wraps himself in a white satin coat, and descends into Ulitza Kievska. He makes his way to the Slonimer shtibl, which stands in a lane not so far from the shadows of the clock-tower. As he enters he is greeted with enthusiasm. 'Reb Aron, give us a tune!', they exclaim.

Flasks of brandy stoke the fire. Arms linked, shoulder to shoulder, they dance in short measured steps that move slowly at first, and then quicken to the pace of the melody. Eyes are closed, faces tilted upwards. Heads sway from side to side. The circle closes, and an ancient fear evaporates. They are the heirs of the Baal Shem Tov, Master of the Good Name, who had appeared not so many years ago, in a village not so many miles away, after the people had emerged from a great calamity. And he had proclaimed that to sink into gloom is to invite the presence of the Evil One. Counter him with ecstatic prayer, he had counselled. Oppose fear with dance, he had advised. Find your way back to the Creator, he had urged.

Another sip of brandy and Reb Aron is spinning. All faces have dissolved into one face, ascending between earth and heaven, beyond conflict and struggle, beyond a scarcity of bread and tedious hours of work; beyond drunken peasants on a rampage; beyond rival armies and contending empires; beyond history's abrupt twists and shifts; and beyond an incessant undertow of fear and suspicion, until merged, within each other, in a whirling circle of light.

In the pre-dawn darkness Reb Aron wanders the silent streets of the Chanaykes, his feet pounding the cobblestones, his head soaring above the roofs, somewhere in the higher heavens. And, as she tells the story, mother's eyes shift upwards, as if fixed upon a waning mirage called Bialystok.

Yet again the fate of Bialystok is heralded from the skies. Before dawn an unsuspecting populace is suddenly awoken by the sound of shattering glass and the shrill scream of Luftwaffe fighters engaged in aerial battles with Soviet planes. Columns of smoke billow towards the heavens as bombs fall upon a military base and civilian suburbs;

and one of them explodes upon the home of Reuben Zak, his wife Feigele, and his daughter Liebele.

Feigele, father's youngest sister, was the very same Feigele who had gone missing on the day the Zabludowski household was hit by bomb fragments at the outset of the first War. She had been one of the first and youngest of the wounded. This time she was one of the first to be killed. Reuben, his wife, and child were wiped out in that very first raid, in the early hours of Sunday, June 22, 1941.

An aunt, uncle, and cousin accounted for. A fragment falls into place. The mosaic is taking shape. This is a tale of fragments. There is no other way to tell it. This is my inheritance: shreds of family fate seeking recognition. It can only be pieced together.

Those with transmitters heard the news on Berlin radio: at four a.m. the Nazis had crossed the western borders and had launched an invasion of the Red Empire. The Soviet-Nazi pact was in tatters. The Jews of Bialystok were overcome by a chilling fear. They ran to each other's homes seeking reassurance. They clung to the hope that the Reds would repel the attack. At noon they heard the Soviet foreign minister, speaking on Moscow Radio, remark that Hitler had invaded in the same month as had Napoleon. An even darker fate awaited Hitler, he predicted.

His words were of little comfort to a Bialystok under siege. It was soon evident the Red Army was in complete disarray. Officers and commissars were seen loading their wives and children into military vehicles. Grabbing their most precious possessions, they fled east. The panic spread quickly. Trains were choked with passengers. The highway to Minsk overflowed with thousands on the run, clutching packs and sacks, driven by one thought: to escape as fast as possible from the plague about to infest Bialystok. Everything was reduced to a cold sweat, or so I imagine it, from a childhood experience, when a neighbourhood bully gone berserk took after me with a knife — houses seemed to sway and recede out of focus; the ground beneath my feet appeared unsteady.

And so it may have been as they ran on that Sunday, and throughout Monday, their numbers swelling, pursued by planes swooping low to rake them with bullets. The roads were littered with burnt-out tanks, maimed horses, crushed bicycles, overturned wagons and autos. The dead and wounded lay on country paths and in fields of corn. The living dug holes in which to shelter during the night. German soldiers were parachuted in behind the retreating Soviets. East and west were ablaze. Burning trees buckled like bodies in fierce heat. There was nowhere to run.

A city in a vacuum. Days of anarchy and chaos. Red Army guards desert their posts at the Bialystok prison. The building is set alight, and its inmates charge into the streets ransacking stores. They grab crates of liquor, food, clothing, tobacco. For three days the looting continues. An abandoned populace wanders about like animals detecting the scent of an approaching calamity. By Thursday 26 June, a deathly silence has settled over Bialystok. And somewhere within this brooding city there waits Reb Aron Yankev and Chane Esther Probutski, Bishke and Sheine Zabludowski, with their families and friends — their restless dreams coloured by a terrible foreboding.

Chapter Eleven

AS A CHILD, father had been afraid of the Great Synagogue. He would detour on the way home from cheder to avoid the shadows that loomed from its towering walls. At nights, it was claimed, spirits of the dead came here to pray. They would swarm inside draped in white shrouds. Anything white — a coat, a hat, a cat flashing by — would make the child hasten his steps home. He would glance over a shoulder to see if he were being chased by an imp, an ogre, a mischief-maker from the netherworlds.

'Tales of demons and dybbuks wove through our folklore', father muses. 'They lived in chimneys and crept in under doors. Perhaps we enjoyed the thrill. Or perhaps they embodied the real fear that lurked in our lives. After all, at the outset of the first war, the synagogue was damaged by bombs. I came across the smouldering ruins as I roamed the streets next day. But at least, after that assault, the synagogue had been restored, and the phantoms had resumed their nightly gatherings.'

It had always been the centre, the heart of Jewish Bialystok. A succession of prayer-houses had stood there since the days of Count Branitski. The area became known as the Shulhoif, the courtyard district. Compact neighbourhoods radiated from the prayer-house as if clinging to it for protection. The original wooden shul had been destroyed by fire. Its replacement had fallen into disrepair. Cobwebs clung to corners and could not be removed. They were regarded as sacred. When the progressive Abraham Blumenthal became the sexton, he got rid of the cobwebs, despite the objections of town elders.

The Great Synagogue replaced the shul to meet the needs of an expanding city. 'Its tin-plated dome could be seen from afar', father recalls. 'The building seemed vast, with high ceilings, stone steps and arched entrances. But the Shulhoif remained a jumble of wooden cottages and artisans' workshops, the domain of shoemakers, tin-smiths and impoverished tailors. Their dwellings mingled with fish markets, stables, and study houses. Here stood Reb Aron Yankev's Slonimer shtibl and the Talmud Torah I attended as a boy.'

Mother had also known the Shulhoif intimately. She had been employed as a seamstress in the workshop of master tailor Israel Milander. The workshop was a cramped room attached to Milander's cottage. It was cluttered with wooden sofas and work benches. Fox furs hung from the ceilings. Leather skins lay piled in the corners. From the open doorway could be seen the dome of the Great Synagogue.

At night the workshop was converted into living space. When mother arrived for work in the early mornings she would find some of Milander's seven children asleep on makeshift beds. All day clients filed in to be fitted. Peasant women dragged in reluctant husbands to order suits. Gossip mingled with the growl of sewing machines. Alter Chalele, the well known wedding jester, lived directly opposite, and would often come by for a cup of tea. Mother describes him as a plump man with a jovial face; a permanent laugh had engraved itself upon his features. He made his living entertaining at bar mitzvahs, engagements, and circumcisions. Even in Milander's workshop he continued his familiar patter of quips and old wives' tales.

As in so many of mother's anecdotes, there are sudden flashes of harshness; and, when she comes across them, her smile of reminiscence fades. The workshop sweltered in summer and froze in winter. Work began very early and finished well after dark. The pay was low and irregular and, although she had become a member of the Seamstresses' Union to agitate for improved conditions, she finally left to find a better life elsewhere.

Mother's mood lightens as she recalls the leather coat Milander had designed for her as a going-away present. The coat still hangs in my parents' wardrobe. As a teenager I had wanted to remodel it for my own use. But the pattern was set too tight, the shoulders cut too narrow — shaped to fit the slim build of a young woman about to travel to the New World. 'Milander was an honest man', mother emphasizes. 'He made clothes that would last. In those days artisans made things to endure.' And the rare animation in her voice betrays a regret that will never be extinguished.

June 27, 1941. Morning. Nine o'clock. Silence. Deserted streets. An outburst of gunfire. The first Nazi divisions break into Bialystok. The resistance put up by remnants of the Red Army is quickly suppressed with a barrage of incendiary bombs. The victors make their way into residential quarters hurling grenades. Jewish men are hauled out and shot in front of their wives and children. Nine-year-old Witold wanders the streets. He sees men and boys dragged into the Great Synagogue. The building is set alight. In the smoke and confusion the Polish watchman Batoshko manages to open a side door; a mere handful escape. Flames leap through nearby homes. The timber cottages are quickly consumed. Milander's workshop is reduced to a heap of ashes. Alter Chalele, the wedding jester, is among the many hundreds who perish in the synagogue. One third of Jewish homes in Bialystok have been razed. The forest can now be seen directly from the town square. All in a day's work. The first day. In years to come, June 27, 1941 will be remembered and mourned as 'Red Friday'.

Witold drives me to the outskirts of Bialystok. It never takes long to move through a city that has not quite severed itself from field and forest. I am reminded of how primitive Bialystok remains despite its urban facade. Within easy reach are pastures flecked with haystacks. Teams of peasants are burning grasslands. Flames give way to veils of smoke pierced by shafts of afternoon sun.

A path veers off the road into Pietrasze forest. Witold, a forester by profession, loses his quiet reserve as soon as we are among trees. He stops the car occasionally to point out various features: clumps of bilberries, resin oozing from the trunks of conifers, mounds of earth teeming with ants.

The path conveys us to a large clearing. A notice indicates that this was a site of execution. The trees here are seventy, perhaps eighty years old, Witold tells me. And I too can share information about this site, despite coming from an entirely different part of the globe. I have traced it in memorial books, and intimate histories written soon after the war for survivors and former Bialystoker who, like father, would scour them for a familiar name, the fate of a family, or at least a hint, a possibility of knowing.

Father had underlined the crucial passages in red biro: names of friends, streets, and events of personal significance. In accounts of 'Martyr's Thursday', for instance, it is Ulitza Kupietzka which is underlined, the street in which the Zabludowski family had lived for many years. Kupietzka was one of several streets the Nazis cordoned off on July 3, 1941. A thousand men aged between sixteen and sixty were lined up for 'selection'. Workmen and artisans with callouses on their hands were freed. The physically weak — those deemed unfit for slave labour — were detained, tortured by drunken Gestapo officers, loaded onto trucks, driven to this site, and machine-gunned into pits. Nine days later, on a Saturday, five thousand Jewish men were dragged from their homes, ordered to march and sing as they were beaten, and ferried to an unknown destination. All day long the trucks kept returning, empty, in readiness for the next load. Some time later, peasants living on the outskirts of Bialystok told of massacres they had witnessed on that day. Yet again the murders had taken place here, within the Pietrasze forest.

'Red Friday', 'Martyr's Thursday', 'Black Sabbath'. Dates inscribed in memorial calendars. Within weeks of the initial onslaught a grim folklore was emerging, an epitaph for each day of the week, dates for future generations to absorb and be condemned to remember, and mass graves that would one day draw grandchildren to them to clarify their confused dreams.

Witold moves quickly, closing the gaps for introspection. We drive from Pietrasze onto country roads. The grassfires glow crimson now, and merge with mists that bring on the night. Villages flash by in a whirl of cottages snuggling against each other for company. They disappear moments after we first sight them, consumed by a voracious darkness. With similar abruptness the streets of Tykocin are upon us.

We come to a halt by a cottage and are greeted by friends of Witold. They are young, the oldest perhaps no more than thirty. I am welcomed as a guest to a gathering of their local history society.

After supper the lights are dimmed. Hasidic melodies play on a gramophone as we watch slides of former Jewish settlements on the Bialystoku flatlands. Roses and sunflowers blaze in country lanes. Whitewashed farmhouses glow amidst luscious gardens. Bearded rabbis sway in ecstatic prayer. A water-carrier balances buckets on a pole slung over his shoulders. Windmills whir against sullen skies. Furriers and cobblers, their spectacles fallen low over their noses, cut cloths and skins. Lost worlds are resurrected to skim across living room walls, idylls of Jewish life culled by young Poles from books and archives, images which radiate the intensity of those who once lived on the edge of extinction — or so it appears in the obscure light of hindsight.

My hosts glance at me as if seeking approval. I discern in them a flicker of unease, an incompleteness, a gap of which they too are acutely aware. The presence of a vanished tribe lurks all around them. Who were these strange people who once lived among us?

Out on the streets, we walk towards a white phantom which hovers in the night until it clarifies into the shape of a synagogue. Tykocin is the source, my young hosts impress upon me. It predates Bialystok as a Jewish settlement, and centuries ago held jurisdiction over its community. They are enthusiastic about their knowledge, anxious to please. 'The synagogue was completed in 1642. We have restored it. We are preserving it.' One of them hurries before us so that, by the time I enter, I am greeted by the voice of a cantor, soaring above the chant of massed choirs.

The chant emanates from a tape deck. The synagogue of Tykocin is a museum. Chandeliers cast speckled shadows on the upper reaches of walls on which are painted fragments of psalms in Hebraic script. Encased in glass booths are embroidered skull caps, brittle parchments illustrated with biblical scenes, and rams' horns that were blown to herald the New Years of many centuries.

My hosts seem anxious to show me every corner, every restored detail. They guide me up a spiral staircase to a garret. It is small and rounded, a dome in which a table stands fully prepared for the Passover seder. The plates, the soup bowls, the ritual containers are of fine porcelain. Carved wooden chairs await the family. Two candles stand ready to be lit and blessed. A seventeenth-century Haggadah is open, ready for the patriarch to commence the ceremony. Elijah the prophet's silver goblet glitters with polish. Everything is exact, perfect; a still life. We dare not touch. We dare not disturb. We descend into the night, shivering.

Mid summer 1941. The final days of July. The streets of Bialystok are overflowing with men, women, and children: a community uprooted, dragging suitcases, heaving makeshift sacks, pushing carts laden with belongings, lifetimes of effort, generations of heirlooms, intimacies exposed in broad daylight like raw wounds; a people flushed out of their homes and driven towards an enclave cordoned off near the heart of the city. Here they have been forced to erect a wooden fence, three metres in height, under Gestapo supervision and the threat of deadlines that drive them to work furiously well into the night, constructing their own prison, a disease-prone isolated jail for over fifty thousand dispossessed Bialystoker Jews.

It is a time for vultures, easy pickings, hit-and-run thefts. Hooligans attack and rob the defenceless. Polish peasants exact jewellery, furniture, currency, in return for assistance. For soldiers of the Third Reich it is a time for celebration, an occasion for photos to be taken and sent home to family and friends depicting the great triumph of the 'Master Race'. Years later these photos will resurface in memorial books; and as a child I will gaze at them, mesmerised by ethereal figures drifting through a ghostly dream, stars of David sewn on their upper garments. When I look closely at individuals within the crowd, I catch glimpses of that inconsolable panic which erupts when a prisoner realises with finality that he is about to be locked in, the key turned, a destiny sealed.

August 1, 1941. The ghetto fence has been completed and crowned with barbed wire. For the Jews of Bialystok, the outside world recedes and becomes a distant apparition.

One dream barely evaporates and we are speeding towards the next. The moon has broken free of the mists and hangs in the mid heavens, an orange ball, just days before its fullness. Witold's eyes are fastened on the rapidly curving roads as he grips the steering wheel, the sight of the synagogue ablaze on 'Red Friday' permanently creased on his forehead. And more than ever I feel it — this land is possessed. Everywhere, it seems, there are lost souls seeking refuge. See how we once lived, they seem to whisper. See how we huddled against each other, clutching at our houses of worship, yet forever exposed, never knowing when warring tribes would return to stalk our cobbled streets. Yet on nights like this we were entranced. Moonlight pierced our windows. We lay in bed with visions of redemption. Messiahs and ancient prophets visited our dreams. Besides, it was not so easy to escape. So we stayed, and awaited the end of days.

Witold and I cannot let go of the night. We leave the car parked outside his flat and stroll through the Chanaykes against a distant backdrop of modern flats. At night the dwellings seem more askew, at acute angles which glove the contours of winding streets. They lean precariously, as if thrown together at random and told to fend for themselves. Perhaps this disorder is their curious appeal. They emanate an intimacy, and it is easy to imagine mother and her friends, walking arm in arm on the way home from a Bundist gathering, a choir rehearsal, a concert, seduced by the stillness of the night and the warmth of each other's company.

The streets of the Chanaykes unwind into the broad thoroughfares of a more affluent Bialystok. Mother and father are strolling, on a Saturday evening in the summer of 1932, along treelined Sienkiewicza Avenue. The city hums with weekend revelry. Queues are forming at the Apollo cinema. The dance halls are shaking to fox-trots and waltzes. In the Café de Luxe ladies sip coffee while in the back rooms young men play billiards and chess. Shops in the Macedonian quarter are doing a brisk trade in halva and Turkish delight. Kondruchuk, the White Russian, sells ice cream from a two-wheeled cart. Horse-drawn carriages dash by, conveying merrymakers to parties, and from the distance can be heard the faint sound of an orchestra in the city gardens.

'It was as if we were moving on a common stream', father tells me. 'One couple among thousands, bound to a common fate. And then I heard your mother's voice as though from afar, from another realm: "Would you join me if I left for a new life in Australia? My sister Feigl can arrange a permit." '

'In that instant', says father, 'we were jolted from the crowd. We became a couple detached, thrust in another direction. We saw vast oceans opening up before us and new worlds hovering on distant horizons. The strollers on Sienkiewicza Avenue receded. I saw them as marionettes activated by strings from which we had broken free. We had become exempt from their common fate and hurled into an unknown but alluring future. At least, that is how it appeared then.'

By 1941 my parents had lost touch with Bialystok. At best they were able to obtain snippets of information from Wellington newspapers: the occasional paragraph on a minor page, unconfirmed reports of massive pogroms. Yet so long as they were reported as rumour, there remained a degree of hope.

Some time in 1942, father cannot recall exactly when, there arrived in Wellington the first eye-witness, a refugee by the name of Shapiro. He had been in Warsaw during the Nazi invasion and had lived through the early weeks of occupation. A frequent guest of my parents, he would stay late into the night, recounting fantastic tales of his escape, while glancing from time to time at photos of the wife and daughter he had left behind. He had fled east, across the length of the Red Empire, and beyond, through Siberia into Japanese-controlled Manchuria. Wherever he went he was pursued by war. The world had gone mad, or so it seemed, until he made his way by boat via Shanghai to New Zealand, to the quiet haven he had come to believe no longer existed upon the earth.

But refuge had been exacted at a high price, for within its silence Shapiro had time to brood over the fate of his wife and child. He had left them with the hope of rejoining him when he found asylum. Day and night he was haunted by their faces. He talked about them incessantly. Had he abandoned them?, he asked himself. Should he have stayed with them?, he agonised. As father describes Shapiro's obsession, it becomes apparent that to my parents he had seemed like a spectre, an apparition from a lost world, an uneasy reminder to those in the world of the free that they had become helpless, far removed from their loved ones in their moment of greatest need.

This sense of unease was to increase, and become deeply embedded, as the full impact of the Annihilation was gradually revealed; and in time it would become clear that, despite their voyage to the ends of the earth, they had not truly broken free.

Chapter Twelve

I HAD KNOWN HIM in early childhood as 'the Partisan'. He was a regular visitor. He would come on weekends, especially during the summer, as I recall it, dressed in shorts and sleeveless cotton shirts. He seemed large to me then, far bigger than father. I remember him as a man of muscle and bulk leaning back on a sofa, legs sprawled out in front, body sagging into cushions, while he spoke in a light tenor that highlighted the melodic flow of Bialystoker Yiddish.

His stories wove in and out of forests, hamlets, and glistening swamps, leaving in their wake a fantastic 'other' realm: bands of partisans roaming the countryside; thefts of arms and raids on enemy bases; miraculous escapes from barns surrounded by soldiers; and battles that left bullet scars in arms and legs. His anecdotes were told with a slight smile, a sense of irony, and dark humour. The irony was lost on me then, of course, but my glimpses into that other realm remained, always recalled against the clutter of endless cups of tea. It is part of my picture of him: a modest man, balancing a cup of tea on a saucer as he sank into the sofa, the cup rattling as he changed position. I also recall frequent references to a place called Pruzhany, although it would be many years before I came to know why it had been so important to my mother and the fate of the family she had left behind.

September 1941. The Gestapo orders the evacuation of 12 000 ghetto inmates. They are to be transferred, it is claimed, from Bialystok

126

to Pruzhany, a townlet one hundred and fifty kilometres southeast, not far from the Bialowieza forests. The order provokes widespread panic. There have been rumours of death squads, tales of massacres in Vilna, the Ukraine, White Russia. Surely Pruzhany is a ploy, a pretext, a fiction.

The Judenrat, the Jewish councils imposed by the Nazis to carry out their demands, is instructed to make the selection. Debates rage for hours over who is to go. It is the devil's calculus they have been forced to engage in. Councillors agonise. Arguments erupt. And, as the deadline draws near, criteria are drawn up: retain the able bodied, the skilled, those thousands who trudge to work every morning, to factories controlled by German industrialists, both within and outside the ghetto. Provide slave labour, pay the arbitrary fines, keep the ghetto productive, and we can buy time, argues Judenrat chairman Efraim Barasz. He emerges as the dominant figure. His views are persuasive: what choice have we but to select from the poor, the unemployed, the widows and their children, and from families crowded in the most squalid of quarters?

On the eve of Rosh Hashonah the first notices are delivered: tomorrow you are to assemble at five in the morning by the gate on Ulitza Fabryczna. Among those whose names are on the dreaded lists are Reb Aron Yankev, Chane Esther, my Aunts Liebe, Sheindl, and Tzivie, and Uncle Joshua with his two children Chaimke and Itke.

Five a.m. Darkness. On the streets a heavy frost, a steady drift of snow. Only hand-luggage and shoulder packs are allowed. Furniture, mementos, heirlooms are left behind. Reb Aron parts with his holy books, Chane Esther with mortars and pestles, Aunt Sheindl with some of her many dresses; and like shadows they move through the streets, feet slipping in mud and snow, shoulders bent and hunched under packs and sorrow.

By Fabryczna gate, the lists are checked. There are last-minute attempts to plead for exemption, to flash forged work-passes, to bribe Judenrat police. Occasionally someone makes a dash for a side-street. Fate flits softly, a mere straw on a breeze. The crowd huddles in the cold, against the mute falling of snow, the muffled screams of Nazi guards, the quiet crying of a child.

A fleet of trucks moves through the gates. The evacuees are herded aboard. Packs are lost in the confusion. The convoy lurches off over ice-glazed roads. Many hours later it comes to a halt by a cottage

on the outskirts of Pruzhany. The prisoners are ordered in, one at
a time, to be stripped naked and searched. Lining is ripped apart
for hidden gems and currency. Possessions lie scattered over the
floors. Those caught concealing valuables are beaten. For hours the
evacuees wait outside, exposed to the frosts.

Pruzhany looms across a field of snow: an oasis, a relief, an unexpected welcome. Jewish doctors wait to treat the bruised and frost-
bitten. Hot meals are served by the ghetto Judenrat, and the evacuees
are escorted to their new homes: cramped timber cottages confined
within electrified fences.

And so it was, as accurately as I have been able to recreate it from
scant information, that eight Probutskis from mother's family and,
over a period of weeks, an estimated 5 000 Jews of Bialystok made
the journey to Pruzhany ghetto in the winter of 1941.

The Partisan made his way to Pruzhany under very different circumstances. It is years since I last spoke to him; but apart from areas
of private pain that are clearly off limits, he recounts his experiences
quite willingly. He appears considerably smaller than I had imagined,
his shoulders now hunching. Yet traces of a once powerful build
are still evident; and, as he speaks, that half-smile dimly recalled
from childhood encounters hovers upon his face. I am never quite
sure which way the smile is going — towards a grimace that conceals an inner torment, or towards genuine laughter. In time I realise that his smile contains both possibilities, constantly at play. The
events he describes are at once so bizarre and menacing that his
mild demeanor and humour act as a counterpoint, a means of containing the absurd within the bounds of normality. The Partisan
brings the voice of the ordinary to events of the extraordinary.

'You have no idea. How can you? You were not there', he emphasizes, echoing a refrain I have heard from many survivors. At times
he pauses in the middle of a story as if he himself finds it difficult
to believe that he had actually been 'there'. 'It is impossible to understand. Somehow I survived. I always seemed to make the right move.
Or was it that fate always favoured me?', he muses, and shakes his
head in disbelief.

In the early days of August 1941, soon after the Bialystok ghetto
was established, he was approached by a Judenrat member, escorted

outside the ghetto to a timber yard, and introduced to the German manager. 'He had been mobilised to build roads. He needed someone to build garages. I said, "Okay. I can do it. But I need workers". "How many?", he asked. "Six. Perhaps eight", I replied. "Choose whoever you want", said the boss. I returned to the ghetto. People were desperate for work. Many clamoured around me, pleading for a job. I chose some friends, acquaintances. What could I do? I was the only true carpenter among them.'

I have come to enquire about Pruzhany and my relatives, but the Partisan jumps from story to story, following a thread of his own; and he draws me in, increasingly spellbound, into a web of tales, 'a thousand-and-one nights', he calls them, and again shakes his head in disbelief.

'He was a fine man, the boss. He called me "Herr Goldman". Do you understand what that means? At a time when his fellow countrymen were calling us worms, vermin, the lowest form of life, he would greet me as "Herr Goldman". He fed us well: bread and liverwurst, a rare piece of meat. One day he called me over and held up a bucket of jam. "Chief", I asked, "how much should I pay?" *"Dummkopf"* he replied, "this is a present!" He even agreed to help me smuggle it into the ghetto. As we approached the gates, he saluted the guard: *"Heil Hitler!"* A few steps beyond the entrance, he spat on the ground and cursed: *"Scheisse Hitler".*

And Pruzhany? How did the Partisan meet up with my family? 'There is a lot to tell', he says. 'Until this day I still cannot believe I had the chutzpah to do the things I did. One morning, as I arrived for work, I saw Gestapo officers approaching the shed. I quickly realised that they suspected some of us were involved in underground activity. Actually, we had only just begun to talk and to scheme. There was a Polish mechanic in our group, a Russian, and several Jews. When I saw the Gestapo coming I acted quickly, on impulse. I jumped through a window and hurried back to the ghetto. On the way I met one of the members of our group, "Shloime the Geler", the fair-haired one, and I warned him not to come to work. He lives today in Germany. We correspond from time to time. A clever man. Resourceful. He even survived Treblinka, where he became one of the barbers who cut the hair of those condemned to the ovens. Aron! You have no idea! A thousand-and-one nights, and many more!'

That evening the Partisan stole over the ghetto fence and made his way to the city square. Two Jewish workers were loading a truck. They had been ordered to transport wool to Pruzhany, where it was to be used in lining boots for the Wehrmacht. 'At first they refused to take me. So I held up something that looked like a pistol. It was nothing. Merely a bluff. A piece from a dead grenade. But it was enough to persuade them', the Partisan tells me with a grin.

'I hid in the back, under the wool. Late at night, as we passed through Bielsk, we were stopped by a Nazi patrol. They probed and prodded. I crouched in a corner. Just as I was about to be detected, they gave up the search.'

'Pruzhany was a Yiddishe shtetl, a small crowded ghetto, far more intimate than Bialystok. It was possible to endure.' The Partisan speaks matter-of-factly about the struggle to survive. There was a certain point at which one lost the will to live. Over one-third of Pruzhany inmates did die: of hunger, disease, despair, especially in the early months. But those who weathered the initial onslaught toughened, adjusted. They were able to smuggle in food. White Russian peasants were willing to trade. In the spring of 1942, it was even possible to bake matzos for Passover.

Nevertheless, Reb Aron Yankev refused to eat it. He preferred to go without, rather than eat suspect food. What could be kosher under the rule of the devil, he argued. He would rather stick to a meagre diet of tea and potatoes. In Pruzhany Reb Aron appears to have turned away from the absurdity called life, to retreat inwards, to the refuge that had sustained him through previous crises. A 'black plague' on a world that had fallen victim to the 'evil impulse'. The past was repeating itself. As he had during the first war, Reb Aron withdrew to his dream of God and Tzaddik, while Chane Esther, the matriarch, remained firmly rooted in matters of daily survival. 'She was old, worn out, embittered', observes the Partisan. 'But she was also tenacious, persistent, a fighter.'

The Partisan came to know her well. He was a frequent visitor in the Probutski household, for it had become a meeting-place for a cell of the Resistance. During their secret gatherings, on her own initiative, Chane Esther would tie a kerchief over her head, stroll nonchalantly outside, and stand lookout by the fence which ran close to the house.

Potapoffke 33. The Partisan recalls the exact address. Every detail is welcome, every little aside that throws light on an aunt, a cousin, anything that elevates them above a welter of facts, statistics, and collective destiny. Potapoffke 33. A peasant's cottage. Of timber. A small garden. A kitchen and one large room in which lived Reb Aron Yankev, Chane Esther, Liebe, Sheindl, Tzivie, Joshua, Chaimke, and Itke; and, in addition, two young men. One was a goldsmith who made rings on order, for German clients. He would hand over the meagre profits to comrades in the underground. 'His hair was grey', recalls the Partisan. He still marvels that one so young could look so old.

The second boarder was Yanek Lerner. He was a key member of the Resistance. The Partisan had known him for years. A tall man, with blond hair, he spoke the earthy dialect of a peasant. In Bialystok he had dealt in dairy products and livestock. The Partisan laughs as he pictures him walking through the streets of Bialystok driving gaggles of geese. He was a regular guy, a reliable comrade; and in Pruzhany he had become Sheindl's lover.

'Your Aunt Sheindl was beautiful', claims the Partisan. 'A true krasavetse.' Whereas the youngest sister, Tzivie, appeared fearful, a haunted soul afraid to venture out into the streets, and Liebe had become bent with labour and resignation, Sheindl remained proud and defiant. She ran the household, provided spine to the family, infused everyone around her with energy; and at night she lay with Yanek Lerner. 'This is how it was', says the Partisan. 'One could be fearful, another defiant. No better, no worse. Merely different. After all, who are we to judge them?'

Sheindl was such a beauty. They all say it: mother, father, Aunt Feigl, Uncle Zalman. I had not visited Uncle Zalman for many years. A distant uncle, related through in-laws of Feigl's, he had left Poland in the late 1930s to settle in Melbourne. He greets me enthusiastically, and remarks: 'You are a true Probutski. I can see it in your eyes: a grandson of Reb Aron Yankev, a nephew of my best friend Joshua.'

He is in his eighties, a frail man with Parkinson's disease. It is eating into him at the edges. Yet there is a gentleness, the poignant dignity of an elderly man struggling to keep his faculties intact. Zalman's vision of things around him is blurred, constantly disintegrating. But when he focusses on the past he moves into clear waters, and within this transparency he regains sight of a city and of friends he has not seen for fifty years.

Zalman had grown up in the Chanaykes, next door to the Probutskis. His friendship with Joshua had persisted beyond childhood; as young men they had often sung together in the renowned Chor Shul. 'Joshua was a tenor. He had a voice that could fly', claims Zalman. 'And your Aunt Sheindl was very beautiful. I had my eye on her for many years but, alas, she never wanted me. She was a true krasavetse. She looked like a famous film star of those times, but I can't quite remember who. And Joshua, he was my best friend', he repeats with tears in his eyes.

'When he cries, it's a sign he feels well', Zalman's wife assures me. She is a no-nonsense woman who fusses around him, wipes the saliva from his mouth, attends to his every need.

'Bialystok was a city with a heart', mutters Zalman.

'And you went barefoot and hungry', interjects the practical one. She brings us cups of tea and continues to fill them to the brim.

The table is overflowing with drinks, strudel, honey cakes, apple compote, and albums featuring family parties and picnics, bar mitzvahs and weddings, children, grandchildren, a recently born great-grandchild; and pasted between them, in stark contrast, are obituaries to relatives who have died in recent years. 'All of them Bialystoker', points out Zalman. 'Those who managed to get out in time.'

'The doctor says he shouldn't talk so much about the past', interrupts the prudent one, forever observant of every fluctuation in Zalman's moods. But increasingly time loses meaning as we sit around the kitchen table, flipping through family albums in which past and present, celebration and obituary, seem to dissolve into one shared moment of silence. Suddenly Zalman glances up and remarks, 'You look exactly like Pushkin, the Russian writer'; and he begins to recite one of his poems. But he stops abruptly, mid sentence and, like a cheeky child, he grins and announces: 'I know a verse far more profound than any written by the great poets. We used to stand on the streets of Bialystok, your uncle Joshua and I, and recite it as we gazed up at the stars:

A Jew looks up at the sky.
Is he looking for God?
No — he's just scratching his beard.'

Fate is not a grand design. It is made up of slight twists and feints, impulsive decisions, hesitations, unexpected detours. Sheindl had many admirers and boyfriends. In one photo she is pictured with her first fiancé, Chilek, in 1930. She is wearing a black dress with white frills on the sleeves. Chilek is dark complexioned, curly haired, his face lean and tense. He migrated to Palestine, and in mother's album there is a postcard in which his portrait is circled and linked with Sheindl's, above a montage of Tel Aviv scenes. He was organising a visa for her, he wrote. Soon after, letters ceased. He had found someone else.

Several years later, Sheindl was engaged to a Bialystoker called Laizer. On the eve of his departure for Chile they married. Sheindl sent a photo of the occasion to her sisters in Melbourne and Wellington. Laizer is appropriately handsome, exuding confidence, a man of the world. He wears a pin-striped suit, a black shirt, an embroidered silk tie. He is looking away from the camera at some distant point, while Sheindl, as usual, gazes directly at the lens. Yes, she reminds me of a film star of the times, but I am not quite sure who. Perhaps it is that she embodies the look of the era: she is of the future, rather than the past, far removed from the shtetl outlook of her parents, and unafraid of her beauty.

She had always been strong willed, mother has told me. She was the sister who fought the fiercest of the battles against Aron Yankev and his strict orthodox ways. He had tried to forbid her from associating with the bohemians, freethinkers, and visionaries who had captured the longings of Bialystok youth. Sheindl drifted in cafés and dance halls about town. On one occasion she had brought home a statuette of a naked woman, sculpted by a friend. 'I will smash it', raged Reb Aron. 'Smash it and I will set fire to your holy books and never return', retorted Sheindl.

She had her way. The statuette remained standing on top of the living room cupboard, and Reb Aron withdrew one step further from his daughters. Yet, in the final days, he was to be reunited with Sheindl in a fashion far more potent than formal religious bonds, and Sheindl was to prove a source of loyal support in the darkest of times.

The photo of Laizer and Sheindl is dated February 6, 1939. By the time Laizer had organized a visa, in Chile, it was too late.

He called him simply Probutski. He could not recall his first name. He was aware that he had been a master weaver in Bialystok, and that he was Chaimke's and Itke's father. But it was not until after many conversations between us that the Partisan mentioned that uncle Joshua had been one of the tenants in Potapoffke 33. It was as if in Pruzhany he had become a nonentity, unrecognizable as the spirited Joshua of Zalman's reminiscences. I have to press hard for information. 'What can I say', the Partisan replies. 'He had become a shadow, always standing to the side. His sunken eyes gazed only at his children, as if afraid for their every move. That is all I remember.'

Yet usually the Partisan can recall the most minute of details. 'There are incidents that took place yesterday I forget', he tells me. 'After all, I am almost eighty years old. But of the ghetto and the forests, my memories are so clear. For instance, I am standing in the kitchen of my White Russian boss, a man I worked for in Pruzhany. He ran a factory in which wooden kegs were assembled. Sometimes I would be directed to work on his house. There was a pan of peas, frying in pig fat. It smelt so inviting. I was very hungry. In the ghetto there was a severe shortage of food, and the boss didn't feed us well. For a moment I was left in the room alone. Mmm! I couldn't resist it. I approached the stove and grabbed some peas from the pan. Of course, instead of getting a tasty morsel of food, I burnt my fingers.' As he tells the story, the Partisan winces and blows on his hand, as if he had grasped the food a mere moment ago.

The winter of 1942 was approaching. The earth lay buried under snow and ice. '*Jude! Jude!*', the Wehrmacht officer ordered. 'Take this wood to the third floor!' The Partisan hauled the heavy load up three flights of stairs to the officer's quarters.

The order had been barked in typically abusive tones. Yet when the Partisan entered the apartment and stacked the wood, the officer thanked him. He had to maintain appearances in front of the others, he claimed, and apologised for having nothing to offer except some biscuits sent to him from Germany.

The Partisan gave the biscuits to seven-year-old Itke on his next visit to Potapoffke 33. Her radiant joy on receiving them he can picture vividly to this day. Again the Partisan laughs, this time fully and spontaneously; and it is obvious that when one lives in Gehenna a spark of joy is a revelation, a flash far brighter than the snows that covered the earth in the winter of 1942.

In the cottage at Potapoffke 33 the Partisan and his comrades discussed reports from the Russian front, and worked out ways of obtaining arms. The Partisan chuckles as he recalls one of their smuggling ventures. 'I built a concealed deck into a sled. One of us had obtained a pass to bring firewood into the ghetto. We stole arms from a nearby barracks where some of us worked, and hid them in the false deck under a pile of wood. When we reached the ghetto gates we asked a Nazi guard to accompany us. We convinced him it was his duty to ensure safe delivery of our load. He was flattered. Instead of searching the sled, he rode with us, seated upon the wood, drawn by horses across the snow, the proud protector of Wehrmacht property.'

The underground in Pruzhany was divided over whether to move to the forests or remain within the ghetto to foster an uprising. The debates were fierce. Those with family tended to favour a final stand within. Others insisted that effective resistance could only be waged beyond the fences that kept them trapped and encircled. 'At times we came to blows, and even worse', mutters the Partisan, and lets it go at that. 'After all', he adds, 'either way we were confronted by a ruthless enemy determined to destroy us.'

Yanek Lerner and six comrades left for the forests in December. The Partisan was to steal out later with a second group. Yanek had asked Sheindl to accompany him. There was no future in the ghetto, he argued. There were rumours the end was imminent; sooner or later the camp would be liquidated. But she could not be persuaded. She would not desert her aged parents and family. Perhaps she would join him later; but not just yet. She was needed at Potapoffke 33.

After they crept out of the ghetto, Yanek's group raided the barracks, obtained arms and a typewriter, and disappeared into the forests. 'You will never understand such things', says the Partisan, allowing himself a smile at the thought of a typewriter being lugged into a forest.

On January 27, 1943, two partisans stole into the ghetto and approached the Judenrat offices to discuss Resistance matters. As they entered they unexpectedly encountered the Gestapo commandant. Upon seeing he was confronted by armed fighters, the commandant turned and ran. Fearing reprisals if they shot him, the fighters held fire. 'In such situations', asserts the Partisan, 'we acted from instinct, seeking above all to survive. As I see it, most of us become brave only when it can no longer be avoided; and our heroism conceals an immense terror.'

The Judenrat was accused of aiding the Resistance. Next day the deportations began. 'Some claim they were in direct response to the events of the previous day', the Partisan says. 'I am more inclined to believe that the trains were already waiting. Besides, what difference does it make? One way or another, this was the fate they had planned for us all.'

All the next day the Partisan hid in a bunker with a group of about forty. The warmth generated as they crowded against each other caused a vapour to rise into the rooms above. This could have given them away, since outside the Nazis were beginning their round-up of the ghetto inmates.

That night the Partisan and his companions crept towards the ghetto cemetery, where they had hidden their arsenal of weapons. Within metres of the fence there stood a carpentry workshop. The Partisan entered to make last-minute repairs to some of the guns. The noise almost alerted German guards. 'I still don't know how I had the nerve', he tells me, yet again.

The electric wires were cut with insulated pliers. After scaling the fence they moved away beneath white sheets, a camouflage against the snow. For hours they walked without any sense of direction. At dawn they realised they had wandered to the edge of a Nazi airstrip. Falling snow had wiped out their footprints, and they were not discovered.

They lay under the sheets until evening in groups of three, beneath trees merely metres from a road. Military vehicles flew by. Peasants whipped horses to draw their sleds faster. On the second night they waded into swamps and through water that rose up to their shoulders until, at last, they reached the forests. They now faced a life of scavenging and hunger in bitter conditions, in snow and in blizzards. Yet it offered, at least, a means of survival.

Four days it took, from January 28 until January 31, at 2 500 inmates per day, to clear the entire ghetto. The Probutskis were ordered out of Potapoffke 33 to assemble in the central square. Lists of names were barked out interminably as the ghetto inmates were loaded into horse-drawn wagons driven by local peasants.

'Between Pruzhany and Linowe station was a distance of perhaps fourteen kilometres', the Partisan tells me. Snow and sleet drifted in a veil of mists. The convoy stretched for miles, a procession of phantoms enveloped in ghostly white. Occasionally someone jumped off and made a run for the forests through a gauntlet of bullets.

At Linowe station the trains were drawn up by the platform, waiting. The time-tabling was precise, the organisation efficient. The doors of the cattle wagons slid to a close on entire families, crammed together, robbed of light, air, and hope. Soon after they were on the move: a journey of several hundred kilometres southwest, across the breadth of Poland, to a town called Auschwitz.

Yanek Lerner and the Partisan established separate bases. They constructed zemlankes, earth huts, one sizeable room dug underground. The floors were cushioned with pine needles; the roofs covered by branches and twigs, topped by a camouflage of dirt and grass. In some of the hideouts, primitive stoves provided a semblance of warmth.

Various groups roamed the forests. 'There were Ukrainians, White Russians, Poles, and Jews; even the occasional German deserter', the Partisan explains. Alliances were formed; others remained determinedly separate to emphasize their national allegiance. And there were gangs of bandits, intent on survival at any cost.

Within days of taking to the forests, the Partisan heard shots echoing nearby. On investigating, he came across Yanek and his comrades lying in a well near their zemlanke. They had been shot by bandits who had masqueraded as friends. The bandits had made off with guns and boots, grenades and food. 'Boots were our most prized possessions, especially during winter', says the Partisan. 'One of Yanek's comrades survived and gave an account of the attack. He lives today in the United States. Just a few years ago I visited him.'

Our fate is so fragile. A mere straw on a breeze. What shall we do? Stay in Poland or leave? And when the doors are sealed, the New World cut off: which way shall we go? To the trains or the forests? And at the end of the journey, at the gates of Auschwitz, Doctor Mengele waits, white gloves on his hands, as he points left or right, the ovens or slave labour. As it turned out, Yanek Lerner and Sheindl Probutski perished at about the same time — Yanek with his comrades in the forests, Sheindl with her family in the ovens of Auschwitz. Children of the Annihilation, we know it well: life is so fragile. A mere straw on a breeze.

Chapter Thirteen

ABOVE ALL, FATHER RECALLS the seasons. Take, for instance, the first winter snows; the remembrance remains clearer than the most recent of dreams. Mother Sheine is singing him to sleep. Lullabies fade to darkness and, as if no time has passed, he awakens to the sight of ice clinging to window panes above the bed. The morning light silhouettes fantastic shapes of ghostly figures, wild images painted by overnight frosts, while outside the first snows are falling.

When Bishke came home from work during the winter months, he would bring the ice with him. It clung to his beard, clothes, and bundles of unsold newspapers. He would arrive fresh, cold: an iceman returning to the family, to be greeted by a simmering samovar and the heavenly warmth of that first cup of tea.

Snow caressed the earth as far as the eye could see. It filled the streets, permeated the forests, froze over lakes and rivers. From its softness, father and his playmates built babushkas, only to smash them soon after. They hurled snowballs at each other, while on the iced surface of the Biale they raced sleds down inclines in a whirl of whiteness. And in the many decades since, father's memories of the harsher aspects of winter, of its biting winds and relentless chills, have softened. What has been retained, with increasing lucidity, is the surface white, the purity of Bialystok covered in snow.

In the winter of 1942-43 the fate of Bialystok careered like a drunkard on thin ice. Letters flew between Nazi headquarters, in Berlin and

Koenigsberg, the capital of East Prussia, where Erich Koch, one of Hitler's most trusted cronies, ruled over his little patch of the Reich. SS and Gestapo factions, local bureaucrats and commandants, debated whether the ghetto was to be liquidated or allowed to survive, for the time being, because of the productivity of its skilled slaves. With the destruction of all provincial Jewish settlements in the early days of November — among them my ancestral shtetlech, Bielsk and Bransk, Orla and Grodek — Bialystok had become an oasis, an island of refuge towards which escapees from the death trains made their way. Yet all the while the gas ovens and crematoria were working overtime to fulfil Hitler's vision of a Europe rid of Jews, the 'Final Solution' to an age-old curse.

Still, Bialystoker hoped. Perhaps they would yet be spared. Judenrat chairman Efraim Barasz berated them: Work! Attain your quotas. Produce furniture and coats, chemicals and suits, uniforms and boots for your overlords. He dashed about in the Judenrat carriage as if possessed, galloping to Gestapo headquarters on Sienkiewicza Avenue, and along the wide pathways that led to the Nazi administration in Branitski palace. In these offices of the Reich he pleaded for concessions and stays of execution.

Within the ghetto, beggars huddled against wind and frosts. Makeshift stoves belched smoke into crowded rooms and apartments. Inmates shivered in the dawn light as they shuffled to work; and, for the fortieth year in succession, Bishke Zabludowski ran the streets, the disseminator of news, the distributor of Judenrat posters with the latest Nazi ordinances and demands. He pasted sheets on walls and fences, within courtyards and against buildings, in alleys and lanes, day in and day out, bound to his lifelong vocation like a man in a trance. In a collection of documents, unearthed and published after the War, I have been able to trace the last poster that grandfather conveyed: number three hundred and eighty-six, dated January 29, winter 1943.

Bishke first took to the streets as a vendor of news in the winter of 1903. In January 1913 communal leaders, editors, writers and journalists, printers, and friends gathered in his apartment to celebrate his tenth anniversary. It was the great event of father's childhood. Tables were crammed with delicacies: herring and caviar, chopped liver and chicken pieces, salamis and strudels. The guests sat at tables playing cards, talking politics and gossiping, sipping liqueurs and spirits. A phonograph whirled with waltzes, polkas, cantatorial chants and the latest hits from the Yiddish theatre. The Zabludowski children dashed between guests, crawled under tables, listened in on conversations and resisted attempts to put them to bed. Father refused to sleep unless he was given a glass of cognac. Whatever drink Sheine brought him, the seven-year-old would grimace and exclaim: 'That's not cognac! I want only genuine cognac!' How could cognac be just a bitter drink? It had to be something extraordinary, exotic, comparable to the wild stallions that reared from the labels.

One quarter of a century later, in the winter of 1938, prominent Bialystok Jews gathered in Rabinowitz's A La Minute restaurant to celebrate the thirty-fifth anniversary. The banquet was reported in all the Yiddish dailies, and father learned of the event from cuttings sent to him in New Zealand. Editors and agents had delivered glowing tributes. 'Who in Bialystok doesn't know Bishke?', they had declared. 'He is a city landmark — a short, lively, energetic Yiddele, running with bundles of newspapers tucked under his arms, his tongue always on the move, his voice at full pitch from dawn to dusk, proclaiming the latest news, our Bishke, an artist in his trade. In his hands newspapers realise their full potential. When he announces the headlines, they come alive; and when there is an event of particular significance — a disaster, an assassination, a declaration of war — Bishke takes flight. Crowds gather, electrified, carried along in his wake as he hurtles through the streets, trumpeting the event as if it were the coming of the Messiah, no less.'

While we discuss these articles of praise, father recalls Armistice Day 1918. Bishke had flown through the streets with special extras, screaming: 'Cease fire! Cease fire!' People had burst out of their homes and apartments, broken off their prayers, emerged from alleys and lanes, charged out of shops and factories, to tear after him. Newspapers spiralled through the air, passing from hand to hand. The crowd jostled like a congregation of excited Hasidim straining to gain a glimpse of their Tzaddik. The news erupted and spread through the city, while in the centre of the commotion stood Bishke, the town crier, the messenger, the medium through which news flowed and dispersed in all directions until every home, every yeshiva boy, housewife, rabbi, and priest was informed. After all, a war had ended. A catastrophe was over. 'No more wars!' was the catch cry of the times. 'Peace! Bread! Liberation!' was the expectation of a war-weary Europe. And for a moment, at least, caught up in the throng, even pessimists were drawn along by the cry of Bishke on Armistice Day 1918.

In January 1943, disturbing rumours circulated throughout the ghetto. Cooks, cleaners, and secretaries working in Gestapo offices told their resistance comrades of plans for mass deportations. A German factory manager warned his workers of imminent disaster. When denounced by ghetto informer Judkowski, he was thrown out of Bialystok and five of his workers were tortured and executed.

At the beginning of February, Sturmbahnfuhrer Ginter, an envoy of Heinrich Himmler, arrived in Bialystok with a squad of SS men experienced in mass murder. Efraim Barasz was ordered to compile lists of 17 000 inmates for 'resettlement'. In frantic negotiations with Gestapo bosses the numbers were whittled down to 6 300 — liquidation on the instalment plan.

On February 2nd, Gestapo officers inspected the fences. All escape routes were sealed. On February 4th, the passes of those who worked outside the ghetto were confiscated. A Gestapo delegation toured the factories to assure workers that nothing out of the ordinary was about to take place. Mass murder requires a certain degree of psychology. The Nazis prided themselves on it. A minimum of panic would ensure a maximum of efficiency. Go quietly. This is merely a transfer to greener fields.

Nevertheless, on the night of February 4th, the ghetto inmates were restless, nervous, ready to take to the hideouts they had been preparing within false walls and chimneys, in garrets and under floorboards, in cellars and bunkers — a secret city of burrows and tunnels to which they feverishly added last-minute extensions, water outlets, electricity connections, stockpiles of food — while cells of the Resistance surveyed their limited arsenals of primitive weapons, and waited.

Raphael Raizner was a printer by trade; and, like so many Bialystoker connected to the newspaper business, he had been a friend and admirer of Bishke Zabludowski. It was Raizner who first informed father of the events that had taken place on February 5, 1943.

Both father and Raizner had arrived in Melbourne in the late 1940s — one as an immigrant from New Zealand, wanting to live in a city where there was a strong community of former Bialystoker, the other, as a refugee from the displaced persons' camps of Eastern Europe.

In Melbourne they lived just a few blocks apart, in the same neighbourhood, since this was a suburb where many Jewish migrants first settled on arrival. When introduced to each other, there had been an uneasiness, a hesitancy, an avoidance of eye contact. 'Don't ask. Don't think about it. You shouldn't dig too deeply', Raizner had said. 'It doesn't bear telling.' And father admits that he too had been anxious, reluctant to pursue the details, in fear of the renewed sorrow they would cause. But Raizner had been a witness, an inmate of Gehenna. He had no choice, it appears, but to pass on what he had seen.

Raizner talked for many hours during their first encounter, describing in particular the events of February 5. Yet they never discussed the incident again, despite the many times they visited each other before Raizner passed away some five years later.

At 2 a.m., on Thursday February 5, a convoy of trucks carrying Gestapo and SS men, security police, and Ginter's evacuation squads entered the ghetto and approached the Judenrat offices at Kupietzka 32. Gestapo boss Gustav Friedl directed Efraim Barasz and the Judenrat police to accompany him with their lists of deportees. Several blocks were surrounded and raked with machine-gun fire. Nazi commandants screamed instructions; Judenrat police pounded on shutters; residents were ordered into the streets. But no one emerged.

When Friedl's men broke into the apartments they found them empty. Enraged at having been foiled, he tore up the lists and ordered random attacks. Those who resisted were immediately shot. As news of the Aktion flashed through the ghetto, many of its inhabitants vanished into hiding.

At about 4 a.m. evacuation squads made their way into Ulitza

Kupietzka to continue their onslaught on the crowded apartments that lined both sides of the street.

Kupietzka 38. I first saw this address on the backs of envelopes containing letters father sent to his wife in Wellington during their three-and-a-half years of separation. The Zabludowskis lived on the second floor. There were two bedrooms, one of which father shared with Bishke and Sheine; a large kitchen where Sheine and her eldest daughter Etel ruled supreme; and a dining room in which stood a book cabinet, a sofa, and six chairs around a table covered with a waterproof cloth. On the walls there hung portraits of the renowned philanthropist Moses Montefiore, and a group photo of Yiddish writers. Among them stood Mendele, the 'grandfather' of Yiddish literature, and the popular humorist Sholem Aleichem. The others father cannot recall, but he thinks they were on the deck of a boat, sailing on the River Dnieper . . . or was it the Black Sea?

Father has always preferred rooms with a view, exteriors to interiors. To this day, when he enters a building for the first time he is drawn immediately to the windows to gaze at wide vistas and their intimations of what lies beyond. The window fronting Ulitza Kupietzka overlooked a tangle of rooftops and squares, courtyards and lanes. In the distance, Ulitza Jurowietzka stretched towards the international section of Bialystok station. Once a day, the Moscow-Paris express would draw up by its platforms. Children ran beside the rails as it slowed down. They waved at faces peering through the windows and dreamed of jumping aboard to travel far beyond the confines of their landlocked lives.

The window to the left overlooked the inner courtyard. It was a world in itself, a miniature village stirring with constant activity. Within it stood a bakery, a dyer's workshop and the Polish caretaker's hut. He was an irritable man who worked hardest on Saturdays, as the 'Shabbes Goy', attending to odd jobs and manual work — thereby enabling the Orthodox to observe their day of rest. The dyer spread furs and leather on the cobblestones to dry, and their acrid smell permeated the neighbourhood. Wagons entered by an arched gateway with supplies of flour and pelts. Peasants hawked potatoes and firewood, their wives delivered dairy products, and their children played between horses, merchants, and drying skins.

The window to the right was father's favourite. It overlooked the Biale which meandered just metres away. A strip of wild grass and shrubs threaded between the building and the river. Nearby there was a field in which stonemasons shaped tombstones from blocks of granite. Ulitza Kupietzka continued on over the river across a bridge, supported by columns between which birds often congregated. As he stood by the window father would sometimes hear the notes of a piano drifting from a nearby apartment. The pianist was the daughter of a wealthy balabos, the proud owner of factories and property. She had once been in love with father's eldest brother, Zachariah, but he had ignored her. Besides, he had long since disappeared in the Red empire with the theatrical troupe Sniegov and Dubrolov, and the girl next door had become a spinster who harboured romantic illusions of a pure love that would rescue her from loneliness and boredom.

Every year, on the first day of Rosh Hashonah, late in the afternoon, a crowd of Hasidim would gather by the banks of the Biale. They would stand in the field facing the river, between slabs of granite and half-completed tombstones, fringed shawls draped over their heads and shoulders. Chanting and swaying, they cast their sins into the Biale waters. Throughout the 1920s and well into the next decade, father would observe this ritual from the window, and he would remain long after, until the new moon rose towards its zenith and cast a thin glow over the rooftops of Kupietzka.

Itzchok Malamud has been described as reserved, a quiet man, somewhat withdrawn. When the February Aktions began, he was living with his wife and child at Kupietzka 29. During the previous year he had fled the town of Slonim, a witness to the murder of his parents in massacres that had wiped out thousands of Slonimer Jews. After hiding in the forests he had smuggled himself into Bialystok ghetto. He obtained work in one of its factories and had become a brooding participant in the early-morning meetings conducted there by resistance leaders. When the February Aktions drew near, he had obtained bottles of sulphuric acid distributed by members of the factory cells.

In the early hours of February 5, Nazi police rushed into the corridors of Kupietzka 29 and ordered the residents outside. Malamud responded by hurling acid into the eyes of one of the officers. Severely burnt and blinded, the officer fired into the crowd and succeeded in killing one of his cohorts.

The body was carried to the Judenrat offices and placed on Efraim Barasz's desk. After conferring with Gestapo boss Heimbach and SS envoy Ginter, Gustav Friedl ordered the Judenrat to deliver Malamud or face severe reprisals.

Father remembers Prager's garden as a vacant block, with gnarled fruit trees, weeds and ivies — formerly the walled grounds of a wealthy merchant. Nearby stood the Neivelt house of prayer. Father had attended cheder with the son of the cantor, and they often played together in the neighbourhood.

Soon after the ghetto was erected, Prager's garden became the site of a market. Residents gathered to barter: an overcoat for bread, a bar of soap for butter. Children would steal over the ghetto fences to smuggle in whatever they could to augment their parents' meagre stocks. When Nazi patrols happened to be in the area the dealers would scatter, leaving behind their paltry goods, their sole means of survival.

At two in the afternoon of February 5, over one hundred hostages were herded from the courtyard at Kupietzka 29, marched to Prager's garden, lined up against the wall of the Neivelt prayer-house and shot, in reprisal for Malamud's deed.

Father recalls the exact moment when Raizner described the shooting. Raizner had paused and faltered, unable to continue his account. His face had paled; and, when at last he resumed, his voice had fallen to a whisper. On the evening of February 5, 1943, Raizner had seen the shallow graves, the protruding hands and feet, the arms stretching upwards — the last movements of those who were still alive. Among those murdered in Prager's garden were my grandparents Bishke and Sheine.

'Do not dwell too much upon the past', father warns. He blots out disturbing dreams and prefers that which he can touch and see while wide awake. 'A fractured past and muddled dreams are synonymous', he claims. 'Obliterate the crippled visions that emerge from the darkness', he stresses. When father awakens, he deliberately breaks free of the night and reminds himself: The sun rises in the east, sets in the west, and life goes on.

For eight days, except Sunday, the Aktion continued unabated, with relentless punctuality: at six in the morning the sudden roar of trucks, the gleam of steel helmets, the heavy tread of Nazi boots entering the ghetto to resume the hunt. Cramped in their hideouts, the inmates waited in terror — stifling every cough, a baby's cry, the slightest sign of life. Floorboards were ripped out, false walls smashed in, and bunkers dynamited. Jewish police were forced to go first into suspected hideouts, to act as shields against potential resisters. On the second floor of Kupietzka 10, Jews fought with iron bars, axes, and knives, before being shot and hurled through the windows. A family poured boiling water on their assailants and were executed. Feingold the madman laughed and cursed as he was beaten to death. Mothers clutched their dead babies long after they had suffocated. Many suicided before they could be taken. Others spat and swore in their captors' faces. The ghetto was engulfed by mayhem and rage.

Raphael Raizner surveyed the scene from an attic on the third storey of a garment factory. The floors were crowded with workers' families exempted from the transports. Frost and biting winds slipped through gaps in the walls. In the streets below, huddles of women and children, old men and bent grandmothers, whole families clutching each other for support, staggered by. Those who could no longer keep moving were shot on the spot, their bodies left lying in the mud. Occasionally someone would attempt to escape, only to be gunned down as he ran. Two women broke away and hurled their children through factory windows. Soldiers dashed in, retrieved the children, and dragged them back to their mothers. A woman begged to be shot and an SS man obliged. A dog scampered towards him. He picked it up, patted its back, and asked sympathetically: 'Haven't you eaten today?'

At six the troops would retire and march from the ghetto. Some made for Kupietzka 32, the Judenrat offices, to drink and celebrate until the early hours of the morning; while outside, in the darkness, figures emerged from their hideouts. Like trembling shadows they darted about to scavenge for food, exchange information, and prepare for the next day of terror. As they searched for their loved ones they could hear in the distance the whistle of the last train fading into the night, bound for Treblinka.

I probe, press for details, seek out witnesses, scan documents. It becomes an obsession; and always at the core hover mother and father. What did they feel at the moment of revelation? Father recalls Raizner's eyes, unfocussed, remote.

'His pauses were frequent', father tells me, 'his silences prolonged; and within them I saw Bishke being dragged to Prager's garden, to the shrill commands of his captors. They pushed and prodded, bayonets at his shoulders. Bishke stumbled and ran, not knowing why or for what. His cheeks were hollow, his face gaunt, the eyes vague and haunted. Then I saw them at Bialystok station, on the day I left Poland. It was the first time in my life that I had kissed Bishke. Who kisses a father with a beard that itches and a face beaten hard by wind and rain? Beside him stood Sheine, wearing a blue silk dress, with a white bow over the bodice. It had been a present from my youngest sister Feigl and her husband Reuben Zak. They loved her very much, and no wonder, for in the days of their court-ship she had encouraged their romance and allowed them to be free.

'When Sheine wore the dress for the first time they had taken her out to the theatre. She looked radiant. The dress matched her blue eyes. My blue eyes come from her, as does my great love for life. She was good natured; she believed in people. Until I was ten I would sleep next to her. I was permeated by the scent of her being and awoke to her blue eyes.

'Raizner talked. Bialystok raged. Bishke and Sheine had to dig their own graves. I saw it clearly. Then I said, enough. Pain is a luxury; sentimentality an indulgence; the lure of life far more powerful. I had to shut out the remembrance, my visions and dreams. Other-wise I would have succumbed to grief and shame.'

A reward of 25 000 marks was offered for the head of Itzchok Malamud. The Gestapo threatened to shoot thousands if he were not found within twenty-four hours. Malamud gave himself up, although there are some who claim he was betrayed by an informer.

On the morning of February 8 a gallows was erected outside Kupietzka 29. Detachments of SS men and police lined up before the execution site. Gestapo boss Heimbach pronounced the sentence, and Malamud was led to the gallows. As the rope was placed around his neck he spat in his executioner's face and screamed: 'Criminals, you will pay! Your end is near!' His words are said to have echoed throughout the length of the street.

Malamud remained hanging for forty-eight hours. In Bialystok today a small plaque indicates where the execution took place, and Kupietzka has been renamed Ulitza Malmeda.

On the morning of Saturday February 13, shocked and bewildered inmates began to emerge from hiding. Bodies lay scattered about the streets. Cows and horses stalked through the rubble. Grief-stricken men and women wandered in search of kin. Staring wildly in disbelief, mothers clung to their dead children. Work brigades collected the dead from courtyards and cellars. Winter frosts had fused the corpses. The bodies in Prager's garden were exhumed and carted to the ghetto cemetery in Zabia Square to be buried in mass graves, men and women separately, Bishke and Sheine apart.

In the afternoon rain fell and washed away the blood. Zabia Square became a quagmire of churned mud and ice; and years later, when I came across poster three hundred and eighty-six, I noted the postscript that had been added: 'February 5th to the 12th. An Aktion. 900 shot within. 10 000 sent to Treblinka'. Short. To the point. The first item of news disseminated in Bialystok after the death of Bishke, the newspaper man.

Chapter Fourteen

TOWARDS THE END OF WINTER, frozen lakes and rivers would crack apart and release fast-flowing ice that swept downstream. Cool breezes fanned the countryside and, on the river banks, hunchbacked willows swayed reflections in rejuvenated waters. The landscape around Bialystok seemed spellbound, poised between seasons, about to break beyond its winter dreaming.

When the nights became moderate, father would be invited by the Polish shoemakers for whom he kept books to go fishing overnight, on the outskirts of Bialystok. While they walked in the darkness owls moaned, and fireflies streaked by in showers of gold. The shoemakers fished until dawn and, as they trekked back to the city, they would meet peasants leading their oxen and horses to work. All was renewed energy, enthuses father, and he clenches his fist to stress the power of spring: a sharpened plough, a team of horses, a dew dissolving, the sun ascending, the earth ripped open to receive a scattering of seeds.

Soon after, the first herons would appear, winging their way from southern retreats, majestic in the skies, but awkward when they stumbled on their ungainly feet. To father they appeared ghostly, their claws sharp and threatening. Yet they still remind him of the scent of lilac, or 'bird's milk' as it was called in Yiddish. It would be gathered clinging to twigs, and taken home to permeate the evening with its fragrance. As for the chestnut tree of Zwierziniec, the memory of its massive canopy in silver bloom remains startling. It hovered over a forest floor studded with wild flowers, within a resounding silence in which everything seemed slenderly balanced, imminent, about to cut loose.

On the banks of the Biale by Kupietzka bridge, within sight of the window where father once stood on Rosh Hashonah nights, the corpses of three informers hung from gallows erected by enraged mobs. They roamed the streets in search of those who had saved their own skins by leading Nazis to hideouts. When a cry of 'traitor' was heard, crowds rushed to the scene. They would tear and claw at the suspect, and lynch him on the spot. In the ghetto hospital on Fabryczna lay the crippled and maimed. Many had lost limbs through frost-bite and exposure. A bitter thirst for vengeance mingled with despair in those first days after the February Aktion. Ghetto inmates moved about in a daze, a community bewitched by a collective fate that seemed endlessly and inevitably to be leading to oblivion.

Then slowly, with the lengthening of days, the faintest of hopes began to stir. Clandestine radios hidden in cellars transmitted the grim optimism of London and Moscow. The Reich had retreated from Stalingrad and suffered defeats in North Africa. The Red Army was advancing. Divided factions of the underground met to analyse their February shortcomings. Bitter schisms that had lingered since pre-war years were dissolved. A united front was established, led by the Zionist-inclined Mordechai Tennenbaum, with the veteran communist Daniel Moscowitz his deputy. The Judenrat expanded it factories. Thousands clamoured for jobs. The ghetto gardens came to life with spring planting and experiments to improve yields. Ghetto kitchens were restored, furtive prayer meetings held and, on April 19th, Bunim Farbstein organised a communal seder in Shmuel Cytron's house of study. Rabbis recited the Haggadah; and while Bunim spoke of freedom as the symbol of Passover, guests wept over the loss of loved ones and their desperate sense of isolation.

Some time towards the end of May 1943, Shapiro hurried to my parents' Wellington flat. Ashen-faced and trembling, he clutched Yiddish journals he had just received by mail from New York. The Warsaw ghetto was burning. A revolt had erupted on April 19th, the first night of Passover. The journals also reported the suicide of Shmuel Artur Zygelboim, in London, on May 11th. As Bund representative of the Polish government-in-exile, he had become aware, via couriers and underground contacts, of the fate of his people. European Jewry was on the brink of annihilation. Every day they were being railed en masse to death factories. He had tried to convince British media and politicians. He had contacted the Foreign Office. He had met with US envoys. Bomb Auschwitz, he had pleaded. Save the remnants, he had begged. But the tale he told seemed too incredible. And those who believed him claimed that little could be done; their aircraft and personnel were required elsewhere. As a last resort, Zygelboim had taken his own life and left a note with his grim tidings. Perhaps with his death, he concluded, he would be able to arouse the 'conscience of humanity'.

He was soon forgotten, except by the likes of Shapiro, who now stood in a Wellington flat, anxiously reading aloud Zygelboim's last testament. As he listened, father was overcome by a sense of dread. What had been but a vague apprehension could no longer be denied. 'Over there', in the world he had left behind, his dearest friends and kin were dying; while here, under southern skies, he moved free as a bird. Every day, to and from work, his bus emerged from rolling hills into sudden views of sparkling seas. As Shapiro read, one thought echoed within father: I am of the living, while they, Bishke and Sheine, once devoted to my every need, are in Gehenna, and all that I once knew is on fire.

Shmuel Artur Zygelboim had been an integral part of my childhood folklore, a principal actor in a world of rebels, fighters and defiant souls who hurled themselves against the enemy with audacious abandon. The refugees who became my storytellers brought with them a universe of fire. Figures darted through the flames. One grabbed a grenade in mid-air and hurled it back at his executioner; another blocked the entrance of a bunker and was riddled with bullets. Children smuggled arms through sewers. Women jumped from collapsing buildings, screaming last words of defiance. I listened wide-eyed. The tales entered my dreams. They were enshrined in song. We sang them in choirs, at memorial services, at summer camps, at Yiddish school concerts:

> Birds are coming, close your eyes my child,
> They circle your cot in a world gone wild.
> God has locked the doors and everywhere is night,
> It awaits my child, in terror and fright.

Father draws distinctions between the dreams which emerge at night and what he calls 'living dreams'. Such dreams, he explains, are sparked when fully awake. They are memories triggered in the present to form something new — a poem, an insight, an original idea. Take his latkes, for example. The recipe had come from his mother, Sheine. She would beat together grated potatoes and eggs, shredded onions and flour. Father follows the same formula, to which he adds raisins, perhaps almonds, something of his own imagining. The latkes thereby become a 'living dream', a live reflection of the past. As such they transcend mere nostalgia, he is at pains to stress.

In Bialystok, Sheine's latkes had been very popular among his friends. They ate them with great relish on their many picnics in local meadows and forest clearings. To this day there are in Melbourne former Bialystoker, survivors, who mention Sheine's latkes and find themselves dreaming of summers in Bialystok. The streets burned and melted underfoot. Heat waves could persist for days on end. The air was thick, the earth perspiring with heat. 'We longed for a drink', recalls father. Every well was an oasis, and he came to know the location of obscure springs in the forests.

Father has always preferred the immediate reward, the moment of heaven on earth, however brief, to the promise of an afterlife. So he took to the forests whenever he had the chance; after work he would often stroll from the city to the family dacha in Zwierziniec. He walked as night descended. The air was vibrant with the chatter of insects and bats. He glimpsed the stars between trees and, as he describes the scene, he suddenly pauses. Ah yes, he recalls, there was a Yiddish poet who in the 1930s travelled the Australian deserts and observed that the new moon rose in a reverse crescent to its counterpart in northern skies. Now that is a perfect example of a 'living dream', adds father, beaming with the pure delight of a child; and again he stresses, this is not a mere wallowing in the past, but a poetic jewel, an original image, a new moon rising over ancient worlds.

Lag ba-Omer is celebrated on the thirty-third day after Passover. Legend has it that in the first century of the common era, while in revolt against the Roman occupation, 24 000 disciples of Rabbi Akiva died of plague because they did not sufficiently honour one another. On Lag ba-Omer the plague ceased. The period of mourning was over. Music and marriage were again permitted. And on Lag ba-Omer 1943, in accordance with custom, over thirty couples were married in the Bialystok ghetto.

Perhaps the fate of Bialystok has become my 'living dream'. The more I delve, the further I travel across Polish landscapes and into the tales of my elders, the more I seem to be moving in an hallucination, a warp in time and space, a netherworld in which slaves scurry about, clinging to life as the summer heat beats down upon them. And within that heat I catch dazzling glimpses of resilience. In the summer of 1943 there are love affairs in the ghetto, women daring to be pregnant. The underground operates with increasing audacity. Experiments are carried out in munitions workshops hidden in cellars and bunkers. Guns are smuggled in loaves of bread, under dresses and coats, or hurled over ghetto fences at pre-arranged locations. Resistance cells are formed to defend factories and streets. Partisans steal out to set up forest bases. Young women powder their faces, rouge their lips, disguise themselves as gentiles, and rent rooms on the Aryan side. With forged papers they obtain menial jobs in Nazi homes and offices, while acting as secret couriers between ghetto and forest. Underground radios report the fall of Mussolini. Children march around the courtyards proclaiming the news. Ghetto gardens are in bloom, tomatoes growing fat. Factory orders are flowing in from Berlin and Koenigsberg. The ghetto inmates are producing, preparing, sharpening their survival skills as the eastern front edges closer.

In back alleys, drooping over walls, bunches of red cherries glistened like rubies in the summer sun. Street boys would steal by to snatch their fill. For relief they took to the forests and strung up hammocks between trees. Father sways with the memory of the hammocks and the redness of dawns and dusks. Red permeated everything. It covered fields of corn and shoots of grain. It streaked through windows and doorways, seeped into courtyards and lanes.

And it occurs to father that, no matter how hot it became, Bishke remained outside, between dawn and dusk, pausing only when he noticed one of his sons approaching. In an instant he would forget the business, his livelihood, the heat. He would open a newspaper and point excitedly to an article: 'Have a look! Read this! It's written just for you!' He loved finding something of relevance for them to read. Even on Sabbath afternoons, during his hours of rest, he would read aloud to Sheine the latest episodes of serialised novels — 'soap operas for the masses', father calls them. And he confides that, to this day, he regrets his former tendency to look critically upon his Bishke, the news vendor, the eccentric, the small Yidl who dashed through the streets like a man possessed. It was only much later, well after he had left, that he came to realise Bishke plied his trade simply because he was trying to provide for his family, to make ends meet. 'So explain', says father, 'why did he and so many like him, have to come to such an end? Why do people have so much hatred for those they don't even know?'

In July, Gestapo commissions inspected the ghetto with alarming frequency. The fate of Bialystok was again being debated in Reich headquarters. Odilo Globocnik, SS commandant of Lublin, a ruthless pioneer and advocate of the Final Solution, arrived to co-ordinate plans. Secret meetings were held in Branitski palace. The February Aktions and the Warsaw uprising were analysed to learn from past errors.

By August the signs were ominous. German clients collected unrepaired watches from ghetto jewellers. Factory orders were being cancelled. Gestapo bosses Friedl, Dibus, and Klein were seen checking ghetto fences. Unfamiliar troops and detachments of SS men roamed the city streets.

Wehrmacht officers and Judenrat leaders tried to assure nervous workers that there was nothing to fear. On Sunday, August 15, the ghetto was quiet. That evening many of its 40 000 inmates went to bed with a glimmer of hope. Perhaps the rumours of impending Aktions were unfounded.

Who remains in the ghetto on August 15th? Uncle Isaac? Aunt Etel? Uncles Motl and Hershl? A Probutski? A Zabludowski? A Liberman? A Malamud? I have been sucked into the hunt. I scour lists of names, devour eye-witness accounts, sit in libraries, sift through archives, rummage through cupboards. And however scant, there are revelations. Take, for instance, a board of three-ply, two feet square — a still life. It had always been in the house, but I had never seen it. Perhaps it had been hidden, or neglected. Or kept out of sight. Perhaps I had glimpsed it in a dark corner and taken no notice. It was father who eventually brought it to me. He had received it in 1936, when he left Bialystok. It was a present he was to deliver to his wife, in New Zealand, painted by her youngest brother Hershl.

The three-ply has cracked in the sunlight. The board is warped. Yet the oils have held fast. I adjust it on my desk, exposed. The fruit are fully ripened; the colours remain strong. Against a backdrop of pale emerald stands a straw basket with apples, a pear, a bunch of dark grapes. Beside the basket lie three plums, a pineapple, green leaves. Rising above, behind the basket, is a slim crimson vase. The flowers are chrysanthemums: white, yellow, pink. The brushstrokes are bold. The fruit is thick to the touch; painted when Hershl was about twenty-one.

What can mother tell me about Hershl? 'He was talented', she replies, and falls silent. She too has become a still life. The kitchen clock ticks. She clutches a shawl around her shoulders. She nods her head gently, backwards and forwards. Her lips loosen. She begins to smile: 'He used to sleep in late. So we had to rouse him from his dreams, my sisters and I.'

I want to know more. 'What more is there to tell?', replies mother. 'He was a quiet boy. Became a house painter. Gave his wages to the family. Spent many hours drawing. Did no one any harm.' She lapses back into stillness. Yet he must have been special. He gained a namesake. Of the three brothers, the eldest is named after Bishke, I after Aron Yankev, and the third after Hershl. 'Why Hershl?', I ask mother. Her answer is simple. Matter-of-fact. Obvious. 'Because he was the youngest. And he did no one any harm.'

August 15, 1986. Zabia Square, site of the ghetto cemetery, is deserted, except for old men who sit on park benches under a mild afternoon sun. Dogs sniff about the stone monument that stands in the square. A van with loud speakers comes to a halt nearby. A bus arrives conveying former Bialystoker who live in Warsaw. People now outnumber dogs. The local Party boss and mayor of Bialystok alight from chauffer-driven cars. Their bodyguards remain by them throughout the ceremony, motionless, their eyes cold and impassive. Short speeches are made. Words evaporate in the stillness. A queue forms in front of the monument. One by one we come forward to lay wreaths. Chrysanthemums, marigolds, and ferns predominate. A small crowd of bystanders looks on, caught in passing, neutral observers of a subdued ritual. It is all over within an hour, a pantomime performed by survivors locked into remembrances of the day the ghetto began to burn.

On Sunday, August 15, 1943, a full moon rose over Bialystok on a warm summer night. Soon after midnight the ghetto was encircled. An inner cordon armed with light automatic weapons stood close to the fence. A second cordon with machine guns formed behind them. An outer circle of cavalry and artillery completed the three-pincer movement. The Judenrat offices were commandeered as campaign headquarters. Electric wires were strewn through the streets, and field telephones installed. Couriers on motorcycles stood by to circulate orders. All escape routes had been blocked, the operation meticulously planned.

At 2 a.m. residents near the ghetto fences were awoken by the tread of Nazi boots. The news spread quickly. Thousands emerged from sleep into a world gripped by fear. Neighbours milled in the darkness, frantically asking each other: 'Is this the end'?

By 4 a.m., SS posters plastered the walls. In the red light of dawn the message was clear: All were to assemble by nine o'clock, in Ulitza Jurowietzka and the Judenrat gardens. They were to bring hand luggage. From there they would be transported, with all factory equipment, by train to Lublin. Those who disobeyed would be shot immediately. Move quickly. Do not resist.

'Do not dwell upon the past', father warns. He rebels against nostalgia, against dreams and even sleep itself. 'A waste of time', he declares. When his energy begins to sag he reminds himself: focus on your daily tasks. Adhere to routine. Use everything in your power to keep moving — even that terrifying refrain, so familiar to loved ones in their final hours: '*Raus! Raus! Juden raus!*' He imagines it deliberately, sometimes, in the early mornings, as he lies in bed, trying to emerge from strange dreams and temporary paralysis. '*Raus! Raus! Juden raus!*' He brings to mind the infamous words, to drive himself into another day of existence. Even such a dreaded command can be put to use, father insists, and transformed into a tool for survival.

'*Raus! Raus! Juden raus!*' In a swarming mass they move, through corridors and courtyards, clutching pillows, eiderdowns, coats and furs, their last treasured possessions, weighed down by blankets and packs, stumbling and struggling to arrive on time, to avoid being beaten; they surge over bridges, across the Biale, like a herd of cattle, towards an enclave of narrow streets and lanes, unpaved and lined with wooden cottages, vacant blocks and vegetable gardens. The Nazi plan is simple, effective: to have the residents out in the open, far removed from the protection of solid factories and tenements.

The underground is forced to change its tactics. It must move with the masses, smuggle weapons across bridges. Tennenbaum and Moscowitz set up headquarters at Ciepla 13, a cottage within the enclave. Young fighters stand on street corners urging revolt, one last stand, a dash for the forest. An eleven-year-old girl, Bura Shurak, leads a band of teenagers, pasting posters that cry out for revenge: 'Blood for blood! Death for death! The road leads to Treblinka. There is nothing left to lose!'

'*Raus! Raus! Juden raus!*' Resistance cells move into position. Explosions mark the beginning of the revolt. Factories erupt into flames. Haystacks are set alight. Cottages catch fire. Smoke billows towards summer skies. Horses rear in panic. As one fighter falls, her comrades charge forward hurling primitive grenades. The Nazis counter attack. Mothers clutch their children as they dive to the ground. Ghetto inmates crouch in the gardens, caught between shrapnel and fire. The earth burns underfoot. The sun blazes in mid heaven. The Nazi charge mounts. Bullets spit from windows and balconies. Tanks barge through the streets. Planes swoop low to strafe trapped masses. Resisters hurl themselves at the fences, but are beaten back by cordons of troops. Cornered and isolated, their ammunition running out, they take to axes and crowbars in a rage fuelled by futility and a bitter thirst for vengeance.

By mid-afternoon the initial battle is over. Five thousand lie dead. Columns of inmates are being herded through Jurowietzka gate. They are driven by truncheons towards Pietrasze field. Those that try to escape are shot as they run. Raphael Raizner, in hiding with his family in a cottage on Chmielna Lane, looks out upon a scene of utter devastation. The Judenrat gardens are littered with corpses and abandoned packs. The wounded are crying out for water. Children crouch beside dead mothers. Their moans rise up in a discordant chorus of terror. The bridge over the Biale, beneath Kupietzka 38, is crammed with bodies. As darkness falls, a sudden downpour floods the ghetto, smothering the cries of the wounded.

'Do not dwell upon the past', father warns. Yet the past intrudes regardless. 'It can happen any time', he tells me, as if finally pushed into the admission by my incessant probing, my persistent questions, my urge to penetrate his inner world. Gradually at first, and then with increasing rapidity, the floodgates are prised open and, yes, he confesses, it can erupt without notice, a sudden flash, a stab of regret, a glimpse of a face — a Bishke, a Sheine, a Zundel Mandelbroit, tangible, three dimensional, their eyes startled, confused. He can be working in the garden, immersed in daily chores, strolling in streets or neighbourhood parks, any time, anywhere. As soon as they appear a battle ensues: between tears and desire for life, between chaos and a longing for light.

The tears began a long time ago, on the very first day in fact, at the time of departure. March 5, 1936. Father stood on a platform at Bialystok station, a small man in a large overcoat, clutching a suitcase in each hand as he entered the train. He looked back towards the faces of Bishke, Sheine, and intimate friends, hovering by the windows. Then they were gone, and everything he had known had vanished beneath the horizon. And in that moment he knew he would never see them again.

The faces that still come to father with such startling clarity are now a blur. I cannot make them out among the twenty-five thousand who huddle on Pietrasze field. I can merely describe their collective fate second-hand, in vague outline, as I pursue them into their final days. They are surrounded by heavily armed guards who scream abuse in drunken stupors under a scorching sun. The captives are driven to and fro, fleeing from beatings and bullets fired at random. Many are trampled as they run. Rings are ripped from their fingers; watches torn from their wrists. Parents smear children's lips with urine to ease their thirst. Many buckle under in despair and give way to the mud, to be released from their ordeal.

On the second day the selections begin. SS men stalk the assembled mass, hooking the U-shaped handles of their canes around those deemed fit for slave labour. Any who refuse to leave wife and children are dragged away. The elderly and ill are hurled into carts and taken back to Zabia Square, where pits have been prepared. Gustav Friedl drives by in an auto, leaps out, fires the first shots, and directs his murder squads to finish the job.

On the third day the captives are lined up five-abreast and marched to Bialystok station. The stronger are prodded with cattle prongs into the forward wagons. The remainder are herded to the rear wagons. They are unhinged when the train arrives in Malkin station, and attached to a second locomotive which disappears into a forest — destination Treblinka. The forward carriages continue on to Lublin, where the prisoners are distributed among the work camps of Blyzin, Paniatowa, and Majdanek. On arrival in Paniatowa the newcomers are greeted by camp commandant Tumin, astride a white horse. He surveys them and shoots, on a whim, anyone whose appearance annoys him.

As he travelled west, across Poland, father's disorientation persisted. He had been thrown into a vacuum in which all around him —

passengers, gliding landscapes, country stations — remained distant, remote, while within him flashed scenes of a Bialystok he would never see again. These were precious moments, he tells me, in which he could reflect, take stock, weigh the good against the bad. There was the poverty he was glad to be leaving, the narrow streets of child-hood that had cramped his expansive dreams; the constant undertow of menace that had always permeated his life; and the growing threat of renewed pogroms he was relieved to have escaped. And there were the regrets, he reminds me, the moments he could have done this or that differently, been more considerate, said something softer to Bishke, to Sheine, a brother or sister.

Yet the Bialystok he was leaving had also been imbued with com-munal warmth, a sense of unity and purpose: 'We grew up as chaverim', father emphasizes. 'We were mirrors in which we reflected our shared aspirations. There were many who emerged from poverty as loving companions who were happiest when they served the needs of others. The essence of the Bund ethos to which I was drawn was our chavershaft, our loyal friendship. Our lives become possessed by a form of magic, an indelible bond, a common song. We sang it as we walked through lanes and alleys, and effortlessly beyond, along country paths, until abruptly all was still. And from that still-ness there arose the humming of more primitive worlds: swamps, lakes and rivers, untamed, forbidding, yet studded with jewels; slim white beryoskes, chestnuts in silver bloom, and warm nights ablaze with stars hovering over a luminous dream we called Bialystok.'

Ten thousand remain within the ghetto, in hiding. Search squads in groups of ten return day after day. Suspected hideouts are dynamited, listening devices installed, ferocious bloodhounds urged on, buildings torn apart: one by one, family by family, bunker by bunker, the quarry is hunted down. Once detected there are only two alternatives — an immediate death by bullet or the journey by cattle wagon to Treblinka.

When father arrived in Gdynia he saw the sea for the first time in his life. Yet, despite the exhilaration, his sense of regret remained. It pursued him as he set sail for New Zealand. What he had left behind continued to hold sway over what was to come. The open ocean was an awesome universe that surpassed his wildest imaginings. As the earth dropped beneath the horizon it seemed as though the foundations had been torn from under his feet. The boat cut through the water like a plough, and reflected in its wake were elusive images of Bialystok, of those he had so recently farewelled. And it was during these early days of the voyage, from Old World to New, that the dreams had begun, disturbing visions that have persisted to this day.

They come to him often, Bishke and Sheine. They stand by the bed and ask him how he is, while father asks them, 'Where are you now?' And in the mornings his sense of disorientation is overwhelming. 'This is why I must deny my dreams', father insists. 'Otherwise I would suffocate. A father. A mother. Bathed in blood. A beloved city. A community of friends caught in an ocean of flames. And I was so far away.'

A need for workers to cart and bury the dead, and to load factory equipment for transfer to Lublin, enables a stay of execution for several hundred porters, mechanics, and Judenrat officials. They are issued with special passes as a number of buildings are cordoned off and ringed with barbed wire to create an inner ghetto. Efraim Barasz is warned not to permit intruders. Random inspections are carried out every few hours to check passes. The Nazis are intent on leaving nothing to chance as they pursue their mission to make Bialystok Judenrein.

From the moment I first entered Poland, across the Soviet border, I was struck by one overriding thought: *this landscape is Judenrein.* I had never before been so confronted with the enormity of this fact. I became remote from the other passengers, my eyes riveted on the countryside. Here my ancestors had lived in a vast network of settlements which teemed with a way of life that had evolved for a millennium; they had created a kingdom within kingdoms, a universe pulsating to its own inner rhythms. Then it had vanished. Wiped clean from the earth. Judenrein. My journey took on a shape of its own, an inner logic, a relentlessness which has propelled it forward, regardless. Facts and stories have arisen of their own accord, demanding recognition, no matter how disturbing. And even now, as I near the final days of liquidation, this inner momentum drives my chronicle towards a completeness, to the remnants now roaming the forests as partisans, to the dwindling bands of fugitives holding out within the ghetto ruins, to the last pockets of resistance. One larger group of seventy-two fighters hides in an extensive bunker with well-concealed entrances — one through a disused well, the other in a cottage on Chmielna Lane. At noon, on August 19, the bunker is suddenly surrounded. The entrances are blown apart by grenades, the prisoners led away to the corner of Kupietzka and Jurowietzka. From a distance, in hiding, Raphael Raizner hears the defiant singing of revolutionary songs abruptly silenced by bullets as the fighters are executed.

Trains criss-cross the Bialystoku province. I gaze through the windows, absorbing every scene, sucking the marrow from Judenrein landscapes as if hidden truths lie buried within them. We were born in the wake of Annihilation. We were children of dreams and shadows, yet raised in the vast spaces of the New World. We roamed the streets of our migrant neighbourhoods freely. We lived on coastlines and played under open horizons. Our world was far removed from the sinister events that had engulfed our elders. Yet there had always been under-currents that could sweep us back to the echoes of childhood, to the sudden torrents of rage and sorrow that could, at any time, disturb the surface calm: 'You cannot imagine what it was like', our elders insisted. 'You were not there.' Their messages were always ambiguous, tinged with menace, double-edged: 'You cannot understand, yet you must. You should not delve too deeply, yet you should. But even if you do, my child, you will never understand. You were not there.'

Inevitably, we were drawn into their universe — the regrets, the nagging grief, the wariness and suspicion, and the many ghosts they fought to keep at bay as they struggled to rebuild their lives. And given the tale I seem compelled to tell to the end, could we have expected it to be otherwise?

The last major battles are fought on August 20. The Fabryczna Street cell retreats to the grounds of the ghetto hospital. Doctors, nurses, and patients join them in a desperate attempt to defend the court-yard. Squads of SS men break into the wards and, in a fury border-ing on hysteria, they hurl patients — newborn babies and elderly alike — onto footpaths and into carts bound for pits in Zabia Square.

Tennenbaum and Moscowitz retreat to their headquarters on Ciepla Lane. Surrounded on all sides, with ammunition running out, they set fire to the cottage. Legend has it that the two leaders took their own lives rather than fall into the hands of the enemy.

Mother and father fight to keep their ghosts at bay in radically different ways. They are opposites, and have been for as long as I can remember. For mother, especially in the years of her ageing, it is the silence that predominates, broken occasionally by a quiet humming, a snatch of ancient melody which evaporates back into silence. Sitting with her, for hours on end, by the kitchen table, I have come to understand the variations of that silence. At times it resonates with defiance; at others it suggests an irredeemable loss. Sometimes it is softer, a surrender, a letting-go. Yet the anger and rage I knew in her as a child can flare up, without warning: 'What did you dream about last night?', I ask. 'Nothing', she replies. 'And besides, is dreaming going to bring them back to life?'

By early September, all machinery and merchandise have been removed from the factories. The inmates of the inner ghetto are led to Bialystok station. In the front row walks Efraim Barasz, suitcase in hand, neatly dressed, proud in bearing, silver hair glowing in the sunlight. Behind him stretch long columns of Judenrat officials, com-munal leaders, Jewish police, factory managers. Their footsteps echo on the cobblestones. They move in silence through a shattered ghetto, their faces set, resigned, beyond hope, beyond tears.

A passenger train transports them to Paniatowa work camp. On November 3rd, along with thousands of fellow Bialystoker, they are slaughtered into mass graves while a camp orchestra plays the waltzes of Johann Strauss.

Father avoids silences. He resorts to his first and most enduring love: words. Through words he strives to make sense of the world. When a dream of Bishke and Sheine recurs, or a vision of a former friend suddenly invades his being, he fights ferociously to regain control by overwhelming them with words. The words mount, become more strident, more insistent, as he talks his way to survival.

We sit together on a park bench, in Curtain Square, our favourite meeting-place, on a Saturday morning, eating father's most recent variation on Sheine's latkes; and there is little for me to do but to be a spectator of his inner drama, to absorb his barrage of words, and to wonder why I have become so obsessed with pursuing the past, and why I have pressed so hard to extract the dreams he has so effectively suppressed. Or is it rather that the camouflage has always been transparent and that, within both parents, I have always known a simmering sorrow, despite their efforts to disguise it?

On September 16, the Bialystok Aktion was officially declared at an end. A squad of older Nazis remained to root out the few Jews left in hiding. They maintained daily patrols and marched their captives to Krashevski Street prison. When about fifty had been assembled, they would be driven beyond the city to be shot. Others were retained as slaves. They were led out daily to exhume corpses from communal graves in the forests. The bodies were thrown onto pyres and incinerated. As the eastern front edged closer, the Nazi mania for obliterating the traces of their crimes spiralled.

In October, a German firm arrived in Bialystok to transfer Jewish belongings from the ghetto. Everything of value was declared to be property of the Reich and was shipped back to the Fatherland. Nothing was to be wasted. Houses were stripped down to their skeletons. The entire ghetto area was looted.

When their work drew to an end the slaves were led out to be shot. As they approached the pits, they made a sudden break for the forests. Nine of them survived the gauntlet of bullets. Jewish Bialystok, five hundred years of vigorous effort and communal prayer, lay behind them, effectively Judenrein.

Hitler's shadow extends from the grave and darkens lives far removed. It reaches around the globe into a home where a child sees in his father's eyes, beyond the veil, an ocean of regret and bewilderment;

and in his mother's eyes, a distant stare of non-recognition. She is a prisoner of inner voices screaming, '*Raus! Raus! Juden raus!*' And just as she skirts the edges of madness, she reasserts herself, yet again, with relentless work and melodies. She sings for hour upon hour, as she cooks, scrubs, sews, and fights to keep the household afloat, her sanity intact. Her songs are in Yiddish, her repertoire vast, sung in a soprano trained by renowned choirmasters of Bialystok. There are lullabies that speak of white goats setting out on miraculous journeys; ballads about folk heroes and rebels on barricades. She sings worksongs of cobblers and weavers, tales of wonder rabbis and Hasidim on pilgrimage. She sings of families gathered by the Sabbath table and of gypsies gathered in forest clearings:

> Play gypsy, play me a song,
> On the fiddle all night long.
> On the fiddle, green leaves fall.
> What once was is beyond recall.
> What once was and what will be,
> Red is blood and red is wine.
> A star falls and then another,
> And our hearts reach out to each other.

Chapter Fifteen

'FROM MOSES UNTO MOSES there had never been such a Moses', the epitaph proclaims. 'Light of the West, greatest of the generation's wise men': words inscribed on the tomb of Moses Isserles, sixteenth-century scholar and preacher, renowned Rabbi of Krakow. It remains standing to this day in the Rema cemetery, within the grounds of the oldest living synagogue in Poland; and to this day the congregation continues to assemble here. They are arriving now, Shabbes eve, for the service. One stumbles through the gate with the aid of a walking stick; others are wheeled in. They approach singly or in pairs, the heirs of Moses, through the streets of Kazimierz, their childhood playing grounds. Shoulders stooped, frail, they walk slowly, berets perched upon their heads, thick overcoats wrapped around to protect them from the autumn chill.

At the entrance to a crumbling tenement a fat bubka sits on a wooden stool and knits. She gazes at me intently as I pass by, and mutters: 'Yiddish? Ich ken etleche verter Yiddish.' Yes, as it turns out, she does know a few words of Yiddish; five lines, in fact, which she had picked up in childhood from the Jewish neighbours who had lived within these tenements one generation ago. As I wander the streets of Kazimierz the bubka follows me, reciting her well-rehearsed Yiddish lines as one would intone a verse from the scriptures:

I am not afraid
I have no money
I have no compliments to offer
Kiss me on the behind
Go away you black devil

Bubka's face is circular, and the frames of her spectacles are similarly shaped; two moons within the larger moon. Her eyes glint with a hint of mirth, as if on the verge of cascading into uncontrolled laughter. Moon lady has, it seems, become my self-appointed escort. She follows me through Szeroka Square, muttering her Yiddish lines as we approach the Rema. For over four hundred years it has stood, this inconspicuous greystone building. Weeping willows droop over its walls. Moon lady stops at the arched gate, beyond which she does not venture. Her Yiddish verse trails after me while I enter the courtyard: 'Go away you black devil'. The words hover in the stillness as Moon lady disappears.

It is cool and quiet in the walled courtyard, protected from the winds. We sit on benches awaiting the Sabbath. One by one they pass beneath the arched entrance, the minyan gradually assembling in the waning light. 'You come from Australia?', an old man sitting beside me asks. 'So why didn't you do something? Why didn't you tell the world what was happening?'

'How could I do anything?', I reply. 'I was not even alive at the time.' But my words do not seem to have registered. 'Why didn't you do anything? Eh? Why didn't you scream? Why didn't you let the world know what was happening to us?' Only when we have entered the prayer-hall does he cease, for a while, to pursue his obsession.

There is no longer a rabbi in Krakow, and no cantor to lead the prayers. Members of the kehilla take turns at the pulpit. Of the fifteen assembled, several sit in the back row reading newspapers, others hold whispered conversations, while half a dozen or so concentrate on the prayers. Yet a sense of intimacy pervades the hall, and from time to time we unite in a common chorus of amens.

Some way into the service a young man enters the hall. He is tall, lean, his physique sharp and angular, his face pale and tense. He reaches into a pocket for a black skull cap, and hovers behind the back row of lacquered pews, scanning the congregation. He observes the proceedings from the fringes, like a stranger who wants to come out of the cold and close to the fire.

After the service the narrow foyer inside the entrance of the shul is thick with the din and hubbub of quick introductions, cries of 'Shabbat Shalom', and rapid-fire exchanges of the latest communal gossip. The young man remains on the perimeter hesitantly, as if looking for an opening, a polite way of entering the animated circle of well-wishers.

When I approach and introduce myself he is visibly relieved at having made some contact. We converse in English, although it is not his mother tongue. He seems reluctant to reveal where he is from, and constantly deflects the conversation away from the issue. He is in Krakow for a quick visit, he informs me. He has arrived today from nearby Auschwitz. He will return on Monday to continue work as a volunteer in the camp museum. There is a small group who do so every year, for several weeks at a time. They sift through archival material, help assemble exhibits, clean and dust, and do whatever is needed. The facilities are undermanned. Workers are urgently required to maintain the camp for the many thousands who come on pilgrimage from all parts of the globe.

It is obvious where he is from, and it has been from the beginning. Now he confesses, with embarrassment. He was born in Germany, soon after the War. His story tumbles out quickly, in staccato-like whispers, as if he wants to tell it before I can judge him. I have to strain to hear him. His father had been a soldier during the War. 'What did you do, father, during the War?' And year after year, the same answer. 'I was a soldier. I did my duty. There is no more to be said.' But the son had stumbled upon clues, documents, photos. He had made enquiries, talked to family acquaintances, and had pieced it together. Father had been an SS man. He had served in Poland. He had worked in Auschwitz. 'What did you do, father?' The questions became more insistent. The answers were always the same. 'I did my duty. I was a soldier. I had orders.'

'If only he would have admitted it. That would have been at least something. And mother. Always a hausfrau. She had seen nothing, known nothing. Merely maintained a household while her husband was away on duty, for the Fatherland. I grew up in a house of denials and secrets.'

The son atones for the father. He goes on a journey to Israel. He lives in Jerusalem for two years and works among the elderly, as a nurse's aide. Since then, for several years now, he has journeyed to Auschwitz with a group he has formed — the sons and daughters of former SS men. Together they make the annual pilgrimage to atone for the crimes of their elders: 'I cannot comprehend how an Auschwitz could have existed. It eludes me, constantly. But I will continue to work there. We must maintain it for everyone to see what our elders once did.'

We keep talking in the courtyard, long after the others have gone. Feigl Wasserman, the caretaker of the Rema, has turned off the lights and is locking the synagogue doors. 'I cannot comprehend how they could have committed such deeds', Werner muses, as if conducting aloud an inner dialogue he has pursued for years. 'But in the work, in my travels throughout Poland, I escape my father's cold silence, my mother's pursed lips and, for a while at least, I am free of the shadow that has clung to me since birth.'

Feigl Wasserman ushers us through the arched gate into Szeroka Square. I shake hands with Werner, and he disappears into the darkness. From Moses unto Moses, there had never been such a Moses; and his shrine, within the walls of the Rema, stands enveloped in silence, mute witness to the shadows flitting through the crumbling tenements of Kazimierz and beyond, not so many miles from here, in a town called Oswiecim.

Feigl Wasserman guides me from the synagogue. The moon is bloated, approaching its fullness, and in its light can be seen the names of streets glued to tenement walls on wooden plaques: Jakuba, Isaaka, Jozefa, Miodowa, Krakowska, legendary streets of Kazimierz, Jewish quarters since the fourteenth century; and at this hour, after the Shabbes service, families would have been assembling in their homes, about to eat the Shabbes meal.

We enter an apartment block and ascend several flights of stairs. On the first- floor landing, on guard in front of an apartment, an emaciated dog barks and howls. His fury echoes along the corridors as we ascend to the higher floors. There are three sets of locks on Feigl's apartment door. When it is finally opened, the Sabbath candles can be seen burning upon a table which stands just inside the entrance. We are home at last: *Shabbat Shalom.*

The royal city of Krakow is veiled in mist and rain, a steady downpour which persists for many hours. The streets of Kazimierz are overflowing. The gates to the Krakow Jewish cemetery are locked. Nearby stands a three-storey brick building. I climb the stairs to the first landing. Windows overlook the graveyard. Ivies, creepers, wild grass, and tombstones seem entangled in a single dripping mass.

Ascending the stairs is an old man. His face is yellowed, the pallor of parchment, his bullish neck sunken between the shoulders. His eyes are squinting as he draws closer, scrutinising me with suspicion. My Yiddish greeting reassures him somewhat, although he keeps his distance as we talk.

I am never quite sure, during this first encounter, whether he is playing a game of some sort, or if he is indeed, as he claims, the caretaker of this burial ground. 'My name is not important', he insists. 'It is enough that I am alive. In my life I have had more luck than joy.' He is an enigmatic creature, the old man with the waxen face, and reveals only carefully chosen glimpses of himself. Suddenly he grabs my hand and pulls it to his cheeks. 'Here! Over the left eye! Can you feel the empty space? Beneath the skin? There are no bones there. And here, at the back of my jaw, there are pieces missing. In my life I have had more luck than joy.'

After indicating that he lives in an apartment on this floor, the old man leads me downstairs to a back door which opens directly onto the cemetery. I offer to share my umbrella. 'It's not necessary', he says scornfully. 'I am an old soldier. I was for many years in the Soviet army. We fought in mud, snow, and bitter frosts. I don't need umbrellas. The heavens are merely spitting on us.'

On the ground floor there is a large hall in which bodies are prepared for burial. Passages from the scriptures circle the upper reaches of the walls. 'This is where we all come when all is said and done', mutters the old soldier. 'Our bodies are stripped, cleaned, tidied up, carried through the door and, so, it is over; we become mere memory. The memory fades and is transformed into history. In time the history is distorted, denied, impossible to believe, and we are reduced to absolutely nothing, zero, not even a figment of the imagination.'

The caretaker leads me over mud-splattered paths to a segment of the cemetery wall. On it can be seen an extensive mosaic, pieced together by survivors from fragments of marble and granite, with cracked names and epitaphs — the remains of desecrated tombs which the Nazis had intended to use in building roads. 'On this wall you see the whole meshugas', claims the old soldier. 'We spend our lives breaking each other's bones; then we try to patch up the mess. I too was patched up. I left Krakow in 1939, fled to Russia, joined the army, drove tanks, struck a mine, and awoke on an operating table in Moscow. The best doctors worked on me. They assembled the bones, a piece here, a piece there. I am like this mosaic. Yet I was the lucky one. I left Krakow a community of 69 000 Yidn, returned six years later with half a face, and was greeted by one huge burial ground. In my life I have had more luck than joy.'

Oblivious to the rain, the old soldier continues to spin tales spiced with sarcasm and spite, although as he talks a tinge of warmth, a fatherly tone, creeps into his voice. Yet he remains guarded about his name. 'I am a mosaic', he says. 'Take a letter here, another there, and you have my name. If you wish, you can call me "der vant". And what can one do with a wall? It provides protection, and to your enemies you can say, "Go beat your head against the wall!" '

A middle-aged couple carrying yellow chrysanthemums walk along the flooded paths of the cemetery. They stop by a grave and set to work. Weeds are removed, the stone wiped clean of dust, the marble surface polished. Oil lamps are lit and arranged with flowers by the base of the tomb. A pair of hands held up in a gesture of blessing, engraved on the headstone, indicates that here lies a descendant of Cohanim, the priestly caste.

Today is the tenth anniversary of David Schaffner's death and, by chance, I have become a participant in the occasion. His son Henry claims it is no coincidence that we have met at this time. He sees life as a series of interrelated events, all of which have significance against a wider scheme of things. 'There is no random chance', he claims, as he tends David's grave, 'but patterns: some evil, others beautiful. The goal of life is to intuit beyond the apparent chaos an infinite order of things, a higher intelligence at work.'

Henry's flat is on the Royal Way, in Ulitza Grodzka. The building is six-hundred-years old and stands near Rynek Glowny, the mediaeval market-square that occupies the centre of the walled city. Henry and his Polish wife live in two small rooms. Everywhere there are clocks, piles of clothing, and short-wave radio equipment. The clothes are repaired by Mrs Schaffner to augment her husband's sickness pension. The clocks sit on tables, mantelpieces, bookshelves and cupboards. Others hang on walls, while grandfather clocks squat on the floor. On the hour, every hour, bells chime, cuckoos fly out of cages, trumpets blow, and drums beat. One clock, disguised as a painting of an idyllic rural scene, comes to life with chimes synchronised to the movement of buckets being drawn from a well by village women.

Clocks are one of Henry's two grand passions. He collects and restores them. He scours market-places, remote hamlets, antique shops, and will travel many miles to follow up the slightest rumour that a clock is languishing somewhere in an attic or barn. He has transported them in taxis, buses, trains, and on foot, back to the cramped apartment in Ulitza Grodzka. His father had been a clock-repairer and had passed on the skills to his only son. 'Clocks are a constant reminder', Henry affirms, 'that there is a way to create order out of chaos. No matter how insane the world may seem at times, the chiming of a clock reminds the executioner, if only for a moment, that he too will one day be forced to move on.'

Henry's other great love is the short-wave radio which sits on the living-room table. It is a massive apparatus, always awake, crackling in the background, lights blinking a multitude of signals, the occasional voice filtering through with a call for 'Hotel Sierra', Henry's radio code-name. He is in regular contact with operators in seventeen European countries. They send each other cards and letters. Many can be seen stacked high on the mantelpieces, between clocks. 'Hotel Sierra' shows me a card he has received this very day from Viking Radio in the Shetland Islands. They had made contact for the first time a fortnight ago. The card is inscribed with the motto: 'Vikings raise the wind on the air', and beneath is printed their anthem:

> On distant seas their dragon prows
> Went gleaming outward bound.
> Stormclouds were their banners;
> Their music, ocean sound.

The radio card of 'Hotel Sierra' features a drawing of Krakow's walled city, against a background of red and white, Poland's national colours, inscribed with the motto: 'Though we are miles apart we are not strangers, but friends who have never met.'

Today is the tenth anniversary of the death of David Schaffner, who lies buried beneath a vase of yellow chrysanthemums. In the kitchen of a six-hundred-year-old apartment on the Royal Way, near the heart of the walled city, I listen to the bare outlines of his life story, told between the chiming of countless clocks and the faint voices of radio operators from all corners of the continent.

David was born in Krakow in the last decade of the nineteenth century. During the First World War he fought in the Polish army. Taken prisoner, he was sent by the Russians to Siberia. On his return he left his native city and settled in Germany. It would be safer there, he believed, far from anti-Jewish pogroms that had flared up in Poland at war's end.

His son Henry was born in Germany fifty years ago. During the Kristallnacht pogrom, on November 9, 1938, Nazi stormtroopers broke into the Schaffner home. They rampaged, looted, and over-turned David's extensive collection of antique clocks. 'Time stopped', says Henry, 'and for the next seven years we were continually on the run, seeking refuge, a place to hide.'

After deportation from Germany the family made their way back to Krakow. Within three months, the Nazis had invaded the city. When the Jews of Krakow were driven from their ancient quarters in Kazimierz and herded into a ghetto on the opposite banks of the Vistula, David urged his wife and son to escape. They hid in a village not far from the city. With the help of local peasants they survived.

David Schaffner was shunted from camp to camp. Somewhere within that vast network of terror, doctors of the Reich used him in their experiments. They pulled apart his immune system as one would take apart an antique clock. But they were not so concerned with reassembling the parts.

At war's end the Schaffners were among the few Krakow Jewish families to return. David remained a sick man, his constitution irretrievably broken. He passed his last years silently immersed in restoring clocks. 'It is no coincidence we met today', insists Henry. 'As a result you are recording my father's story. Every being craves recognition, someone to bear witness. Only then can a soul be finally put to rest.'

'Hotel Sierra', keeper of clocks and guardian of the airwaves, one of the last members of the oldest Jewish community in Poland, rides the waves of time and space in a landlocked apartment on the Royal Way. He receives messages from distant kingdoms, restores timepieces, and creates order out of chaos. 'This is the least I can do to combat evil forces', he claims. 'Heed the passage of time, listen carefully to a story, a cry for help, and restore that which has been damaged or broken.'

Feigl Wasserman is small and rotund. Her greying hair remains strong, and is tied in a series of buns which sweep upwards to a rounded summit. She ties her hair as she does everything else — with precision, care, and a sense of symmetry. As caretaker of the Rema she keeps watch over its dwindling congregation with a stern eye. 'They are useless', she declares. 'They cannot do anything by themselves. They need a mother to look after them.' She dusts off their coats, adjusts their ties, scolds and fusses and, at closing time, bundles them out of the synagogue.

Between chores she sits in the courtyard and chats to tourists who come to see the tomb of Moses Isserles. In return for advice and information she receives tips. American dollars, in particular, are most welcome. The visitors relieve her isolation and she is bemused by them, especially travellers such as myself. 'What are you looking for?', she asks. 'You think you can bring the dead back to life?'

In the evenings I return to her apartment. On the kitchen table stand rows of candles which she makes for synagogue services. When she retires to bed she moves the telephone to within arm's length. Calls from her two children are always imminent. There is a daughter in Israel, a son in Russia. She often talks about her grandchildren, shows me photos, describes their many virtues. Except for Shabbes eve she remains at home every evening, alone, awaiting the next call.

'Why don't you join them?', I ask her. 'And who would look after my husband's grave?', she replies, removing the crumbs from the table. When there is absolutely nothing left to clean or dust, she sits by the telephone and knits. 'He was a pious man, my second husband', says Feigl. Fifteen years ago he was invited by the Krakow congregation to become the sexton and cantor of the Rema. With their two children grown up and married, Feigl and her husband moved from their native Russia and took up the post in Krakow. And the first husband? That is another story altogether; to tell it, we need a cup of tea, several slices of almond cake and, if you wish, a glass or two of vodka.

The year is 1941. In a village somewhere within that vastness called the Red Empire, a man says farewell to his wife and one-year-old daughter. He sets off with his Red Army unit and vanishes from their lives. As the Nazis advance into Russia, the village is razed. The woman and her daughter move from town to town, always one step ahead of advancing armies. To recount the details of that epic journey would take many hours. Let us just say they survived but, despite Feigl's many attempts to locate him, it seemed as if her husband had disappeared without trace.

In 1950 he abruptly reappeared. He had been badly wounded, he explained. Shrapnel had lodged in his lungs. For many years he had been dangerously ill: hospitalised, listless, without any interest in life. Finally he had regained enough will to insist that, with whatever strength remained, he would search for his wife and child. 'And you think this story is unusual?', Feigl adds with a shrug. And indeed it now seems I have been listening for months to one common tale, with slight variations, a common chorus from which individual voices emerge to take centre stage for a moment, before retreating back to the wings.

'We were reunited for a mere ten months', continues Feigl. 'His lungs were on fire until the day he died. I was seven months pregnant at the time. It was only after I raised my children that I remarried. And when my second husband died, two years ago, I decided: enough, no more wandering, this is where I will end my days.'

Her knitting needles move fast. A pattern emerges. There is a touch of steel in Feigl Wasserman. 'It is not wise to dwell too much upon the past', she warns me. 'Do your job and stay one step ahead of trouble.' She is sharp, shrewd, just a touch angry, extremely wary, and very kind, in a motherly fashion. The keeper of the Rema, protector of the tomb of Moses Isserles, Feigl Wasserman is a wise and irritable babushka, mother of the last congregation of Krakow Jewry. 'Do not dwell too much upon the past', she insists. 'It will be of no practical use.'

On the wall there hangs a portrait of Jessica and Shylock, the merchant of Venice. His face is suffused with fatherly love; Jessica is radiant. Monika stands in front of the painting and stares at it intently. Her eyes are large and wide open. They blaze with such intensity that other features emerge slowly, as if advancing from the shadows. She is plump and wears a cotton dress with fading floral patterns. It hangs down loosely to her ankles and verges on shabbiness. Her face is a balloon, the cheeks tinted with rose patches which flare into fiery blotches when she becomes excited. At moments she relaxes into a childlike smile, and the permanent dimples in her cheeks deepen into rounded troughs. But most of the time she remains taut, alert, with her eyes taking on an existence of their own as they flit nervously between fear and extravagant hope.

I am never quite sure whether the story she is telling is true or the fantastic fabrication of a disintegrating mind. It does not seem to matter either way. The core of what she is recounting burns with something that extends beyond fact and fantasy. It is the myth by which she lives, the obsession which induced her to study the Hebrew language and scriptures, and to acquire a passion for a people who had almost vanished from the soil of her native land. Her passion had been disciplined into a vocation and had provided her with this temporary niche in life as an assistant in the Krakow Jewish museum.

The room in which we are talking is a garret in the museum, which in turn is housed in the Alte Shul. It sits above a narrow wooden staircase that spirals up from a cold, cavernous prayer-hall in what had been, for over five hundred years, a house of worship.

Construction had begun in the late fourteenth century, and the Shul was completed in 1407. It is a low building, squatting intact off Szeroka Square; and, from a distance of a mere fifty metres or so, it seems perched on the edge of the horizon, about to sink out of sight. On an adjacent side of the square stands the Rema, where I had first met Monika on Shabbat. She was swaying in the courtyard in her shabby dress, her eyes glowing, while the men were praying inside. 'She is a meshugene', Feigl Wasserman had whispered. 'There are enough lunatics here to make up their own minyan. Their heads are full of wild dreams and phantoms. Some of them claim to be Messiahs but can't even do up their shoelaces.'

She was twelve years old at the time, Monika tells me, living in a village on the outskirts of Katowice. She had been taken on a school excursion to the Auschwitz camp museum.

'There were no Jews in my village, although I had heard stories about a time, not so long ago, when they had lived crammed together in a neighbourhood by the stream. In the museum I saw Jews for the first time, in photos. For months I could not shake off the image of naked women running in fright towards death, trying to protect their dignity with their hands. Not long after, I became aware of the rumours. Whispers echoed through the streets of the village. "Your mother is one of them. You are the daughter of a Yid."

'Father laughed when I told him. He could not understand what had led me to imagine such a story. Mother remained silent. I felt they were both concealing the truth. I detected a fear in their eyes. When I persisted they became angry, especially father. Yet there were people in the village who told a very different tale, and my soul burned.

'Mother died when I was sixteen. I followed the Jewish custom I had read about in books. I tore my garments, and for seven days I sat on a low stool in mourning. By the seventh day I felt so light, like a child, an embryo in my mother's womb.'

Monika tells her story with a fervour which betrays a relentless compulsion. She fluctuates feverishly in mood, one moment caught up in a fear, naked and naive in its transparency; the next, swept along by a longing so overwhelming that she breaks beyond fear into a state of exaltation. As her story unfolds, her passion assumes an hallucinating quality which draws me into a private world of shadows and luminous visions. Before me, in a garret where the elders of the kehilla once discussed the affairs of their people, stands a woman who walks a tightrope between revelation and despair.

'After the period of mourning was over, I searched for a house of prayer, an active Jewish community. There was a shul in Katowice where a handful of people would gather on Shabbat. When I first heard their Hebrew chants, I recognised them instantly as my mother tongue. Among those who attended the shul I found one who was willing to teach me. In his apartment I felt more at home than in my father's house.

'Whenever I returned to the village I would plead with father. He remained resentful. Sometimes he broke into a rage. "Do not insult the memory of your mother", he would say. "Do you think I would marry into that race of heretics and Christ-killers you have fallen so in love with?"

'For three years the devil danced in our house. We lived in perpetual distrust. But I persisted. I would light and bless the Shabbat candles despite his disapproval. In time the glow of the candles softened our home. It soothed father's heart and dissolved his simmering rage, until one Shabbat night, without warning, the story I had longed for emerged; and as he told it, I saw for the first time in years a gentle smile play on his lips.

'When the Nazis were about to evacuate the Jews of our village there had come to our house a man known to the family. He had begged them to hide a daughter of his. She remained in the house while everyone she had known in childhood disappeared. The villagers knew where they had been transported to. The secret had seeped into the countryside. In the not-so-distant town of Oswiecim, factories of death were at work. After the war father had married the girl. A love of sorts had evolved between them in her years of hiding; and besides, there had been nowhere else for her to go. She took on his beliefs, converted, and never again mentioned her origins.

'That was all he ever told me. But it was enough. In the remaining year of his life he rarely spoke. I accompanied him to church on Sundays, while on Friday evenings I continued to light the Shabbat candles. When he died I left the village, and I have never since returned.'

On the wall there hangs a portrait of Shylock and Jessica. His face is suffused with fatherly love. Jessica appears radiant. Monika stands in front of the painting and stares at it intently, as if seeking within it an idealised view of herself, the reflection she longs for, a unity between father and daughter, a reconciliation of the warring factions within herself. This is the vision to which she clings. Without it there is no place for her on this scarred landscape; without it she stands alone in a no man's land forever shrouded in shadows.

In the evening I ask Feigl about Monika. 'Who knows who she is?', she replies. 'A Polack? A Yid? A meshugene? She speaks a few words of Hebrew; she works day and night in the museum. She comes regularly to the Rema. When the men are at prayer she stands in the courtyard and sways. She is not quite one of us; yet she does not seem to be one of them. Who knows? And what is so strange about this? We are all tainted by madness here. When you visit

Oswiecim you will see why it is we spend our lives looking after museums and graveyards.'

Like a shadow, I move through the camp entrance under the infamous words, '*Arbeit Macht Frei*'. The sign is smaller than I had expected, partly obscured by a background of trees. The black letters carved in steel weave and twist as if dancing in the air. Welcome. You have nothing to fear. Work liberates.

Just inside the entrance stands a massive kitchen complex, and beside it plays the camp orchestra. Flowers are in full bloom outside the manager's office. The finger, gloved in white, points left or right: instant death, or death on the instalment plan.

Auschwitz was no makeshift camp made of timber where the job had to be done in haste, out of sight, beyond memory and conscience. Auschwitz is of solid brick and mortar, with blocks several storeys high, constructed to house a hospital, research scientists, permanent camp personnel. It was to be a durable feature of the Reich, a continuing enterprise with an assured future. Its barracks now serve the purposes of display. A museum of the impossible exists here.

In recent months I have come to know many levels of silence. It is a language with an extensive vocabulary. There are silences which echo ancestral presences; silences in which it is possible to observe the slightest movement of dust, an insect in hiding, a pod floating from a dandelion with the faintest promise of rebirth; and the awesome silence of forest clearings where mass executions took place against mute backdrops of stunning beauty. Yet here, in the headquarters of the Reich terror network, the vocabulary of silence reaches beyond its own limits. It overwhelms with the sheer force of numbers: and the fact that here, lived and worked a company of technicians and bureaucrats who went about the task of efficiently and quickly annihilating over a million human beings.

The scope is too vast. I can only register glimpses. At random. Electrified wires. Watchtowers. A wall where twenty thousand were executed. Cellars one metre square where prisoners stood without light for weeks on end. Rooms in a hospital where experiments were carried out on infants. Each glimpse offers an insight into an eternity of suffering.

There are children bearing flowers, schools on excursion. The flowers glow: golden chrysanthemums and marigolds, blood-red roses, emerald-green ferns. Guides repeat grim stories in a babel of languages. Yet all I hear clearly is the beating of my heart, the tread of my own footsteps, and the rustle of clothes against a backdrop of infinite silence.

There remains just one crematorium standing in Auschwitz. I am struck by how small and innocuous it looks. The only harsh feature outside is the chimney, which juts upwards in a jagged thrust towards the heavens. The impact is softened by trees and lawns which have been planted around it.

Inside: a dimly lit cave. Trolleys, which had conveyed the bodies along rails directly into the flames, stand still, as if frozen on a tightrope in time. At the entrance to one of the gaping ovens burns a single candle. A wreath of fresh flowers lies beside it. Glued to the the oven door is a sheet of paper which is headed: 'Voices of the Children Saved from the Ashes.'

Written for the most part in cool anger, the notice lists demands for retribution, increased reparations, and the apprehension of war criminals. But it is only the final pledge which fully resonates within me. It is a miracle of poetry; a slim but potent reminder of my goal in coming here. The Voices assert: 'We promise to show our children where their grandparents hugged us for the last time.'

As I walk back towards the entrance I feel alert, nerves stretched taut like finely tuned wires — antennae ready to pick up the faintest of signals. I pass the block of apartments where the commandant had lived. There are potplants on several window-sills. A woman trudges home with a bag of shopping and disappears into the building. A car is parked in the driveway. A man exercises his dog. It is bizarre to see the rhythm of normality beating in Auschwitz.

Moving between rows of barracks I catch sight of a ring lying on the ground: a silver band with a black stone. The ring fits easily. So often I have seen the tattooed numbers on the lower arms of family friends — their indelible signature from the kingdom of darkness. It seems appropriate to have found this token, a permanent

reminder of my brief stay, the black stone of Auschwitz. Yet I feel
uneasy. Does it belong beyond the perimeters of this sinister universe
so tightly contained within barbed-wire fences? Should I carry with
me a constant reminder of the power of evil? Why be so obsessed
with maintaining the memory?

It is late afternoon. The tour groups have departed. The museum
is about to close for the day. Above the camp entrance leap those
words which make such a mockery of reason. The silence is a vortex
drawing me back towards the first intimations of clarity. I approach
the fence, hang the ring on a barb of wire, and walk out of Auschwitz.

It is three kilometres from Auschwitz to the sister camp, Birkenau.
This was the killing field, the end of the line. The tracks are now
covered in weeds and are rusting. They snake towards a towering
red-brick structure known as the 'Gate of Death'. A lookout rises
above a spacious arched entrance. The tracks continue into the camp
past a sprawl of barracks constructed to house over 200 000 inmates
at a time. Several kilometres on stood the gas chambers and
crematoria. Only the ruins remain, and a lake in which, it is said,
ashes still float to the surface. Here, thousands could be disposed
of in a single day; as they were, day after day, month after month,
the victims conveyed by train from countries throughout the
expanding Reich.

The sky darkens. A row of poplars stand guard behind a monument on the far edge of the camp, the leaves softly rustling. The
air is cool, penetrating, chill. In the distance the 'Gate of Death'
fades into night, enclosing a field where so many precious souls were
wrenched from life.

Krakow bursts from the mists into a glorious autumn day, as if
revealing its beauty for the first time. The Royal Way threads into
the walled city through St. Florian's Gate and proceeds along what
was once a much-travelled trading route. Merchants, pilgrims, adven-
turers and foreign armies were drawn to the renowned marketplace
in the central square, and beyond, up a steep ascent to the summit
of Wawel Hill. Overlooking the Vistula River loom the palaces of
former Polish kingdoms. Underground, beneath Wawel Cathedral,

the vaults of the royal crypt contain tombs of kings, bishops, and eminent dignitaries. It is too impersonal, grandiose, too cold, this citadel of royal corpses. I descend to the familiar streets of Kazimierz and to the Krakow Jewish cemetery, whose crumbling stones seem far more accessible.

The flowers on David Schaffner's grave have withered. The front door of the caretaker's apartment is opened by an elderly woman. Her greying hair is tied back tightly into a bun. She glances at me warily, retreats into the apartment to consult the hidden presence within, and returns minutes later with a welcoming smile.

He is seated in the kitchen, hunched over a table beside a desk lamp which sheds light over a transistor radio in an advanced state of disarray. Screws, nuts, wires, and strips of plastic lie scattered about. The old soldier probes the innards of the transistor with miniature tools. He is, in his sceptical, hard-bitten way, pleased to see me. 'I'm just playing, passing time', he says. 'What else is there to do?'

His Polish wife hovers around us quietly. She prepares tea and sandwiches with slices of salami and tomatoes. 'At least she doesn't expect me to be a millionaire, as most Poles do. And there is always something to eat, a clean shirt to wear.' She smiles faintly at his words. There is an obvious bond between them, a softness that could be called love, despite . . . or is it because of his wary cynicism?

'I'm just playing out time in this mad world', the old soldier muses. 'People torture and kill each other. They don't know what to do with their insatiable desires. Yet we all end up there.' And he gestures towards the window through which can be seen the object of his remarks — a burial ground of decaying stones fading in the evening light. '*Azoi iz es*', he says in his sing-song Yiddish as he attempts to reassemble the transistor. 'That's the way it is.'

The bus is climbing upwards, ascending foothills which swell from the Vistula valley, well beyond the walled city and cobblestones of Kazimierz, far above outer industrial Krakow barely visible in a veil of smoke, lumbering into the Carpathians past fields of radiant greens, landscapes flooded with sun, steep slopes criss-crossed with haystacks; and with each passing mile I feel lighter, more exhilarated. Herds of goats and sheep move slowly on the upper reaches. Multi-storey timber farmhouses with intricately carved facades rise amidst vegetable gardens and fodder-filled barns. Interminably upwards the bus moves, towards mountain peaks looming in the distance; and it is not fast enough, nor high enough as yet, to tame the wild images dancing in my mind.

We spill out of the bus into the streets of Zakopane. The air is startlingly crisp; the resort town teeming with tourists, backpackers, farmers; the streets crowded with jeeps and four-wheel drives. I am caught unawares by this sudden gust of affluence, and I keep moving, beyond the town limits, along country roads, onto narrow paths that weave through forests of conifers, of evergreens among autumn annuals engulfed in crimsons and gold. The sun is moving downwards, touching mountain peaks now well within reach. I look out upon an ocean of swaying trees. They give way to barren, rock-strewn slopes which stretch steeply towards summits and beyond, into skies of blue clarity, beyond suffering and despair, beyond past and future, beyond obsession and hope, and far beyond all trace of that blot in a distant valley, that ugly smudge of darkness called Auschwitz.

Chapter Sixteen

PERHAPS IT WAS BLOOMFIELD who gave me the first inkling. He would tramp the streets of our neighbourhood in a worn suit, verging on neatness in a navy-blue tie and white shirt. But the heels of his shoes were non-existent from constant walking, and his clothes were frayed. He would pause only for a quick chat, a few cryptic remarks. Forever restless, he was anxious to resume his rapid strides which headed purposefully nowhere except within a well-defined territory of local streets and parks. It was said he slept in rooming-houses for paupers and single men. In winter a large coat weighed him down, while in summer he would discard the jacket of his suit and walk with his shirt sleeves rolled up. It was then that I would see, clearly exposed, the primitive scrawl of blue figures, his 'pass-port number' as he called it with a nervous laugh. And for as long as I can recall, I associated him with whispered conversations among my parents and their friends: something about him having been a human guinea pig in experiments conducted by a Doctor Mengele, the white-gloved arbiter of life and death in a place they called by its Polish name, Oswiecim. The word would evoke in me a chill, a sense of terror, a feeling of dread.

Or perhaps I first heard it in the annual commemorations which took place, late April, throughout the 1950s , in the Melbourne Town Hall. It would be packed to the last seat, with several thousand East European Jews, most of them recent arrivals from 'yener velt', the other world, or simply 'over there', as they often called it.

As the lights dimmed, six candles would be lit by six children, the sons and daughters of survivors. We all knew very well what the candles represented. But the figure was too vast, incalculable. I would lie awake some nights trying to penetrate the mystery. Six million dead? Or was it six million spirits? If one travelled out into space, what would be the end of it? Could there be an end? Was six million the end-point of all journeys?

In the candle light, standing on a rostrum, alone on stage against a stark black backdrop, a cantor would recite the Prayer for the Dead, a plea to the Master of the Universe to look after the souls of the departed. His amplified tenor would soar in the cavernous hall, mounting in intensity as it flowed into a recital of names, each one pronounced in a voice that seemed to weep, drawing with it a chorus which ascended from the audience, at first softly, slowly gathering force, discarding all restraint, until it seemed as though the whole of humanity was weeping. Oswiecim was always the first name: Oswiecim, Treblinka, Majdanek, Sobibor, Chelmno, Belzec, Buchenwald, Dachau — ghettoes, extermination camps, sites of execution. As I listened, the names were instilled within me as places on a mythical landscape, in a remote Kingdom of Darkness, in which ancestral ghosts stalked unredeemed, eternally condemned to a netherworld of shadows.

Then the lights were on, the chandeliers ablaze, the community swarming out onto the streets, the children even daring to play. We hurtled up and down flights of stairs while our parents talked on the footpaths. The faces of the town clock beamed at us as we crowded onto trams together, since many of us were returning to the same neighbourhood where Bloomfield, the human guinea pig, could be seen even at this late hour, maintaining his restless patrol, his eyes perpetually fixed on a distant and inaccessible goal.

And there was a golden era, which I vaguely recall as weaving in and out of a darkness. Father would sit on the living-room sofa, stand me on his feet, and lift. His feet contained a magical power. 'Oompah! Oompah!', he would say with every lift. 'Oompah! Oompah!', and I was flying, arms outstretched, while his face whirled below me in a ball of laughter. Mother too displayed magical powers, especially when I contracted the various childhood ailments which swept through kindergarten and primary school. I recall them as one extended fever from which I would sometimes open my eyes to see mother always seated by the bed, her face emanating a soft-

ness, a gentle strength, a constancy. Sunday mornings were the best
of times. We were allowed, all three brothers, to jump into the warm
double bed which mother and father had just vacated. We bounced
on the mattress, crawled under the fat eiderdown beneath which
they slept on winter nights, and revelled in the after-scent of their
bodies.

Yet there was always something else. I do not recall a first time,
but there were to be many times. Mother would be standing in front
of me, rocking to and fro, her eyes shifting out of focus, as if everyone
around her, myself included, no longer existed. She was somewhere
else, perhaps 'over there', in that distant world she had left behind.
I did not see it as such at the time. All I could register was the
estrangement, her non-recognition; and I wanted to shake her, to
bring her back, to awaken her from the dream — or perhaps enter
into it, so long as we were together.

But even this seemed preferable — her silent retreat, the passive
withdrawal — to the rage that could erupt at any time, accompanied by a refrain repeated incessantly as a plea, a demand, an accu-
sation. 'I've got a story to tell', she would exclaim. 'No one sees! No
one understands! No one knows who I am!' It was never clear nor
logical, this outcry, but rather a succession of garbled clues, an erratic
monologue strung together between familiar phrases and catchwords:
something about permits, passports, disloyalties and locked doors;
broken promises, broken hearts, betrayals and unjust laws. Her words
were hurled at father, Hitler, the community, the world at large;
and they careered back, over and again, to the refrain, 'I've got a
story to tell. No one sees! No one understands! No one knows who
I am!' Bialystok, Wellington, Melbourne, Oswiecim, this world and
yener velt were all intertwined. Over there was over here, and here
was over there; and I would take to the streets, or retreat to my
bedroom, to seek relief from the storm. And father too would slip
away, as if somehow implicated, unwilling to answer the questions
I had begun to ask with increasing persistence and mounting anger
as I sought to fathom the source of the constant tension which simmered in the house.

There was another possibility: the dining-room cupboard, full of
journals and letters, ageing books and mysteries. Spiders had found
undisturbed corners in which to spin their webs. Cockroaches scurried by. The letters were neatly tied in bundles, the envelopes coated

in dust. I would prise open the doors, retrieve the bundles, and take them to my bedroom. I carefully unfolded the fragile writing-sheets, which were yellowed and riddled with holes. Others were a little thicker, pale blue, more durable. A vague scent of forgotten days hovered about them. The dates seemed ancient, concentrated between 1933 and mid 1936: they were addressed from mother to Meier Zabludowski, Bialystok, Kupietzka 38; and from father to Hoddes Zabludowski, care of her sister Feigl in Melbourne, and care of a Mr and Mrs Morris in Wellington, New Zealand.

It was difficult to decipher the scrawling Yiddish script — written in haste, it seemed, with an urgency I was too young to comprehend. Only gradually did I come to detect the agitation and longing, especially in mother's letters; and also a strength, always expanding in order to contain her growing sense of isolation, bewilderment, and unfulfilled love.

Her early letters, however, were permeated with optimism and high expectations. On the night of February 3, 1933, the passengers on the Wild Mama held a farewell party. A chocolate cake was baked for the occasion, and the French cook was shown how to ice the message, in Yiddish: 'We wish you happiness in your new life.' The passengers sang, made lofty speeches, and danced. Two black stewards, who had served them throughout the journey, joined in the festivities. 'They were fine dancers', writes mother. 'One of them stood on the table and sang the Marseillaise.' And at dawn they had all gathered on deck while the Wild Mama steamed through the gap between the two peninsulas which enclose Port Phillip Bay.

As the port came into view they could see many people awaiting their arrival. A boat from Europe was quite an event, and the infant Polish-Jewish community of Melbourne would treat it as a public holiday, a rare day off work. Among the passengers, Mrs Abrahams and her three young children were the most excited. Somewhere in the crowd, waving from the docks, stood her husband. Five years of separation were coming to an end.

Mother was greeted by her sister Feigl, her brother-in-law Moishke, their baby daughter Freidele, and many former Bialystoker, eager to obtain news from home, a message from a loved one. As for Mrs Abrahams, her husband was nowhere to be seen. Long after the customs formalities had been completed she remained on the wharf with her three children, their trunks and suitcases in a pile beside them. Nine weeks later, Mrs Abrahams was dead of a stroke. Or was it suicide? The children were in a home for the abandoned, and her husband was still living with the woman who had been his mistress for several years. Meanwhile, the gates of the Old World were slowly closing and, in the New, mother had begun the long battle to bring over her husband.

She writes once a fortnight, late at night, or early mornings, before work, in order to post her letters in time for the next mail-run to Europe. For the most part she concentrates on everyday details, her practical vision of reality. Within two weeks of arrival she has a job as a machinist in a textile factory in Flinders Lane, the garment district in the heart of the city. She gets up at seven, walks to the tram stop at 7.30, and enters the factory punctually at eight. There is a ten-minute break for morning tea, half-an-hour for lunch at one, and an afternoon session until five thirty. At night she works at home, in her sister's dressmaking business. She receives a weekly wage of two pounds and five shillings, pays fifteen shillings for food and lodging and, apart from various little expenses, the balance goes into paying back the loan for her ticket to Australia. She looks forward to the day when she can put aside money for her husband's fare and for her impoverished family in Bialystok.

'Work conditions are in general satisfactory', she writes in the tone of the former committee member of the Bialystok Seamstresses' Union. She is grateful for the regular wage, and enthuses about holiday pay and the overtime bonus. She recalls the interminable hours of unrewarded work in the sweatshops at home. The memory tempers her attacks of nostalgia. She is determined to start a new life regardless, under the strange, somehow transparent light of these southern skies.

Nevertheless, Melbourne's isolated Polish Jews learn to bend and mould time and space to soothe their moments of longing. They recreate the Old World in the New. Mother asks Meierke to send pictures of her Bundist heroes, Vladimir Medem and Beinish Michelevitz, and of her beloved Yiddish writer, I. L. Peretz. When they arrive she hangs them on the walls of her room alongside pictures of the Polish countryside. On Sundays she visits Bundist families in the neighbourhood. As soon as she enters their homes she feels enveloped by the warmth of familiarity. There are regular latke evenings, where fiery discussions of politics burn until the early hours of the morning; and when she walks home, she feels lighter, uplifted, as if she were moving through the streets of Bialystok.

And she calculates distances, time-spans. It takes five weeks for a letter to cross the oceans to her Meierke. 'Here it is midnight. I am sitting at a table, in a room in Melbourne, and over there, my dear one, it is early afternoon. Here it is late summer, and for you it is still winter. Be careful you do not catch cold.' Weeks later, when she tastes the freshness of autumn evenings on the way home from work, she muses: 'If only, on such perfect nights, you were the one who greeted me as I left the factory, rather than the strangers who crowd the streets at this hour.' On Mondays, when letters from Europe arrive, she sits at work impatiently, 'as though on pins'. Her head 'spins from thinking about it', and at five thirty she grabs her coat and beret and hastens to the tram. Within twenty minutes she is close to home, running, her heart beating strongly, plagued by the thought, 'What if no letter arrives today? How will I get through the next week?'

There are times when she can barely contain the longing. Especially on anniversaries and celebrations. Take, for instance, May Day, 1933. Mother writes in March, so that the letter will arrive at the appropriate time. She is upset that this year she will not be able to participate, for the first time since 1922. In ten years she had not missed a single May Day march, 'like a pious Jew does not miss his three daily prayers', she remarks. She recalls the arrest, just one year before, of Rivke Hartman. 'I can picture the scene clearly, the police running with batons and upraised bayonets. Meierke, I trust you will describe everything that takes place during this year's march. Send my best wishes to my friends in the Bund, and take good care of yourself during the demonstration. I will be with you, in spirit.'

As winter approaches, the community huddles together. It subscribes to Polish-Yiddish dailies, worries about the rise of Hitler in Germany, establishes news-sheets, a choir, a Yiddish theatre. Mother sings at concerts and at a grand banquet to celebrate the arrival of an eminent Yiddish writer on a lecture-tour of Australia. Funds are raised for Yiddish schools in Poland; and plans are made to establish one in Melbourne, which I will attend decades later, on Sunday mornings and Wednesday evenings. As a result I will learn the 'aleph beis', the Yiddish alphabet, an esoteric knowledge which will enable me to decipher mother's letters and to discover the ebb and flow of her moods, the slow erosion of her faith, and her increasing desperation as she fought to remain in the New World.

Lives hang in the balance in ill-lit offices where, in between cups of tea and biscuits, with a cigarette dangling from the lips — or so I like to imagine it — a bureaucrat sits down, adjusts his glasses, focusses on the papers in front of him, and deduces that she, my mother, had migrated as a Probutski, on a permit made out to a single woman, sponsored by a sister, and the application he is scanning is for a husband with the name Zabludowski. This is a transgression of the law. Besides, there is an economic crisis in the land, jobs are hard to come by, and there are many citizens calling for an end to migration. A letter is sent to Hoddes Probutski, official, polite, to the point: you have one month in which to leave the country.

Mother fights tenaciously to stay in Australia. Accompanied by her brother-in-law Moishke, she approaches rabbis, communal leaders, lawyers, and lodges appeals. She is interviewed by an immigration officer. He is angry at the 'trick' she had played on the government. She had signed her papers falsely. Mother argues she had been single at the time. 'But you arrived as a married person', the officer admonishes. He turns his attention to Meier. 'Can your husband speak English? Does he have skills which are scarce in Australia? Perhaps he has money. With five hundred pounds he could enter without a permit.' Only towards the end of the interrogation, when mother hands him a photo of Meier, does he soften. 'Not bad looking, your old man', he remarks. 'But I'm afraid the decision is not up to me. Your papers will be sent to Canberra. The boys up there will look into it. Trouble is, there are too many people in this country. Even our prime minister, good Catholic that he is, has eleven children.'

'I have become very nervous', writes mother. 'I am running out of patience.' She waits six weeks for a reply. On October 19 it arrives. Her permit has been revoked. She must leave the country. Mother's despair can be felt in every sentence as she writes to Meier of her sense of humiliation on receiving the reply. 'It was like a clap of thunder', she tells him. She has barely paid off her debt for the ticket out: now she must find money for the return journey. The Christmas season is coming. She works overtime in the factory and well past midnight in Feigl's business. 'At least work helps me forget', she writes, 'and as I work I think of you. Your name is always on my lips, your face embedded in my fantasies.'

A delegation is sent to the Minister responsible for immigration. He promises to think it over. Mother's hopes leap. 'It is good to dream', she writes, 'but woe unto the dreamer.' At the same time, she never allows herself to stray too far from the practical. She rebukes Meier for sending letters express: 'An unnecessary expense. Every groshen is valuable. Write on thinner paper. But your letters are a great encouragement', she adds, 'and I await them anxiously, every Monday, my "sacred" day of the week.'

The Minister rejects the appeal, but allows her four months in which to earn the fare home. A new possibility emerges. Rabbi Brody of Melbourne writes to rabbi Katz in New Zealand. Rabbi Katz approaches immigration officials on mother's behalf. She requires sponsors, they reply, and only then can she apply for a permit. A young Bialystoker in Melbourne has relatives in Wellington, a Mr and Mrs Morris. He asks them to act as guarantors. They agree, and an application is lodged. If this attempt fails, mother reasons, she will return to Paris rather than Poland. She can see what is coming. Any alternative, anywhere on this globe, would be preferable to her former homeland.

Yet with each rejection Bialystok seems more alluring. 'Come home', writes Chane Esther. 'There will be a great simche when you arrive.' 'Life is not so bad here', writes Meier. 'Your many friends would love to see you again.'

Their entreaties are tempting; a day of waiting is an eternity. Each night takes its own time before giving way to the dawn. Mother wakes at 3 a.m. in a fever. She stares at photos of Meier. The ticking of the clock is a creeping insanity. Each minute is fraught with panic; each successive tick resounds louder. Letters float across oceans, bearing images of loved ones. Mother gazes at photos of her sister Sheindl, her cousin Freidele, her nephew Chaimke. 'He looks so alive, as if he were actually here', she writes. 'And Freidele is growing up to be pretty. But my sister Sheindl's sad smile gives me no joy. She seems very upset. Chilek no longer writes to her from Palestine. I feel insulted by it.' This is always the possibility which skitters beneath the surface, the spectre of abandonment, the fate of Mrs Abrahams.

Mother lodges one last appeal with the logic of desperation. Or is there a touch of irony, uncharacteristic of her? 'The centenary of Victoria's settlement is to take place next October', writes Moishke on her behalf. 'The newspapers say that over fifty thousand guests are coming from England alone. So why not allow me to stay on? At least until then? What difference will one person make?'

March 4, 1934: the final rebuff from the Minister. Melbourne has just emerged from a heat wave, over forty degrees for nine days in succession. Factory work is almost intolerable. 'The papers say it was the hottest spell in many years', writes mother. 'It had to be now, of course, just for me. It seems as though I am a true shlemiel. Well, let it be the last trial.'

Mother's moods fluctuate with increasing rapidity. She receives a visa for New Zealand, but only for six months. Her Yiddish script takes on greater urgency. The characters are more elongated, stretched taut almost beyond recognition. 'I have become a mere straw tossed around on wild seas, from earth to the skies, from the skies back to earth.' And she hastens to add: 'This is not just pretty prose, but the way it is. Which way do I go? Wellington? Paris? Bialystok? Buenos Aires?' She changes her mind from one letter to the next. 'Why spend my hard-earned money on a fare to New Zealand, where my future is uncertain, where I am without family or community?' Bialystok appears frequently in her dreams as an enticing mirage. She sees herself sitting in the city gardens on summer evenings, strolling in Sienkiewicza Avenue on Sunday afternoons. 'It will be exciting to see everyone again', she writes. Mother appears to have made up her mind. 'There is much to talk about, Meierke', she concludes, ' but it can now wait for when we are reunited in our beloved Bialystok.'

April 11, 1934: mother's last letter from Melbourne. 'It is early afternoon. At four o'clock I will be going to the station. At 5.30 the train leaves for Sydney. From there I will catch the ferry for New Zealand. My situation you can well imagine. I try to reassure myself, but I have fantasies of arriving in a strange and desolate land. I'd be much happier returning to Bialystok. But I know, within me, I must seize this last chance, so that in years to come I will be certain I exhausted every possibility. Otherwise it will always weigh on my conscience.'

On the train to Sydney mother chats with the woman sitting next to her. She is of German descent. When she learns of mother's predicament she offers to look after her in Sydney until the ferry departs. 'Only seven million people in such a vast continent?', the woman muses. 'Surely there is room for just one more!'

The *Wanganui* steams into Wellington Harbour through heavy rain. When the ferry docks customs police check documents. Mother and a group of Chinese are detained. 'We were treated like criminals', she writes. After lengthy questioning, Mr and Mrs Morris are allowed on board. They identify Hoddes as the woman they have been expecting, and assure the police they are her guarantors.

On April 30 mother writes her first letter from New Zealand. She is at her lowest ebb. During the first week she had walked the factory district looking for a job. Within a week she had found work. 'Mr and Mrs Morris are fine people', she observes. 'I sleep on a sofa in their dining room. They treat me as a welcome guest.' Yet this cannot lift her spirits. 'To tell the truth', she confides, 'I would rather be back in Bialystok eating bread and salt, than here, with all the riches in the world. I cannot see either of us fitting into this way of life. You have to look with a lamp to find just one Bialystoker. As soon as I have earned the money for the fare, I'll take my pack on my shoulders and journey home. This single thought sustains me.'

On the eve of her second May Day in the New World, mother can think only of Bialystok. She pictures the Bund locale on Ulitza Lipowe, where last-minute preparations are being made for the annual march. 'How great would be my joy if I were there with you now.'

Many letters are missing. The last one from Wellington is dated May 15, 1934. Mother regrets the weakness she had shown in her previous letter. 'I know you will not derive much joy from it', she writes. 'It was silly of me to have sent it.' She has set her sights again on finding a way to bring Meier over. This is mother — the determined one, the stoic — as I would come to know her many years later, her life narrowed down to the single objective of raising her three children, the remnants of her once-large family. She did this with a quiet persistence, broken only from time to time by her abrupt scream emerging from a dream of villages on fire, or by a sudden rage with her hypnotic refrain echoing again and again: 'I have a story to tell! No one sees! No one understands! No one knows who I am!'

But increasingly I do, as I criss-cross the pages of her letters, and criss-cross Judenrein landscapes of her vanished past to uncover tombstones sinking into mud and dust. Each stone resonates with unfulfilled hopes; and each page of mother's letters resonates with unobtainable dreams. I see her walking the streets of the New World, surrounded by strangers and locked doors. I see her confronted by her aloneness, her yearning for love and reunion. I see her search for a harmony, a sense of belonging and trust, while the years slowly erode her faith. Yet also I see mother acquiring, perhaps unwittingly and at great cost, a subtle wisdom which years later would be fully expressed only in silence.

On May 11, after three-and-a-half years of applications, rejections, appeals, delegations, threats of deportation, last-minute extensions and interventions, and a final plea at the eleventh hour from a friend of a friend, who knew the Minister for Immigration, father arrived in New Zealand. As he checked through customs he caught glimpses of Hoddes, among the circle of friends she had made during her two years in Wellington.

'In that moment she seemed like a searing beam of light', father tells me, 'and as soon as I was able, I rushed towards her in a blur of excitement. But to tell you the truth', he adds with a laugh, 'I think her friends were somewhat disappointed with the greenhorn who emerged from the boat. They looked at me with great curiosity. Was this the Romeo they had heard so much about, the writer of such poetic letters, the object of Hoddes's tireless passion, reunited at last with his Juliet?' Father warms to the story. 'On the same boat, there had in fact arrived two immigrant Jews', he recalls. 'Meier and Abrami. While I was small and wiry, Abrami was tall and handsome. He would have made a far more appropriate hero.'

Nevertheless, it was a time of great simche. From photos of that time I see a handsome couple at parties, on picnics with young friends, seated on beaches side by side: 'A miracle for Bialystoker', father claims. 'We had come from a vast inland to a slender island, where the sea flowed from the skies and shades of blue permeated our lives.' Mother strides confidently through Wellington streets, always smartly dressed. And father seems content. He exudes the heady lightness of freedom, unshackled by Old World obligations and fears.

Their goals appear simple and clear, to establish themselves with some capital. Father becomes an assistant in mother's dressmaking business. They open a small shop, where he takes care of sales. 'We had dreams of being able to send money to our families', father tells me. 'Particularly Hoddes — she was always talking about repaying Chane Esther for her many years of sacrifice. She planned to bring over her nephew Chaimke, her youngest brother Hershl, and her Aunt Rivke's daughter Freidele. We fantasized that we would one day return to Bialystok on a visit, in style, radiating success, our suitcases laden with gifts, just like others we had seen who had made good in the New World. "Alrightniks", they were called. We would be alrightniks on a triumphant return to the Old World.'

Again the soothing rhythm of trains. From the heights of Zakopane, the beginning of a return, one last visit to Bialystok. Day and night I move, through cities of an ancient dreaming, stopping for a day here, a few hours there, in renowned centres of Polish Jewry.

In Wroclaw it rains. The leaders of the kehilla escort me through their cemetery with a familiar lament: 'We do not even have enough left for a minyan.' In Lodz the burial ground is vast, overgrown, the stones hidden under long grasses that bend to the wind. Highrise flats loom on the edges, as if anxious to stake claims on occupied territory. Back through Warsaw at night, the train hurtles past a sprawl of solitary lights, and I glimpse figures stumbling under an avalanche of rain. By midmorning I am on a stone path which bears the name, 'The Black Way'. It curves through a pine forest and opens out onto a clearing. In the centre stands a grey monolith, a mausoleum over ten metres in height, surrounded by a symbolic graveyard of jagged rocks. Each one represents a village, a town, a city, throughout Europe and remote outposts of the Reich, where victims were herded into wagons and railroaded here. Treblinka. A place of country solitude in a land of peasants. By night I am again on the move, southeast; and at dawn I am on the streets of Lublin, city of saints and talmudic scholars, centre of pilgrimage and rabbinical courts to which seekers once flocked from all corners of the realm. And just beyond the city limits I come upon it — a desolate field, surrounded by guard towers and barbed fences — a raw wound called Majdanek.

Towards evening I make my way back to the Old City quarters, a rambling neighbourhood of tenements with pastel-shaded facades. The winding alleys are deserted except for children who play by the wall which encircles the cemetery. Tufts of weeds poke out between cracks. The wall glows a mute crimson as it absorbs the sun's rays. Never before have I felt so strongly the impact of this hour, when day gives way to night and when, for a moment, light and darkness meet in the luminosity of twilight. It seems impossible a Majdanek could have existed. Where have I been today?

The train circles north, towards the Bialystoku region. I doze fitfully through the night, occasionally jolted by the screech of brakes and flashes of light from stations rushing by. Months of travel coalesce in a trail of menacing dreams; and I envisage how it may have been, in the dying days of the Reich, as the Red Army moved in from the east, and the Allies from the west, liberating remnants from death camps, forest hideouts, attics and barns, a handful here, a few there. Like spectres they move, the survivors, across war-ravaged landscapes, in a trance, returning with the instincts of homing pigeons, urged on by faint hopes of finding someone alive: family, a former neighbour, a familiar face, within that vague, half-forgotten mirage they had once known as home.

In the streets of New Zealand delirious crowds are dancing. Yet my parents cannot recall a celebration, a sense of relief, or an ending, but merely a daze and an ominous blight, a 'black stain', father has called it. The search extended for years. They scoured Red Cross lists and personal notices in the columns of Yiddish newspapers, astounded that they could not locate even one distant relative, when thousands were emerging from the wreckage — this one from a refugee camp, that one from a Siberian prison, another from a remote town in Asia Minor, or any one of the many far-flung enclaves where temporary refuge may have been found while the storm was raging. In all parts of the globe lists were being scoured. And increasingly it was becoming obvious how immense, how complete, the Catastrophe had been.

In 1947, or thereabouts — I have never been able to find out exactly when — a notice appeared in a local paper, addressed to father, from a camp for displaced persons; and, in time, I would become aware of bitter quarrels, accusations, evasions, of matters enshrouded in obscure hints and denials, which seemed always, eventually, to hearken back to that message from yener velt, from the kingdom of night.

Many such notices were appearing at the time, signalling the unexpected reappearance of a friend, an acquaintance, a former comrade, as if returned from the dead. 'I am looking for Meier Zabludowski', she had written, more or less. 'I am thinking of moving to Australia or New Zealand.' The note was brief, a mere inquiry. Yet between the lines could be heard a barely concealed scream, a plea for help. Like so many others, she was seeking a means to flee the ruins of a past life in which they had marched together, through the streets of Bialystok, their arms linked, cushioned by each other's warmth and an illusory sense of communal strength.

'Send her money! Our savings! A permit! A guarantee! Send her everything she needs!', father had replied on an impulse. At least these were the words that mother would mimic, at the height of her tirades. 'Send her everything she needs!' This was mother's version, the way she imagined it, or accurately recalled it — I could never tell one way or another. And when I had begun to question father, he had, in those years, never replied. He would quietly retreat behind his bedroom door, to the works of his beloved Yiddish poets, to seek relief from the rage that had overtaken first his wife and then his children.

On one side, a silence; on the other, a tirade. My loyalties wavered, first one way then the other, goaded by father's retreats, bewildered by mother's furies: 'I have a story to tell! No one sees! No one understands! No one knows who I am!'

The year is 1947, or thereabouts. A baby is wailing. Mother is pregnant with the second child. 'Send her money, guarantees, everything she needs!' The spectre of Mrs Abrahams looms large. The fate of Sheindl remains fresh in her mind. Bialystok has been consumed by flames. Father is consumed by his helplessness and shame. Mother is consumed by a sense of having been betrayed. The shadow of Hitler extends from the grave. Father withdraws, a sullen retreat, limping with a loss of nerve and belief. Mother awakens with screams; and years later I would feel trapped in between, seeking desperately to distinguish reality from dreams.

Nearing the outskirts of Bialystok I see peasants gathering potatoes and turnips. They wear thick jackets, scarves, and knee-length boots. On the River Nerev a boatman poles past cottages sinking into the banks. In the yard of a farmhouse an old woman feeds her pigs. Villages whirl by. Crows swirl between church crosses and spires. A hare scampers from the tracks. Old men walk slowly along dusty paths. Wagons laden with the final harvest lurch over country roads. A midmorning sun hovers above fallow fields.

'Those early years, after the Shoah, were a time of numbness, of suppressed grief, a stumbling through thick fog.' This is how father has described it. And it is only now, since my journey has given us common ground, detailed maps that I have come to know like the veins which run blue rivulets through father's worn hands, that I can fully accept his words. 'We did not know it at the time', he tells me. 'How could we? We were like wounded horses, moving by instinct. We kept our sense of guilt at bay. We immersed ourselves in making a living, and in bearing children, three within four years. We moved back to Melbourne, following an urge to rejoin family and former Bialystoker, to find that they too were so immersed in their own efforts to rebuild their lives they did not have time to pause and look at themselves. We kept moving out of habit, driven by blind momentum, for we had little choice — either move forward, create a home, a refuge, or go mad.' And, of course, some did. Like Bloomfield, forever tramping the streets, sleeping in parks and rooming houses, the tattooed arm his badge of sorrow, his engraved pain, his permanent Oswiecim.

Golden autumn, the Poles call it with pride. The landscape flows with a muted light which streaks into the city I am fast approaching. Bialystok appears tranquil, detached, beyond history, a survivor, intact. I see father in a leather jacket and open shirt, his trousers rolled up to the knees, wading across a stream on a trek through local forests: my favourite photo of him. His eyes are, as I have sometimes seen them, beyond doubt and confusion, denial and shame.

They are blue. Clear as transparent skies. And mother's are deep hazel, almost black, the colour of earth, of endurance.

I see them as they are now, in their old age. Father's natural tendency has always been to fly, to soar on impulse and grand ideas. Yet for the fortieth year in succession he looks down upon the same patch of earth, as he composts, digs, plants, and moves towards an inner balance, an integrity. And mother, who has always cooked and cleaned and sewn and served, is softening, her gaze moving upwards, through distances, towards the heavens, towards surrender. And I see my reflection in them both. My eyes are green, in between; while within, I sense the first inklings of a harmony, the first intimations that a long journey is nearing its end.

Chapter Seventeen

A MIND CONSTANTLY ALERT, hands weaving as he talks, ideas bouncing erratically, curiosity expanding with age, body and soul channelled into single-minded attention on his rambling monologues — my father. A survivor. A philosopher.

Of all the seasons, he says, autumn is the philosopher. He had been born in winter: ethereal, snow-veiled, but forbidding and threatening. His basic pessimism had been tempered by spring's naive and buoyant innocence. The summers had, he admits, been satisfying, at times even joyful. But the heat could also bloat the mind and dull the senses.

So it is autumn, after all, he has come to prefer. Autumn is the present stage in his life. A softer melody. A potential harmony. A song of fruition. A thanksgiving. 'Autumn is contemplative', father stresses. 'The season of afterthoughts, when leaves fall with a quiet language of their own.' In the Old World it had been a season of colours, permeated with a copper glow, bronze and blessed.

And it is colour that greets me as I return to Bialystok after one month's absence. The city parks are coated in ochres and lemons, auburns and pale emeralds. Buildings cast stark shadows to the movement of a sun low on the southern horizon. One day it rains incessantly, the next the sun re-emerges radiant and warm. Yet just as unexpectedly, temperatures plunge towards zero, frosts cover the countryside, and sharp winds bite into the skin.

Buklinski and Bunim are waiting as arranged. They sit in the gloom of Buklinski's apartment, late afternoon, subdued, rugged up in gabardine overcoats. After a schnapps we descend the stairs into Zabia Square. An evening chill has settled upon the city. The two men clutch at their scarves and coats as if protecting themselves not only against the chill, but also against sinister forces they sense lurking around them. As we wait in line for a taxi they shuffle nervously. Out in the open, on the streets of Bialystok, my two companions are revealed as frail and vulnerable men on an alien landscape.

On July 27, 1944 the Red Army liberated Bialystok. In mid August Srolke Kott approached the outskirts of the city. He saw peasants in the fields gathering hay. Others stood chatting in front of their homes. A bizarre normality. An autumn harvest. As if nothing had happened. Srolke oscillated between fleeting moments of hope, and a brooding sense of dread and foreboding. Perhaps, yes, there would be some trace of home, a familiar face, a former neighbour.

I have never met Srolke Kott. For many years he has lived in Buenos Aires. Father knew his family as neighbours in Bialystok; but he remembers little of Srolke, since he was considerably younger than father. Mother had known his elder sister and had sung with her in choirs over sixty years ago. In a world of shadows, such connections can be as strong as blood ties. Soon after the war, Srolke wrote of his experiences as a partisan in the forests of White Russia. Father was particularly drawn to Srolke's descriptions of his return to Bialystok. He absorbed them so fully, he could recount them as if they were his own. The ballad of Srolke Kott, the song of his homecoming, became the song of father's imagined homecoming.

As Srolke drew nearer he hastened his steps. The first sight of the city confirmed his worst fears. The railway station was a burnt-out shell. The bridges were shattered. Whole streets had been reduced to rubble, and rows of houses to chimney stacks, a single wall, a skeleton.

Srolke approached the street in which he had grown up. Cobblestones which had once been smooth from the constant tread of footsteps were now overgrown with weeds. Holy books lay scattered about, their pages rotting. Wherever he looked there were broken chairs, doorless wardrobes, fractured beds. Feathers from ripped pillows and quilts mingled with photographs of people who had once lived there — images of men with beards and sidelocks, women with fashionable hairstyles, a child in her mother's arms, a boy seated on a horse, another wrapped in a prayer shawl on the day of his bar mitzvah — the album of a lost people.

All that remained of his family's house were foundation stones and half a chimney. The rest was covered in sand and patches of grass. There were not even the remains of a wall on which he could find support. Srolke tried to visualise where his parents' wedding photo had hung. For the children this photo had been the measure of their growing-up, while their mother would point to it as a reminder of how young she had once been.

Srolke was overcome by confusion. The legs that had supported him through many kilometres of forest and swamp gave way beneath him. The air he breathed seemed choked with the fumes of Treblinka, Majdanek, Auschwitz. All his loved ones, all that had given meaning to his life, had vanished. One question echoed constantly within him: how could man commit such crimes upon his fellow man?

For a long time Srolke sat on the foundations, unable to remain still; yet at the same time, unable to flee. Nearby stood a fragment of barbed-wire fence, a remnant of the ghetto wall. In front of him Srolke noticed a hole in the earth, and recalled that this must have been the hideout he had built for his sister and parents. He bent over and stared at the opening. Inside it was dark, and he was seized by an urge to begin digging. Perhaps he would be confronted by corpses. It would be as if he had entered his own tomb. And in that moment Srolke was overwhelmed by that thought which was to haunt many survivors in years to come: why had he lived whilst his dear ones had been torn from life? How was he to deal with the fear of his own thoughts? How could he answer for himself? Is this what it meant to be liberated?

On the fringes of Bialystok, where the city thins and becomes forest, stands the house of Yankel, the shoemaker. The taxi draws up to his weatherboard cottage. Yankel guides us through the front garden. Sunflowers glow like lanterns in the darkness. A pair of candles light up a living-room table covered in a white cloth. Yankel's wife, the Queen of Shabbes, greets us. She unravels our scarves, helps us off with our coats, and shows us to our seats. 'Help yourselves', she tells us. Buklinski needs little coaxing. He opens a bottle of vodka. 'Time for a schnapps!', he exclaims. 'Time to forget!'

It was well after midnight when Srolke finally moved away from the ruins. The streets were deserted. In the distance, like a shadow, he saw a solitary figure flitting between houses. Srolke hurried after him, drew alongside and asked, in Polish: 'Where can I find Jews?' The stranger stared at him as if confronted by a lunatic. 'I have seen no Jews at all', he replied. 'There are none here.'

Srolke remained stranded, confused, unable to determine his next move. He noticed a light nearby, and was drawn towards a house in which he knew Jews had once lived. A Polish woman sat by the kitchen table. Srolke greeted her and asked if she knew of any Jews living in Bialystok. After a long pause she replied that she had heard there were several staying in Kupietzka 24; but she could not be sure.

As he neared the building Srolke saw that it was severely damaged. The windows were shattered, the foyer strewn with rubbish. He climbed the stairs and entered a darkened room where he could just make out an emaciated woman sitting by a table. 'Yes', she replied in a barely audible voice, 'there are Yidn living here', and she resumed her indifferent stare.

Srolke and the woman sat silently, lost to each other in private thought, unable to converse. Soon after, her husband entered: a bare skeleton of a man. He was hungry for information. Who was still alive? Did Srolke know the fate of this or that person? Did they have mutual friends? The same questions were asked by other figures who darted into the room from time to time, back from a day of scavenging. They were all shabbily dressed, barefoot, tired and, despite their many questions, reluctant to talk, as if afraid of hearing the sound of their own voices recalling the recent past. They quickly selected a portion of floor to sleep on, covered themselves with papers, and placed their clenched fists behind their heads as pillows.

By the time Srolke awoke the next morning, they had all left on their daily search for food and familiar faces.

'He's going to cry! Bunim is going to cry!', exclaims Buklinski as he dances around the table, stopping by each guest to pour another glass. Bunim's crimson complexion darkens with each successive schnapps. Yankel's wife serves course after course of chicken — chicken soup, roast chicken, boiled chicken, chicken pieces — a universe of chicken. 'A Polish wife with a Yiddishe heart', whispers Buklinski, while Yankel sits at the head of the table like a benign patriarch surrounded by an extended family.

Bunim lifts his head and gazes at the ceiling as if about to address the Creator. His voice is cracked, almost broken, but his once rich tenor has retained at least some of its former glory. He hums snatches of Yiddish melodies. 'Białystok was a city with a Yiddish soul', he muses. 'No longer any rabbis, no longer talmudic scholars, no longer a Yiddishe city', he laments.

'And no longer Zlatke, queen of the whores! No longer pimps, thieves, and brothels on the Chanaykes!', interjects Buklinski, as he continues his vodka-inspired waltz around the table.

A sudden tap on the window: Buklinski's Polish mistress has arrived. She sits on his lap while he sings Yiddish love-songs with the cracked voice of a street entertainer. Buklinski's blood pressure is soaring. His uncontrollable energy, his manic zest for life, propel him back into wild monologues and refrains from the lanes of the Chanaykes, where his insatiable longing was first kindled, and where existence had become an eternal pursuit of touch, vodka, and love. Many years later this voracious drive to live had intensified, rather than diminished — even more so after his sojourn in Auschwitz.

'How did I survive those times?', he muses. 'I was sharp. I knew where to be and where not to be. I sidestepped, stayed alert, made myself useful, and remained silent:

> I dreamt of you, my dear one,
> I dreamt of you day and night.
> I dreamt of your dark black eyes,
> And awoke in sickness and fright.
>
> Oh little bird, my dear heart,
> Please be for a moment still.
> Tend to the fire in my heart,
> And do with me what you will.

October 1944. The twisted dome of the Great Synagogue lies charred in a field of rubble. Bialystok is a liberated zone behind the Soviet front. To the west the dying embers of a protracted war continue to flicker as the Allied armies close in on a crumbling Third Reich. Srolke Kott and his companions spend their nights in an abandoned building, Kupietzka 29, huddled against the elements. Cold winds find easy access through broken windows. A wick stuffed into a bottle of oil glows within a dim light. For hours on end they reminisce: fellow survivors keeping each other warm with endless tales of the other life they had known.

On Yom Kippur eve, one of them suggests they attend a Kol Nidre service he has heard is being held in a house on Ulitza Mlynowa. After all there is nothing else to do, nowhere else to go; and the way is easy, direct. Instead of the maze of alleys around which they would have had to wind in former times, there are empty spaces and vacant lots between the houses still standing.

Mlynowa 157. A small room. By the eastern wall stands a table laden with blazing candles. The room is packed with up to forty people, of whom only half a dozen or so are women. There are no children or elderly men. No one is wearing prayer shawls or white kitlech as basic ritual requires. Many are dressed in worn and weathered clothes. The men are unshaven, dishevelled. Among those present are Red Army officers, soldiers of the New Polish Army, and some who have travelled to the service from outlying villages.

A cantor conducts the prayers, but very few appear to be listening. Most seem locked in their private grief. A senior Red Army officer stands sobbing, a prayer-book clutched to a chest lined with medals. Srolke observes a man with a large moustache, leaning on a cane, a crucifix dangling around his neck — in appearance a Pole. He joins the rest of the makeshift congregation in their occasional cries of amen.

The room is swaying in a dream, a mirage in which reason has been turned on its head. Those present are not here to pray for forgiveness, as is the custom, but to conduct intimate conversations with themselves and a God that many had come to believe had abandoned them. One question haunts them all: can the Almighty explain? How was it possible?

Kol Nidre, Bialystok, autumn 1944. The bare remnants of a

community grieve together; and in each other's presence they find, perhaps, a moment of solace.

Everyone is talking of Bialystok: Bunim, Buklinski, Yankel, inundating me with anecdotes, so that at journey's end the writer will record them, tales of the city I am on the eve of leaving, the Bialystok I had dreamed of for so many years; the city my parents had never ceased dreaming of, even as they had wanted to forget.

I have now more than an inkling of what they felt on the eve of their departures, and why it was so hard for them to wrench themselves free, despite the constant threat and undertow of menace. Bialystok was their siren's song, a spell that had bewitched generation after generation, an enticing melody which forever hinted at deliverance; and even when all that remained was a wasteland of rubble, survivors had still returned with the faint hope that they would rediscover their ancient vision, their lost dream.

And to this day the very last heirs cling to their dream, served by loyal Polish wives and mistresses, at a Sabbath table laden with vodka and chicken, entranced, despite all, by Bialystok's lingering presence, the remembrance of their youth, the protective blanket of their dwindling community, the last trace of a mother's embrace. They lament as they celebrate a receding past that has swept by them with the force of a hurricane, leaving in its wake merely a song of longing which they sing repeatedly, obsessively; until, one by one, the Sabbath meal at an end, they depart into the cool autumn air, the last Jews of Bialystok.

Chapter Eighteen

IN CURTAIN SQUARE, the neighbourhood park, stand two rows of Moreton Bay figs, six sentinels on either side of a path. 'They are grand old beauties', father tells me. He taps them with his fists. 'Rock hard', he pronounces. 'Each one is a sculpture, a unique individual. Each one bears its own character, its own being', he enthuses. 'They cling to the earth with their many roots exposed, like snakes slithering into burrows.'

Father asks me to count the roots extending from the largest tree. There are over twenty. 'See how they unite into a thick trunk which gives way to a spacious dome', he points out. 'Observe how the branches reach for the horizons. The smooth surfaces of their leaves mirror the sun and stay evergreen. They are as grand as the chestnut trees I knew in Bialystok.'

He has known these Moreton Bay figs for over forty years, though it is only recently that I have become aware of this 'love affair', as he calls it. During the earlier years, when the tension had been greatest, they had become his refuge, his private temples. He would come here at night and sit beneath them, as he had sat beneath the chestnut tree of Zwierziniec in the early years of this century. 'A man broken in spirit can pass by them and be comforted', father claims.

There is a certain position, by the kitchen table, from which a window high on the wall opposite the bathroom can be seen. Here

208

mother often sits and gazes at the upper branches of a tree. Timber frames divide the window into twelve separate squares, so that the light streams in at many angles and degrees of intensity. Sometimes it is restrained, the branches barely visible. At other moments it blazes a luminous gold. In winter the branches are thin and bare, while in spring they erupt with leaves. In her ageing, mother's life has been reduced to a simple equation, a silence with infinite variations on tranquillity and light — concentrated, framed, contained, yet full of subtle movement and change.

The silence is rarely broken, except for a sudden gust of wind, the distant barking of a dog, the twittering of birds. 'They return every year', mother announces from one of her reveries. 'Birds can speak', she adds. 'They have a language of their own. They probably talk about where they have been for the past year. They perch on that tree and chatter to each other. You can hear how pleased they are to be back.'

'The whole of existence is contained in words', father claims. 'Words are the source. They are more durable than the grass we are sitting on', he stresses, while poking his fingers at the ground. 'This grass must eventually fade, whereas words eternalise our experiences and express the sum total of what we have been in our lives. Words will never die, so long as there are human beings to receive them. All our knowledge and feelings can thereby be retrieved.'

Father is now fully in his element, spinning a long thread of thought to which he clings with tenacity so that it will not escape his grasp. 'Of course there are words which bind us to prejudice and blind faith', he stresses. 'Such words must be stripped naked, so that we can find our way back to the pure meaning of things, to words which do not dictate our lives and condition our thoughts.'

As father talks his whole being is in harness. 'Words will always triumph', he asserts. 'I am talking of words that express our innermost feelings. In words lie their potential to break out and be released.' As he makes this claim, father's voice falters and gives way to tears. But, as usual, he fights them off before they overwhelm him. Yet in that moment we had both glimpsed and felt that which cannot be captured in words.

But, of course, father tries. He tells me that in his tears he had sensed both his greatest happiness and regret. Happiness, because he had realised that, at last, he had been fully understood. His words had been received. Regret, because he knows that soon he must leave this world he has come to love so dearly. And, he concedes, there are moments which move beyond words. 'Perhaps this is what can be called a zisser toit, a sweet death', he muses. 'Perhaps this is what we are striving for after all — a silence, a zisser toit, beyond all memory and words.'

My earliest of memories: a rare gathering of relatives and Old World friends after a day of picnicking. I am feeling my way through a forest of legs. Smoke drifts down between the trees. As I crawl beside them, I come across a white object. I grasp it in my hands and weave my way through the forest until I find mother. She bends over, lifts me up, and carries me to the kitchen where she performs her feat of magic. She drops the dented ping-pong ball into a kettle of boiling water and, minutes later, it re-emerges, smooth, restored, fully rounded, a glowing white sphere.